MUSIC
IN THE
MIDST
OF
CHAOS

MUSIC
IN THE
MIDST
OF
CHAOS

One Family's Saga on the
Human Rights Battlefield

by Jean Conklin

CARICO PRESS • HERMISTON, OREGON

S pecial thanks –

For help in reviewing, critiquing and editing –
Anna Wilde, my faithful friend
Becky Satter, my soul sister
Betty Shanks, Tom's mother-advocate
Charity Bucher, my publisher friend
Christopher Walsh, an exceptional writer and proofreader
Erin Chowning, my good latté friend
Gina Tedeschi, Tia's friend
Jan [Pipes] Kerns, my older (and only) sister
Pastor Michael J. Johnson, D. Min., my wise pastor friend
Scotty Bruemmer, Tom's sister-advocate
Tia [Conklin] Pollick, my youngest daughter

~ ~

For contributing life stories about their special siblings –
Deanna Hasen, Ruth's older sister
Debbie Keimig, Marty's older sister
Mark Williams, Marty's younger brother
Mary Shaver, Lanetrae's younger sister
Scotty Bruemmer, Tom's older sister
Tia [Conklin] Pollick, Trista's younger sister

~ ~

And for his tolerance, support, love and encouragement
during our 32 years of marriage,
27 years of motherhood and parent advocacy,
and many years with my all too consuming manuscripts –
my love, gratitude and respect
to my faithful and longsuffering husband,
Dave Conklin

TAYLOR ROBY PIPES   2-99

To my Dad,
Taylor Roby Pipes –
the most tenacious man I know.

Contents

~ ~ ~

Foreword

BY DR. MICHAEL J. JOHNSON

We never really knew.

Sure, there were signs, but in the midst of pastoring a growing church, and attempting to raise three very active children of our own, the depth of the trials of Dave and Jean Conklin somehow didn't register. After reading *Music*, it all makes sense now. And that is why what you are about to read is so important – to understand the heartache, trials and triumphs of raising a special-needs child. Because of Jean's book, now we will all know the love and tenacity it takes to accomplish what they have achieved.

It was my privilege to be the Conklins' pastor for over four years. During that time my appreciation for them grew in so many ways. Jean, with an eye for décor and color, was a constant in my life as we were continually involved in a church "make-over." Somewhat of a perfectionist, she worked relentlessly until things were "just right."

Yet there was another side. I remember one day in particular that Jean showed up, unannounced, at my office with her espresso machine and ingredients for a savored passion of mine. She proceeded to make my favorite drink, a café mocha. After serving me, she went through our entire church and Christian school staff, taking orders and making espresso drinks for everyone. What is more, I discovered that she had just rendered the same selfless service for the staff at a local school. That's Jean – part bulldog, with a great servant's heart.

Dave, on the other hand, is a fitness buff. I used to give him a hard time after frequently seeing him running through town with little more than sneakers, and shorts that barely hung on his skinny frame. Dave is an encourager, with unusual perception and insight. Several times, we had conversations about struggles in the midst of church life. I always came away with wise and godly counsel. Together they have also founded "Heart for Romania," an outreach for the less-fortunate in the former Soviet-block country.

As you read this book, you'll find that Jean probably was not always so tenacious and Dave was, perhaps, not always so perceptive. Life dealt them a difficult hand, and yet they chose a path that matured them into the admired and respected people they have become. In these pages, you will sense their struggle, frustration and relentless pursuit of the truth concerning the complex medical condition of their oldest daughter Trista. The sections dealing with advocacy issues and the eventual source of their strength are equally important.

Hang on. You are about to be enriched through these pages, in the same way as I have been enriched from knowing these extraordinary people.

Dr. Michael J. Johnson
Bend, Oregon   July 29, 1999

PREFACE · WINTER 1995

I am compelled to write this book.

I have spent almost a quarter of a century trying to work through heartache. It is the heartache that comes with mothering a handicapped child. I am today, every day, just as I was 20 years ago: a blink away from tears.

Sometimes I hurt so intensely that I wonder if I am on the verge of cardiac arrest. I used to wonder why my heart never quit aching; why my compassion for hurting families seemed abnormally tender.

I received my answer last spring.

The Lord sometimes speaks to us in a soft whisper that we hear with our heart. Last spring He spoke to me the word, **"grief."**

Grief is the pain I can't seem to shake off. It's like dog manure on my good shoes. Hard as I try to wipe my shoes on the blades of grass, I can't get rid of the filthy stuff in the seams and cracks. And whenever I slow down or stand still, the rotten smell permeates my entire presence.

Grief is the clawing that feels like its hands will surely jerk my heart out of my chest. Funny there should be such pain. How can someone who feels so dead, also feel so much pain?

Grief is the feeling that wraps its hands around my throat and threatens to choke me when I try to stifle the pain.

Grief is the balloon that feels like it swells in my lungs, preventing me from letting go of the breath that I find myself holding to suppress the tears.

I'm pretty good at hiding these things. Most people don't know about this war zone where I so often find myself trapped.

Grief has taken a physical toll on me. It has scarred me on the outside, where it's harder to conceal. It's been slowly progressive, and I doubt that others see it much. But *I* see it.

Grief is the eraser that has wiped the life out of my face. When I look in the mirror, I am always surprised to see the pain in my reflection. Grief has wiped chalk over my face – the chalk of emptiness, hollowness, lifelessness. Grief forces me to spend extra time at the mirror, putting on fresh foundation and lots of blush, hoping the skilled cosmetic artistry will conceal the death that I see staring back at me.

Grief has transformed my face. I can *feel* grief working; it is as though there are invisible "earth magnets" at the corner of my eyes, and on my cheeks, and in the corners of my mouth. They seem to pull all the "smiley" parts of my face down towards the earth, to make mine a "sad face." I have to work at making my face pleasant-looking. I *make* my face smile, hoping it will migrate to my heart, because the Bible says, "A cheerful heart is good medicine." [1] I could use a good swig of medicine for my grieving heart.

Grief has furrowed my brow. My brow furrows naturally when I'm really concentrating on something, but grief tugs relentlessly at it. When I catch a glimpse of my countenance in the mirror, my lamentation shows. I am mindful to conceal it. I mentally *work* at "facial relaxation" so that people don't see my pain. Sometimes I find myself *willing* my face to look pleasant, as though I could teach my face to smile again.

I caught a reflection of myself in a store window one day last spring. I was stunned at what I saw. As soon as I got home, I went into the bathroom, closed the door, and turned on all the lights. I searched the reflection, attempting to find the image of the person I thought I was. I couldn't believe the sadness I saw. Like a plastic surgeon, with my fingers I pushed up the corners of my mouth, and pulled up the corners of my eyes. I could synthesize peace and pleasure in my face but as soon as I let go, the woeful look returned. I spoke to myself, "Jean, you look so sad!" An all-too-familiar tear rolled down my cheek.

I found myself wondering how long it had been since I had laughed? . . . really laughed? Gut-wrenching laughter. How long had it been since I had felt pure joy? Sheer, uncontainable joy?

I couldn't remember. Over the years, grief had quietly taken over my being. Like a fungus, grief worked its way deep into my soul and my spirit. *Grief* had me. I was being consumed by it.

> " *. . . by sorrow of the heart the spirit is broken.*
>
> *. . . a broken spirit drieth the bones."*
>
> Proverbs 15:13b
> Proverbs 17:22b (KJV)

Having a diagnosis in my grip, I wish I could write that I overcame grief with some fantastic recovery program. I have not. No solution seems relevant. I have read many books and articles about grief recovery. I have concluded that recovering from grief is a process – a metamorphosis that must happen deep within one's being. I have spent many months pondering this revelation of my problem, and I do not know *how* one gets over grief.

I have prayed fervently about this. I frequently tell the Lord that I want to get beyond this grief. I cannot reckon with the idea that one child's disability will ultimately consume me!

It is winter. I have dealt with this grief awareness for nine months now. That is enough time to incubate another child. All I have incubated is the knowledge that God has shown me something that needs fixing, and I haven't a clue how to do that.

How many years does one have to carry grief before grief dies? Or does it ever? Does a person *ever* get over grief? I know people who have lost spouses, and parents, and children – and it seems to me that they eventually get over it. Five . . . ten . . . twenty years . . . the pain dulls and life moves on. Well, it's been twenty-four years, and my grief is *worse*! How can that be? And how do I reverse this process? The hopelessness of this dilemma sometimes threatens to *consume* me.

I have felt for years I that need to write a book about my experiences with our severely handicapped daughter, but I couldn't get it into perspective. In fact, considering the prospect of *publicly* sharing some of the things that would be said – well, that was simply overwhelming. And just the thought of *dealing* with that pain has been sufficient to keep me from even getting started.

But God is faithful! Today the Lord spoke to me again, with these words, "Physician, heal yourself." [2]

Today it became so clear to me. I am to write the things He has shown me. Write about the music of my own life – there was an entire symphony that was composed while we raised two special-needs daughters. Write about our family's continuing saga on the human rights battlefield. Write about what I have learned – about the obstacles we have overcome. And write about Tourette Syndrome.

I sense the Lord assuring me that there is healing in these pages – healing for both the writer *and* the reader. I do not know how that will happen, but I don't think I have to deal with that. I think that is God's business.

So as I write these pages, and as you read these pages, you can trust that the same Lord who created me, my daughters, and you, has provided healing for us all:

> *"The righteous cry out, and the LORD hears them;*
> *he delivers them from all their troubles.*
>
> *'I will restore you to health and heal your*
> *wounds,' declares the LORD"*
>
> Psalms 34:17
> Jeremiah 30:17a

I believe this book will be anointed. Last year, God made a clear revelation of my problem: *grief.* Now God has encouraged me to write this book. With His calm assurance, He has offered to reach down and lift me from the quicksand that has threatened to destroy me. I'm on my way! God never keeps good things to Himself.

I invite you to glean whatever you find useful in this book. I know the words of an old song are true:

> *"Something Good is Going to Happen to You!"* [3]

~ ~ ~

Advocacy 101

I never gave much thought to having a family. Dave and I fell in love and got married. We must have been so enamored with each other, and with love and marriage, that we never got around to talking about the baby carriage. It seems incredibly naïve, but that's the way it was for a couple of college students. Planning our future meant finding Dave a job after he graduated. It meant seeing the completion of my Bachelor of Science and fifth-year degree. And it meant finding a town where we could both have teaching contracts. That was the extent of our "family planning."

Our strategy worked like clockwork for several years. I finished my degree work at Oregon State University while Dave taught at Philomath Elementary School. Then we moved to eastern Oregon, where I had my first job as home economics teacher at Baker Senior High School. Dave commuted every day to La Grande to get his Master's Degree in elementary education from Eastern Oregon College. At the end of that year, we both signed teaching contracts in Hermiston, Oregon.

But reality had already struck. I had not penetrated my teaching career very deeply before I began to realize that secondary school teaching simply was not for me. I did not enjoy kids, little *or* big! Small wonder this was such a surprise: I didn't enjoy babysitting when I was a teenager, I was not overly fond of any of our friends' children, and I hated student teaching.

Not being one to admit failure, I decided that I needed an *excuse* to make a graceful exit from my chosen profession. I'd get pregnant! That was probably the first time I seriously pondered having children.

It's probably a good thing that we didn't analyze this scenario. If I had dissected the decision to have – or to not have – children, I possibly would have opted out. And I would have missed the greatest blessing of life itself – the blessing of being a parent!

I think it is a God-given element of grace that allows mankind to love his offspring. One could hardly call me a doting parent but I deeply love my own children and my two little grandchildren. And yet, to this day I still don't enjoy babysitting other children – I dislike spending time in schools – and one does not need to watch me in a group very long to see that I do not gravitate towards other people's children.

It somehow never connected in my brain that getting pregnant would result in having a baby, which would grow into a child – a child who would dominate and forever change my life. It's probably just as well that I never put all this together because had I realized what I was setting myself up for, I would have cowered at the very thought of becoming a mom. I think that for many young marrieds, the desire to have a family is one of those innocent pie-in-the-sky wishes. If some parents-to-be were to realize the challenges and responsibilities that they have ahead of them for the rest of their lives, they might turn tail and run into eternal childlessness! (My friend Mary, who has had more than her share of child-rearing problems, jokes about people who have just announced their pregnancy: she threatens to send sympathy cards.)

After we determined to pursue getting me pregnant, we discussed my preference. I did not want to be a working mom. My mother was a full-time mom (today's phrase is "stay-at-home mom"). Almost all my childhood friends' mothers were full-time moms. Most of our favorite students had non-working moms. If I was going to be a mom, it was my desire to be a good one. To me, that meant that we should adjust our life-style so I could be a full-time mom. Most children of working moms spend more of their waking hours with babysitters than with their parents. It's a rhetorical question, but I still think the answer is obvious: "Why have children if someone else is going to raise them for you?"

Dave was very supportive of our decision to begin our family because Dave loves children! And he was also in agreement with my decision to resign from teaching. A month after our decision to begin a family, my husband had an extremely severe case of mumps. We feared that he might not be *able* to father any children because mumps in adult males can result in sterility.

After Dave's bout with mumps, I had a miscarriage. I didn't even *know* I was expecting – the bloody tissue was the only indication that I had even been pregnant. We brushed off the event optimistically. I felt great, physically. We rejoiced that Dave had no permanent damage from his illness. We are of the opinion that miscarriages are God's way of resolving unresolvable major problems in an unborn child, and we viewed this early miscarriage as an unfortunate event that happened, for a reason we would never understand.

I became pregnant again shortly after the miscarriage. My due date was December 2, 1971. My spring resignation from a stressful two-year teaching career was received with blessings by those few who knew the *real* reason was that I would soon become a full-time mom.

Leaving the teaching profession was a difficult transition. I felt like a failure. Teaching was the *first* thing I could remember having tried and totally failed. I had *always* conquered everything that I attempted. I felt like I had just thrown away the last six years of my life. And I felt that my college degree was a total waste. Teaching credentials were useless for someone who hated teaching!

On top of this sense of failure, I had terrible morning sickness, which was followed by incessant heartburn. I was not "showing" when school was out, but I was gaining weight because I had the sensation that if I could keep enough food in my stomach, the heartburn would go away. It only worked momentarily but it provided such positive reinforcement that I stuffed far too much food into my mouth throughout my pregnancy.

Summer vacation came and went. It was the hottest summer on record in Hermiston: 31 consecutive days over 100 degrees. Mourning my teaching failure was short-lived; I was offered a job working for KOHU, the local radio station. They wanted me to narrate a one-hour morning call-in program, focusing on issues related to homemaking. My home economics degree prepared me well for the subject matter. It was a positive experience as I discovered that I could offhandedly present facts and chatty instructions quite effectively. But I also learned that I did not have very good people skills. My interactive responses left much to be desired. As long as I had an outline or script in front of me, I did just fine. But I didn't always field impromptu call-ins very diplomatically. Oprah, I was not!

I don't recall why the radio job ended. Evidently it didn't matter. I was busy getting ready for our *baby*! In spite of my heartburn and subsequent physical discomfort, being pregnant was one of the happiest times of my life. I loved participating in the changes in my body. I loved all the attention that gets lavished on pregnant women. I loved the excitement and the anticipation. Planning for the baby was great fun. Our nursery was becoming well decorated and well stocked. I had the ideas, the skill, the time, and the energy to do it all perfectly, or so I thought.

Around Thanksgiving, just a week before my due date, I was craving strawberries. Our good friends, Tyler and Francie Hansell, lightheartedly obliged my latest obsession and brought strawberry cake, with strawberry icing and fresh strawberries. I overindulged, as usual. And then I had an allergic reaction to something in the dessert – hmmm, I wonder what??? I broke out in hives and was miserable. What a sight I must have been, sitting naked in that tub of cool soda water when Francie came back to console me, pregnant and red all over. I was swollen and weeping – desperate for the rash and itching to go away. I ended up becoming so ill that I went to the emergency room. In 1971, such visits were rather unusual. The doctor prescribed Erythromycin. Although my prescription desk-reference manual indicates "pregnant and breastfeeding women may use this product with no restrictions," [4] I suspect this was not a good time to be taking any medicines.

My heartburn continued through most of my pregnancy. I gained a *lot* of weight – far too much! I refused to look at the scales after discovering I had put on 58 pounds by my December 2 due date. I just couldn't seem to do anything about my excessive weight gain. Weight control, which had never before been a concern for me, has been a continuous nuisance since this pregnancy.

On December 10, I was one-week overdue, feeling fully pregnant and very uncomfortable. My good country doctor summoned me to the hospital for the purpose of inducing my labor. In the little Umatilla Hospital, I received small doses of Pitocin, [5] in tablets, placed under my tongue to dissolve slowly. It didn't work. The baby evidently wasn't ready to be born. Disappointed, we were

Advocacy 101

sent home to wait for nature to take its course. I was still suffering some of the side effects of the allergic reaction, and I had a problem with water retention. I was just plain miserable.

Christmas came and went. We couldn't travel to our out-of-town family because I was already overdue, so Dave and I spent Christmas all alone. I cried throughout the holiday, feeling lonely, fat, miserable, and *forever pregnant.*

However, it is true that no one stays pregnant forever! When I woke up at dawn on Monday, December 27, my bed was wet. My water had broken. (That is the *only* time I would be excited over having wet the bed!) Although I had no contractions, the nurse told us to come to the hospital. I had waited almost 10 months for this day! My labor began at 10 a.m. By afternoon, the contractions were close, long, hard, and relentless – although it didn't seem that they were very productive. They took their toll on my pain threshold. I was fighting the contractions too much, so at 8 p.m., I was taken to the delivery room where the doctor gave me a type of spinal block. The 30 minutes or so of relief seemed like a gift without measure. But when the anesthetic wore off, I endured the contractions just as poorly as I had before. I received a second spinal block several hours later. I was beyond wishing I could cooperate with the efforts of my body; all I could do was fight the pain and beg for something to make it end.

Those were early days in the new wave of delivery room protocol that was beginning to sweep this nation. Dave was the first father to be allowed in the Umatilla Hospital delivery room during the actual labor and delivery. It was a tentative agreement: as long as Dave stayed out of the way and upright, he could remain in the room as an *observer.* The addendum to the verbal agreement was that if there was an emergency, Dave understood that he would cooperate with any request to immediately leave the delivery room. Fair enough.

Many of our friends were in the childbearing stage of life. Shari Ford and I were ex-teachers (and our husbands were teaching at Sunset School in Hermiston.) Shari and I were good friends, both enjoying our first pregnancy, with similar due dates. We had selected the same doctor but Shari's choice was conditional: the doctor had to agree to allow Shari to use the "Lamaze" childbirth technique during her delivery. She said the relaxation and breathing techniques would make her delivery easier. The doctor was skeptical. Shari was being taught the Lamaze technique by Gladys Morrison, a mature obstetrics nurse. Mrs. Morrison had *seen* the differences in deliveries that used this new French childbirth relaxation technique, and she had become Hermiston's first Lamaze Certified Childbirth Educator (LCCE).[6] [Many years after her retirement, Gladys remarked that although her introduction of Lamaze to Hermiston almost cost her career, childbirth education and practice was the most rewarding phase of her entire nursing career.] The physician reservedly agreed to allow Shari to "do her thing" during her delivery. I thought her new philosophy was rather strange. However, when I was in labor, I found myself wishing I had paid more attention to Shari's ideas. Dave was there with me, but having my husband *physically* present was of little help – I needed *skills* to actively cooperate with my body's contractions. I needed someone to coach me, someone to keep me focused on my "job." Today it is considered normal procedure to permit, and even encourage, fathers in delivery rooms. But I feel so sorry for the men who are mere observers to the birthing process, with no means of assisting the woman with her delivery. What a helpless experience! (No wonder tradition had them busy boiling water!) Fathers in the delivery room can be a tremendous blessing but the partner needs the latitude to be more than a spectator. I now know that the father, given the proper training, can be a wonderfully helpful coach to the expectant mother during delivery.

All this is significant to me because childbirth was my introduction to the importance of **advocacy.** ***An advocate is a partner, a sustainer; someone who assists; an ombudsman.*** My body needed an advocate that day: someone who would partner with my body's natural efforts to deliver that baby. My body needed a woman who could sustain the contractions, thereby assisting the muscles in their work and encouraging their relaxation. My body had its *own* agenda that day – involuntary efforts which could have been endorsed; progress which could have been upheld. While I was laying there on the delivery table for hours and hours, I was absolutely no help to what was happening in my body. All I could do was fight *against* the pain, and certainly that slowed the progress. I was not prepared for enduring the intensity nor the duration of pain that comes with childbirth. Shari and Gladys were right. Childbirth *is* a natural phenomenon: *we* need to learn how to help, not hinder, our body to do its very natural work. Dave and I could have been a tremendous pair of advocates for my uterus that day; we just did not realize how important that partnership could be!

Our bodies are incredible machines. In spite of no significant assistance from me, our first baby was delivered some 19 hours after the membrane ruptured. On that final much-too-noisy push, a baby girl shot out of the birth canal, into the doctor's big hands, and up onto his arms. And then like a rubber band on the rebound, she immediately was retracted close to the birth canal.

What seemed odd was the baby's short umbilical cord. The physician said the prolonged labor was partially attributed to the short cord, which *did* act like a rubber band. The contractions would push the baby down the birth canal, and the umbilical cord would pull the baby back toward the placenta, in the uterus. In essence, the labor was fairly nonproductive. The cord was so short that it was not clamped and cut until after the placenta had been delivered.

Trista Suzette Conklin was born at 12:40 a.m. on December 28, 1971. The delivery room nurse presented to us an infant that weighed just over seven pounds, with fingernails that curled around her fingertips. She was classified "post mature" but healthy. For many hours I had my doubts that my baby was ever going to be born! I welcomed the routine four day recuperative hospital stay. I learned a little about infant care and breast feeding, and I rested a lot.

Today, I am convinced that had I known how, I could have cooperated with and helped my body during the delivery of our first child. If I would have known how to use relaxation and breathing techniques, I think the labor and delivery process could have been much more productive, much shorter, and much easier – and without the assistance of any spinal blocks. (This premise was fairly well substantiated during the birth of our second child.) Trista was in the birth canal for a very long time. Obstetrical procedures are quite different today. My mother feels that I should have had a Caesarean birth for Trista. I have always wondered if some of Trista's early problems were a result of subtle birth injuries caused by too much stress on the fetus. We will never know.

Once a moment has passed, it can never be reclaimed. But for the prudent person, life, itself, can often be a very fine teacher.

> *"Some of the best places to eat*
> *have no gaudy menu signs.*
> *Some of the best learning troughs*
> *have no glittering facades."* [7]

A delivery room might seem like an uncustomary classroom. But while I was experiencing such discomfort for so long, I learned the meaning of the adage, "When the going gets tough, the tough get going." During childbearing, there is absolutely nowhere to go – so the mother better be prepared to "get with the program," and help all that she can. I promised myself that the *next time* I was on the delivery table, I would be an active participant!

My advocacy training had begun!

Little did I realize how important this revelation would be for *both* Trista and me!

~ ~ ~

HEAVEN'S VERY SPECIAL CHILD

A meeting was held quite far from earth –
"It's time again for another birth."
Said the angels to the Lord above,
"This special child will need much love."

Her progress may seem very slow,
Accomplishments she may not show.
And she'll require extra care
From the folks she meets down there.

She may not run or laugh or play –
Her thoughts may seem quite far away,
In many ways she won't adapt,
And she'll be known as "handicapped."

So let's be careful where she's sent –
We want her life to be content.
Please, Lord, find the parents who
Will do a special job for you.

They will not realize right away
The leading role they are asked to play,
But with this child sent from above
Comes stronger faith and richer love.

And soon they'll know the privilege given
In caring for this gift from heaven.
Their precious charge, so meek and mild,
Is Heaven's Very Special Child.

author unknown

COLORED PENCIL SKETCH BY SANDRA JONES CAMPBELL   8-74

SANDI NOW LIVES IN LAGUNA BEACH, CALIFORNIA. SHE HAS BECOME A
NATIONALLY RENOWN ARTIST.

DEVELOPMENTAL DELAYS & DEPRESSION

There is a certain innocence that accompanies parenthood. New parents wait for the first healthy cry, they count 10 fingers and 10 toes, and they breathe a sigh of relief that the baby is okay. I was so exhausted after Trista's delivery that I don't even remember *noticing* her fingers and toes – my only concern was that it was over!

Because I had not given much thought to raising a family, I did not realize that I had such fantastic educational preparation to be a pretty good mother. I knew my degree in home economics was wonderfully practical. (I had always reminded Dave how lucky he was to have me because I had the best "wife-preparation education'" that any woman could have.) But I didn't realize how much (and, paradoxically, how little) I had learned about parenting skills until we had a child of our own. I was grateful for my basic understanding of child nutrition, child development, child behavior, and on and on. Though it was all college textbook information, it was, at least, a foundation.

When the reality (and finality) of parenthood settled in on me, I had enough background to know that Trista was a difficult baby. She was colicky, often melancholy and aloof, and she had rashes on her face. My greatest fear was that she would grow up with a bad case of acne because my doctor said there was a correlation between infant rashes and teenage acne. As I look back on it, I'm sure we all would gladly have traded the complex neurological problems that she had ahead of her for a bad case of teenage acne!

I loved her infancy, although it used to break my heart when we could not console our newborn. Sometimes she seemed *so* uncomfortable, and there was nothing we could do for her except to let her cry herself to sleep. Rocking and walking her seemed to only *prolong* her distress. We used to set the timer when we put her to bed. If she cried for over 30 minutes when she was dry, fed, and burped, we'd get her out of bed and put her back in the little windup swing. The "automatic mother," as we called it, always worked better than anything *we* could do for her. She refused to be comforted with holding, rocking or walking. I was grateful that I breastfed Trista because that was about the only time she would let me cuddle her and enjoy her. It had to be sufficient for me because that was the way it was with Trista.

I began to notice subtle indications of slow development. Many of my friends were having babies, and all of their children's developmental stages outpaced Trista's. I abandoned our newly-formed babysitting cooperative because I couldn't bear to scrutinize my child's delayed development. Our country doctor kept reassuring me that all children are different. I clung to *his* optimism like a life preserver . . . that hope was all I had to hold onto.

As every month passed, I became more certain that we were dealing with some significant developmental delays. It was useless to try to settle Trista for a story time, or to encourage her to watch "Captain Kangaroo" or "Mr. Rogers' Neighborhood" on TV. Her attention span simply was not long enough for quiet-time activities. Even joining her to play with toys or little games seemed futile. Because her interest in anything only lasted a moment, she would soon be off to something else. I often found myself deserted – reading her book, or watching the children's program, or playing with her toy – all by myself. Having little friends over to play with her was also fruitless because Trista really never advanced beyond the "parallel play" stage, where children appear to be playing *with* one another, but they are really only playing *beside* one another and are not interacting. The little friends usually sought *me* out to play with them because Trista had abandoned them, as she toddled off towards whatever might have caught her attention.

Trista played hard and fast, running all the time between her pursuits of purposeless activity. She was more active than any child I had ever seen! I used to think of her as our "little honeybee," flitting from one attractive flower to another; hovering for a moment to taste, and then darting off to sample from *all* the other flowers in the garden. She was constantly in motion, and her little body always had cuts and bruises on it because her balance was poor and her coordination was delayed. She didn't walk; she only ran. And when she ran, it was with her hands and arms tensed behind her, where they were useless if she fell or collided with something, which she often did. There were so many times that she ran "full-speed-ahead" into the outside corner-wall of our hallway. We recurrently observed her for signs of concussions. And because of Trista's frequent black eyes and lumps on her forehead, we were fearful that someone would turn us in for child abuse.

When she wasn't getting hurt, she was happy enough, just distant. We couldn't corral her to have long tender moments – we got them on the run! She would be *intensely* affectionate for just a moment, and then instantly become totally engaged in something new which had captured her short-lived focus.

My most tender moments were finding her halfway onto her bed. With her torso and one leg on the bed, the other leg still on the floor, she would be sound asleep. Her infant sleep patterns of going to sleep alone had carried over to her toddler stage; when she got tired, she just went to her bed. But she was usually so exhausted that she only made it *halfway* into bed before she was sound asleep. Many times, I would realize that the house was exceptionally quiet, and I would find her, fully asleep, draped over the edge of the bed with one foot still touching the floor. She was loving and sweet as I would tuck her limp little body into bed. And for just a few moments after she awoke from her naps, she would snuggle and cuddle. I was full of love for her. And yet, her "distance" gnawed at me.

It became too painful for me to compare her lag in development. I pulled farther and farther away from most of my friends, whose children seemed bright, assertive and social. My doctor continued to affirm Trista's general well-being. "She's just terribly two," he would say. "First-time parents worry a lot; your second child will be easier." It placated me but my concerns were valid, and the physician's words did not eradicate my trepidation.

The three years which included my first pregnancy and Trista's early childhood were a real "stretch." I was trying to be a good mom, but I never felt equipped to deal with a child who was like none I had ever seen nor read about. I found myself hoping the doctor would diagnose some little problem because in spite of everyone's reassurances, Trista surely did not seem normal to me!

They say a mother knows.

Dave was dealing with his own set of concerns. He also observed the reality of her developmental delays, although he did not discuss them with me. He worked with grade school children every day, and he knew the challenges that Trista would face if our concerns were substantiated. Dave was active in the teachers' union, and he immersed himself in his teaching and civic activities. We were of little support to each other. We had a good business relationship, but we failed to share with each other the burdens of our hearts.

I knew my parents were also concerned about their first granddaughter, and as a result, I felt like I had failed them. All my young-mother friends had already outpaced me; their companionship offered me no solace. I felt jealous anguish when I observed their children who were all normal, some even gifted and astute. My doctor was less than comforting. He wasn't giving me any of the answers that I wanted – needed – to hear. I felt like I had failed in every arena – as a mother, a wife, and a daughter.

Depression was my close companion.[8] I had such love for Trista, but I felt rejected by her. I found myself drinking more and more, buying wine by the gallon because it was expedient and more economical. And I became very involved in prestigious women's groups, climbing my self-serving social ladder while escaping into volunteerism and good civic causes. Nonetheless, my preoccupation with superficial activities did not fill the void. I cried myself to sleep many late nights. I had nowhere to turn.

Thoughts of suicide invaded my head. It was a recurrent theme in those lonely times. If I ended my life, someone else would have to raise Trista. I knew that was selfish. She seemed to need so much – who else besides a mother could give her that extra attention? I had heard people say that there's *nothing* like a mother's love. Those words haunted me. If I gave up, would there be anyone who could be the mother that this special child needed? Could anyone else love her enough? Sometimes I could answer, "Yes." But usually I knew that abandoning ship was a less-than-satisfactory solution. Ending my problems would only magnify Trista's problems. Suicide was not a solution; but the thought tormented me.

control.

run. jump. pull. bite.
>   too young to understand;
>   unable to control
those urges. you seem driven

to talk. whine. run. cry.
>   return. beg · · · attention.
>   I beg · · · Peace!
>   One hour · · · One minute · · ·

free

of your grasp,
of your incessant activity.

Paradoxical: you sweetheart!
>   "i wud du mama."
Oh Trista. How long
can your innocent charm remain?

How long?

Patience. Understanding. Control, mama.
SHE doesn't know.
SHE doesn't understand.
SHE **can't** control!
>   Love her, mama. Tolerate.
She MAY remain.
>   *even if you don't*

1975

I finally found the courage to reveal my suicidal considerations to my husband. Although Dave was genuinely alarmed, outwardly he was calm and compassionate. Urging me to seek professional help, Dave suggested I speak with a pastor.

During my college days, I referred to myself as an agnostic ("to keep the 'churchy' kids off my back"), and I wasn't too excited about going to a man of the cloth. But I always had great respect for Dave's advice, so I went to the local pastor of the denomination where I was baptized as a child. While I was waiting in the pastor's office, the titles of books on his library shelves seemed to leap out at me: *Help for the Hurting*; *When the Pain Won't Go Away*; *Mister God, I Have a Problem*; *God's Answers for the Hurting Heart*. I was encouraged. I wasn't at all interested in "getting religion," but after looking at his bookshelf, I had a sense of expectancy that the minister would offer me the comfort I so desperately needed.

The man listened quietly as I poured out my heartache. When I was finished, he suggested that perhaps I was not stable enough to raise this child who seemed to need so much. He told me that there were state agencies which could "assist" by removing the child from our home, to give me some relief.

I was terrified. I had gone to a minister for counsel. He had every opportunity to introduce me to the Friend who would stick closer than a brother; to the One who loves children more than any mother; to Him who is the friend of the lonely and the oppressed; to the Counselor who holds all the answers and all the power to overcome all my problems. This pastor had a precious opportunity to introduce me to Jesus Christ, so that I would have the power to live an abundant, peaceful life in the *midst* of my problems.

> *Jesus said, "The thief comes only to steal*
> *and kill and destroy;*
> *I have come that they may have life,*
> *and have it to the full."*
>
> John 10:10

Instead, the preacher threatened me with the suggestion that perhaps Trista should be taken away from me!

I did not pass go. I did not "collect two hundred dollars." Stunned, I ran the entire block to my home, locked the door behind me, and begged a God whom I did not know to **not** allow this preacher-man take matters into his own hands.

Perhaps I overreacted. Perhaps the minister was using "shock treatment" to bring me to reality. Whatever the interpretation, I seemed to snap out of my depression for awhile.* I was fearful for a long time that the state Children's Services Division might suddenly appear on my doorstep, and snatch Trista from my grip. My fears refocused my attentions, and my preoccupation with suicide sat on the back burner for about a year.

~ ~ ~

* Editor's notes: *See* APPENDIX — DEPRESSION – MY CLOSE COMPANION for important information about depression.

For the reader's use and convenience, extensive resources may be found at the back of this book:
 √ ABBREVIATIONS & ACRONYMS
 √ GLOSSARY
 √ ENDNOTES
 √ COPING TIPS & TREASURES (alphabetical index)
 √ INDEX

If I Had Known

If I had known what trouble you were bearing;

What griefs were in the silence of your face;

I would have been more gentle, and more caring,

And tried to give you gladness for a space.

I would have brought more warmth into the place,

If I had known.

If I had known what thoughts despairing drew you;

(Why do we never try to understand?)

I would have lent a little friendship to you,

And slipped my hand within your hand,

And made your stay more pleasant in the land,

If I had known.

by Mary Carolyn Davies [9]

BREAKTHROUGH

As a direct result of my nightmarish delivery room experience with Trista, I became very interested in Lamaze Childbirth Education. There *had* to be a better way to experience childbirth! A new "Preparation for Childbirth" course was being offered through our local community college, and Shari Ford asked me to help teach the course. Two nurses gave the Lamaze instruction, and Shari and I taught mother and baby care. It was a wonderful opportunity for this former home economics teacher. I took to it like a fish to water, splashing the expectant parents with all the encouragement and optimism that I felt about pregnancy. Although I had found parenting to be an almost unconquerable challenge, I had loved being pregnant, and nothing could change the enthusiasm that I felt about mother and baby care. The subject matter was totally objective, and I could easily distance myself from my personal parenting challenges.

During the Lamaze portion of the class, I was an active observer, progressively working with the couples in a supportive role. Because I attended Lamaze class every week for over a year, I had the technique down to a fine art. Dave and I were delighted when I became pregnant again. It was a splendid pregnancy. My involvement in the Preparation for Childbirth classes challenged me to stay healthy and active, and to keep my weight down during this pregnancy.

I was an energetic 27 year-old homeowner who enjoyed staying busy. One of my projects in the ninth month of my pregnancy was being a bricklayer – I applied a brick facade to our front porch. My greatest challenge was not bricklaying – it was *bending over* to pick up the bricks! Needless to say, I felt terrific during the entire course of my second pregnancy.

My best friend and I had developed a nice little part-time business hanging wallpaper. Diane Ziegler and I continued our very physical work almost to the end of my pregnancy. The bending and stretching was wonderful exercise, but I can still visualize the workdays when I had become too "great with child" to hang and trim wallpaper in tight quarters. I decided to take maternity leave when I actually got stuck in the tight corner of a client's bathroom!

While we were laughing over my "condition," that client shared some inspirational personal information that proved, years later, to be almost prophetic. She told me about the winter long ago, when little Mary Dale Seaton suffered frostbite on both hands. She told me that during her childhood she was always embarrassed because of her misshapen hands. But as the years passed, she came to regard the deformities as a special gift. Mary Dale had endured much physical and emotional anguish because of her injured hands, although she knew she was a stronger person because of it. She shared that God had made her very strong through her sufferings That conversation would be replayed many times in my memory, as my life as a mother proceeded to unfold.

My partner, Diane, and her mother, Dolores Sedgewick, *often* spoke to me about God. They *frequently* told me that they were praying for Trista and our family. I knew they meant well but I was, nonetheless, offended. Once I responded cattily, "I guess if that makes you feel better, then that is fine with me." That was the extent of my faith. They talked about God and Jesus like they were *real people*. Putting up with their banter about religious things seemed to be the price I must pay for friendship and our partnership. I enjoyed working with Diane. She was my closest, nicest friend, and I liked her mother. I was always annoyed by their religious talk but I was, strangely, drawn to them.

As happened in my first pregnancy, I was overdue – a full four weeks past the due date. But when Tia was born on July 29, 1974, the only reason I went to the hospital for delivery was because that is what I thought I should do! Home births weren't really in vogue yet, although I could have easily delivered my baby at home, without any assistance at all. I was in total control during the entire labor and delivery. In fact, I almost **did** deliver my second child at home! My breathing and relaxation techniques were so effective that I was dilated four centimeters (I checked myself) before I was convinced that I was actually in labor. When I woke Dave and told him it was "time," he rushed Trista to the babysitter and returned to shuttle me to the hospital. During that short 15 minutes while he was gone, I had progressed from four centimeters to the urge to push! That meant I was probably fully dilated (9 or 10 centimeters), and **ready** to deliver our baby! Dave sped me those four short blocks to the hospital, while I used the puffing technique to delay the birth. Although I waited impatiently on the delivery-room table, Lamaze had prepared me well. When my doctor finally did arrive, he didn't have to tell me twice to "push!"

With one very efficient push, Tia Sherrell Conklin was born. I was so skilled in the breathing and pushing techniques that the expulsion was excessively rapid. She was a chunky little baby, with strong vital signs and wonderful color. Years later we learned that rapid expulsion during the birth process is suspected to be a perinatal cause of Cerebral Palsy. [10] Tia would later be diagnosed with Left Hemiplegia Cerebral Palsy (CP) – paralysis on the left side of her body.

I loved breastfeeding and caring for a newborn, and Tia was a model baby who cooed for everyone and loved to be cuddled. This was such a welcome change from when Trista was an infant, we could hardly comprehend the contrast! Trista, age two and one-half, hardly noticed that we had an addition to the family. She was still our busy little hummingbird, flitting from one thing to another, and the new baby was just an environmental adjustment, with little impact on her life.

Tia's doctor was in Hermiston. Trista's doctor was in Umatilla, a few miles away. It was a hassle whenever I needed to take Trista out to her doctor. I didn't like having to hire a babysitter, nor did I like having to wait in the little clinic for what seemed an eternity. The kind, methodical doctor always seemed to have all the time in the world for his patients, but every client paid the price in the waiting room for that kind of office attention! It seemed that he was always *hours* behind schedule by the time we got in to see him.

I knew the Hermiston Medical Center had many doctors, and it had a reputation for seeing patients expediently. So I decided to consolidate our doctoring. I transferred our little family's medical files to one location, at the Hermiston Medical Center. It was a perfect arrangement: I could walk to the clinic with Tia in the stroller and Trista on her tricycle. It was good exercise for me, and we made it a fun time whenever one of us had a checkup.

It always amazes me how seemingly insignificant events often change a person's life. Making a decision based on expediency issues would mark a breakthrough in the challenges we were facing with Trista. I was soon to have the most valuable doctor's appointment of my lifetime!

~ ~ ~

DEEP THOUGHTS ABOUT HARD TIMES

God sends trials not to impair us,
but to improve us.

Storms make a strong tree.

Great trials prepare for great service.

The darker the night, the nearer the dawn.

A smooth sea never made a skillful mariner.

No branch escapes the pruning knife;
No jewel the polishing wheel;
No child the correction rod;
No chosen vessel the thorn.

In times of affliction we commonly meet
the sweetest experiences of the love of God. [11]

FIRST DIAGNOSIS

It was my first visit to the Hermiston Medical Center. Dr. James Henneberg was our community's newest family physician. I was very impressed by this young, handsome doctor, for he seemed progressive, professional and thorough. After he wrote out my prescription, he turned to me and asked, "Is your little girl *always* this active?" I swallowed hard and inquired what he meant. He replied that Trista had not stopped moving from the time he had entered the room. He quipped that while he examined me once, Trista had examined the entire room and its contents *three* times!

Dr. Henneberg suspected that Trista had Minimal Brain Dysfunction (MBD). "We can generally spot these kids," he said. "We have to peel them off the ceiling." Tears flooded my eyes. Finally! Someone finally saw it! I had repeatedly asked a variety of doctors about Trista, and their answers were always the same: "It's just a stage; she'll grow out of it." This bright young doctor saw more than a "stage."

In spite of all my concern for her, it never occurred to me that there could be something *seriously* wrong with Trista. I was relieved, but at the same time I was unnerved by the doctor's concern.

Dr. Henneberg scheduled Trista to be seen by Dr. Schaefer, a respected pediatrician in Walla Walla, 60 miles away. Trista was given a thorough examination during our intake appointment in November, 1974. We tried to tell Dr. Schaefer everything we could about Trista's behavior. I talked about my frustrations with motherhood. We told him how concerned we were about Trista's developmental delays, her high activity level, and her distractibility.

The pediatrician returned the verdict: Minimal Cerebral Dysfunction, Retarded Developmental Pattern, and Hyperactivity.

We were sent home with the new Feingold Diet, a non-salicylate diet that was proving helpful for some hyperactive children. We were instructed to fast from all foods containing food additives, food coloring, refined flours and refined sugars. It seemed easiest to just change the entire family's diet during her trial period, so we all went on the rigid Feingold Diet. The rapid and extreme change in food was such a shock to our systems that each one of us had thrush-like symptoms for a week. I was breastfeeding Tia, and *she* even reacted to *my* dietary change. There was a red rash inside all our mouths. Dave and my mouths were intensely sore, so we *knew* that Trista and Tia also shared that uncomfortable side effect. We felt so sorry for our little girls. They were both under three years old – we were already experimenting on Trista, and it had backfired on *both* girls. It was just a rapid dietary change but it was also an insult to their little bodies. As our mouths healed, we watched with anticipation for changes in Trista's activity level.

To our disappointment, nothing changed. We abandoned the diet after three months, seeing no improvement in Trista's problems.

Dr. Schaefer had also mentioned Ritalin, [12] an amphetamine which he had used with some success on hyperactive children. Ritalin is a stimulant, and for hyperactive children, it somehow stimulates the area of the brain which, in normal people, inhibits excessive activity and increases attention span. For such children, the drug essentially urges the appropriate area of the brain to function at higher performance, which helps the child to be less distractible and less hyperactive. But Dr. Schaefer was reluctant to prescribe Ritalin for Trista because she was so young. And, he could not predict the long-range effects of this fairly new drug.

One month after we abandoned the Feingold Diet, we seemed super-sensitized to Trista's problems. I had been reading about minimal brain dysfunction and hyperactivity, and the future seemed ominous. I was slipping back into depression. And I began drinking heavily again. Dave tried to alleviate my strain by helping out with the children. We were both concerned that Tia, who was only seven months old, would be adversely affected by all of Trista's problems.

~ ~ ~

to Tia: may you not hear.

So sweet.
Your smile explodes, fades, returns;
Your little eyes twinkle.
You must feel our love;
You return it so quickly.

Are you in a shell?   To sister
we plead, warn, command, punish.
I glance at you – not even aware!

Is it only happiness you understand?

Your day will come.
But please. Not like sister's!
Make it slow — quiet — inward.

And may we not forget
how quickly you grow — hear — understand.

Easy on sister.
Easy on sister.
Monkey see, monkey do?

Easy, mama. Be kind.
Tia's learning too!

February, 1975

Trista – 1973

Pen & Ink drawing by Paulette Carter Bartee

I was always amazed that Paulette captured Trista in this wonderful sketch because our little girl, who was so active, could not have stopped very long to play in the sandbox!

From Schaefer to Cylert

I wrote Dr. Schaefer, requesting a trial period with Ritalin. He complied.

hyper!

Fidget, squirm, jump,
run, trip, fall, yell, cry, run,
tug, pull,
beg.   Divert. Sit, fidget, drop,
        down, away,
        back, up, eat, fidget, squirm,
        down, away.
                Hyper . . . indeed!
                hyper . . . and how!
                active . . . all the time.

Proceed with Caution.
Slow Down.
Walk. Don't Run.
Watch Your Step.
        Nonsense. You can't.
        I'm here to remind –
        beg – nag – bribe.
        Something's got to help you . . .
        or is it me?
                You're happy – and
                making me miserable.
                And you don't even know.
                "She seems normal to me . . ."

Ha! They don't know.
I know – I worry – I cry –
I ache to see you normal.
        Please, Ritalin;
        do your trick! Give us
        some time. Freedom.
                Speed her up
                to slow her down.
                I may be gone

March, 1975   before you know it!

After two months of undesirable side effects from low doses of Ritalin, we gave up. There were some positive results: it *had* calmed her. But we were now having to handle Trista with kid gloves. The medication had affected her sleep and her appetite, and her emotional state had become as delicate as mine. It was not fair to do this to any child.

Dr. Schaefer recommended a child psychologist at the Pediatric Clinic of the University of Oregon Medical School in Portland. The high-powered examination was a disappointment. It was a repeat performance of previous appointments that were much closer to home – the same examinations, the same interviews, the same advice. The team of psychologists reiterated that Trista was, indeed, hyperactive; that she was too young for drug therapy; and that we should treat her as a special child, and hope for the best. It all seemed so futile.

To further complicate matters, we discovered when Tia was 13 months old that she had Cerebral Palsy (CP). During her first year, I had taken Tia to her doctor more than once, just for extra examinations. We kept inquiring, "Why is her left fist always clenched so tightly?" "Why does she only roll over in one direction?" And, "Why is Tia having such a difficult time learning to crawl?" When she did finally begin crawling, it was very strange looking locomotion! The doctor always smiled and assured me that she was just "very right-handed!" We were pacified by his interpretation until Dave's mother, Norma, insisted, "There's *something wrong* with that child!" When we took Tia to a local pediatrician, he said that all these problems were "typical for kids with CP." I had never even *heard* of cerebral palsy. He thought we *knew* that she had CP, and he was most apologetic for springing the bad tidings on us so abruptly. The doctor explained that Tia had some paralysis on her left side; she would probably never skip or swing or type, but there was no reason why she could not live an otherwise normal life. CP is a congenital disorder, and we were assured that it is neither hereditary nor progressive. The pediatrician arranged for Tia to see an orthopedist and a physical therapist.

I was numb. I didn't think I could take much more!

The pain of my heart haunted me almost every moment. When I wasn't crying, I was playing mind games – trying to justify my thoughts of running away from my problems. If I did run away, I knew I would eventually have to return. I could not *face* the humiliation of having walked out on my children. (And I felt I would surely be *found* because in all my travels, I had never gone anywhere that I hadn't been greeted by someone who had recognized me!) Even a vacation from my family was no solution – I would still have to return. I was trapped, by my own doing, with no way of escape. It was *my* idea to leave teaching and get pregnant. Failure was not in my personal vocabulary. But with *two* very special children, I was between that proverbial rock and a hard spot. In the autumn of 1975, I made the decision that I must *live* with the consequences of my decisions.

One summer day in 1976, both girls were napping. Naps were a sacred time in our home; we three girls all participated! However, that day I couldn't rest. I tossed and turned on my bed, with an ache in my heart and tears drenching my pillow. I didn't know how to pray. Agnostics don't pray. Finally, I got down on my knees, and I held my hands in the air like I'd seen in movies. I begged, "**God, if you are really real, help me!**"

Several minutes passed. I felt nothing. I didn't know what to expect, so I wasn't disappointed. I dried my tears and called Dr. Henneberg's office to request another referral to the University of Oregon Medical School. But this time I asked for an appointment in a *different* department, the Crippled Children's Division. I took the first available appointment — six weeks away. Someone had mentioned to me previously that we might want to pursue this alternative, but until that moment, I had never even considered making another trip to the medical school. As I sat there with the phone and note pad on my lap, things seemed better already. And I hadn't even left the bedroom!

The six weeks passed quickly. The first appointment lasted a total of **six hours**! Trista was examined and observed, continuously, by a variety of specialists for four wearisome hours. Some of the physicians played with her while others watched her through a one-way mirror. Meanwhile, we were held captive by what seemed like an endless army of specialists who probed every detail of our lives, gathering more information than we knew we had in us. While Trista was having a delightful time, Dave and I felt like we were pulled through a knothole backwards! It was a shattering experience for both of us, but probably more-so for me because I was severely depressed. I had been wrestling with deep feelings of inadequacy – in myself, in my commitment to my family, and especially in my ability as a mother. Tears streamed down my face during most of the day's investigative drills. I secretly wondered if this team would concur with the minister's earlier recommendation – if they, too, would suggest that Trista be placed in another home, where there was a *better* mom.

After the team had a private consultation, Dave and I were invited to join them for a lengthy overview. We were informed that our local doctor was "right on." Trista's problem really *was* Minimal Brain Dysfunction (MBD). They explained that an area of Trista's brain was not operating at full capacity, and that was the cause of her characteristically short attention span and distractibility. Her long-term prognosis was that she *might* eventually grow out of MBD, or perhaps she would learn to cope with it.

Our concern was what would happen in the meantime; what kind of damage would we be doing to Trista by just *waiting* for her to grow out of her disability? In my husband's eight years of teaching fifth grade, Dave worked with several children who had similar problems of short attention span and high distractibility. He *knew* the unfair disadvantage they suffered – how difficult school was for them; how badly they were teased by their peers; how those children often became school and society's misfits; and how marriages often seemed to fracture in the midst of problems with handicapped children. The dark cloud settled over both of us.

A final team of doctors summoned us. Those specialists recommended trying drug therapy again. But this time they suggested a slightly different medication. Cylert [13] was a new drug which some physicians had found helpful with minimal brain dysfunction.

We embraced the doctors' counsel. The next day, five year-old Trista began a progressive dose of Cylert.

Most mothers know that when school starts in the fall, several routines change. Trista would go off to school, and Tia and I would hurry to get our housework done in the mornings so we could spend time together with other young mothers and their children, doing scheduled activities that were fun for both the children *and* the moms. I especially remember one autumn day at Hermiston's McKenzie Park. Sue DeGroote had been there for some time when I arrived. While her little Jenny and Jason were playing on the swings, Sue was working on a woman's Bible study lesson. When I sat down on the blanket, she began to talk about Jesus as though she really *knew* him. Sue had just moved into our neighborhood, and this was our first opportunity to get acquainted. Sue explained to me that she had been a church member all her life, but she just became a Christian. I couldn't *imagine* what she was talking about. Although I often referred to myself as an agnostic to keep people like Sue from being pushy with their religion, *I thought I was a Christian because I was a church member, and because I had been baptized*! I knew this was a discussion I was not interested in pursuing. I changed the subject.

About a month later, I heard about a luncheon that was being hosted by a new group in town – Christian Women's Club. [14] I liked luncheons, I thought I was a Christian, and I was a woman, so it seemed like an appropriate activity for me. I went alone and was seated with women I did not know. We were served a wonderful lunch, we enjoyed musical entertainment, and there was a short fashion show. Just as I thought the event was concluding, a speaker was introduced. The woman was the Justice of the Peace for Grant County, in central Oregon. She shared her heart-wrenching story about the many hard times that she had experienced as an actress in New York and as an engineering-draftsman for my favorite bridge in Portland, Oregon. Plus, she was now residing in the region where my husband was raised so I was especially interested. Judge Jean Zeiler [15] told how she met Jesus Christ as her personal Savior, and how her life had changed after she became "born again." It was evident that this woman had something that I did not!

She was just like my friends, Diane, Dolores, and Sue: they all seemed to know Jesus personally, and that relationship seemed to give those women great strength. I *knew I needed* whatever it was that every one of those women had. As the speaker closed the meeting, she said something like, "If anyone in this room does not know Jesus Christ as your personal Savior, I invite you to repeat this prayer after me." Then she prayed aloud, giving us the opportunity to ask Jesus into our hearts.

After the prayer, Judge Zeiler said, "If you prayed that prayer with me, please tell me by giving me your nametag as you go out the door." I gave her my nametag.

A woman I did not know contacted me the following day and invited me to a Christian Women's Club Bible Study for new Christians. I began the very next week and attended faithfully for months. But the lessons were *so* difficult for me to understand! I did all my homework but I proved to be a very poor student of the Bible. It seemed that *nothing* in the Book made sense! It was a terrible embarrassment to me because I had always been a very good student in everything else. Nonetheless, I did enjoy being around this new group of acquaintances, and I found myself drawn to participate in everything they invited me to do. It was a wonderful time in my life as I discovered a quality of friendship and support with these Christian women that I did not know was possible. Even though I felt confused about the Bible, I had found a level of peace that was nothing short of a miracle! Sometimes I felt such love from the Lord, and such joy inside of me, that I actually found myself skipping and dancing after I prayed privately! I wondered if I had become manic-depressive because I *knew* what low felt like, but I had never experienced this kind of *high*!

The sudden change in me did not go unnoticed. One day I was outside, working in the yard. Dave and a neighbor were stacking wood and visiting, and I overheard Dave tell the neighbor, "Jean sure has changed since she got saved!" It stopped me in my tracks. I didn't realize *that* is what happened to me when I prayed! All my life, I had heard people speak of getting saved but I never knew what it meant. I remember standing there in the shadows, thinking, "So *that's* what happened to me!" I mulled that one over for days.

It was difficult for me to ask Dave if we could start going to church. I had always fought his appeals, and the few times that we had gone to church together were a dreadful experience for me. It seemed we always went to churches where there was unfamiliar liturgy, and where everything was done differently than what I had grown up with. Whenever I had given in to Dave's beckoning, I felt like a hypocrite because I simply was not interested in any form of religion. We ultimately had made a "truce" – we agreed that if Dave wanted to go to church, he should just go, and not pester me about it. And he did occasionally take the girls and go without me. So when I suddenly *wanted* to attend church, of course I felt awkward about the unexplainable turnabout, and I spent *days* rehearsing how I would ask if we could start a new Sunday routine. My fretting was in vain. Dave is so wise, and such a gentleman, that when I asked him if we could take the girls to church the next Sunday, he just casually responded, "Where shall we go?" We talked about all the churches in town, and we selected the one where our friends attended because they had said it had a good nursery. Subsequent to my rather awkward beginnings, church involvement has always continued to be a high priority in our family.

A few months later, Tia and I were at Sue's new house. Sue was such a special person, and I was drawn to her. I knew she was having serious personal problems but, in spite of that, she seemed to be so happy and full of peace. While she was in the kitchen fixing snacks for the children, I noticed a newspaper clipping that announced a meeting for Women's Aglow Fellowship.[16] I asked Sue what Aglow was. She explained that it was a group of Christian women who met monthly. She said the name was coined because the founders felt they were "aglow with the Lord." I could really relate to that phrase because that was how I had been feeling. When she invited me to go with her to the meeting the next evening, I didn't hesitate. The Aglow meeting was incredible! The women seemed so "complete." They weren't striving or social climbing, or deeply committed to some social "cause;" they just seemed to have a firm grip on their lives, and they were so hospitable. They seemed fulfilled and at peace with themselves, even though I knew that many of them were living with some *real* challenges. *And*, they were worshipping the Lord the same way I had been doing secretly! They had *such freedom* to pray and praise. I wanted *more* of that!

The speaker shared her story about her experiences with the Holy Spirit. The "Holy Ghost" always sounded so scary in my childhood church, but this Holy Spirit sounded wonderfully inviting, even though I didn't understand it at all. Although I had already asked Jesus to be my Savior, I had so much trouble understanding the Bible and my new relationship with Christ. It seemed that I was still confused about the *really important things* that help people get through each day. I felt like there was something more that I needed. I wanted *all* I could get from God, but I didn't know what that was, nor how I could get it.

After the Aglow meeting, I asked the women to pray for me. They surrounded me, touched my shoulders and prayed with me as I asked God to baptize me in the Holy Spirit.[17] The transformation in me seemed immediate! It was as though the scales dropped from my eyes *and* my understanding. I began to understand the Bible better, and I had an insatiable *need* to study it. And I became so fascinated with God's Word and His presence that, very simply, my thirst could not be quenched. The only time I had ever experienced anything similar was when I met my future husband – I fell so head-over-heels in love with Dave that I wanted to spend *every minute* with him! I literally fell head-over-heels in love with the Lord. I don't know how that happens, but it was such a remarkable change in my life, that some of my extended family doubted for many years the validity of my transformation.

It is probably because I experienced such *freedom* to share what happened in my life that others, who were looking for the same power that I had received, were drawn to me. In the years to come, I would pray with many women whose problems were far worse than mine. And I would see their lives transformed just as miraculously and as permanently as mine.[18]

I know that God designed this agenda for me because lurking on the horizon were some extraordinarily difficult problems that would challenge me for the rest of my life. My faith is the only thing that has sustained me.

~ ~ ~

ELEMENTARY DAZE

Five year-old Trista took Cylert for several months. We saw some nice benefits from the drug therapy. Cylert (pemoline) stimulates the central nervous system, "although its mechanism of action is not known in children with attention deficit disorder (formerly called hyperactivity)." [19] Our little girl was not quite so busy, she seemed more focused, and she was definitely less distractible. We felt like the University doctors had given us a miracle drug, and we reveled in the welcome reprieve.

Then we began to notice some subtle, strange things starting to happen. At first Trista seemed to just be blinking her eyes a lot. As abruptly as it began, the eye blinking stopped. And then a few days later she started stretching her mouth. After that went away, we noticed she began facial grimacing. The grimacing disappeared, and Trista was back to blinking. But, this time when she blinked she also squeezed her eyes shut really tightly. These odd movements were elusive, and at first we didn't pay much attention to them. Just about the time we would become concerned about one movement, it would simply go away. And then, after a little while – one hour, one day, one week, or sometimes several weeks – something new would start. I can not say these unusual movements were especially bothersome in those early days – they were just a source of concern.

After observing the progress of the symptoms for several months, we decided it was time for another trip to the Crippled Children's Division. After the doctors examined Trista, they informed us that these "facial tics" were probably a side effect of Cylert. The doctors left it up to us to determine our course of action. We could keep her on the medication and live with the tics, or we could take her off the medicine, and the tics would probably go away.

We immediately took her off Cylert. Trista was too young for us to take chances with medication. Medicine has always been our treatment of last choice, and we gave this drug to her only when we felt we had exhausted all our other resources. When we stopped Trista's medication, we expected the tics to go away as subtly as they had appeared.

The tics did *not* go away.

And . . . *new* tics came!

Some of the new tics were little noises. Little grunting noises. And then the grunting stopped. Then she switched to making sniffing noises, as though she had a runny nose. In the beginning, her tics were singular – only one type of tic manifested itself at a time. It would stay around for awhile, and then leave as abruptly as it began. Another tic would start, stay awhile, and go away.

Trista was five-and-a-half when her tics began. As the years marched on, she began to display more than one tic at a time. And we began to observe that the physical movements *and* sounds or utterances were sometimes present simultaneously. Some of her tics were simple, straightforward manifestations; but *some* were complex, ritualistic movements and sound sequences. It was beyond our comprehension how one person's body could do so many things all at once, with that person being hardly even aware of it. She even did those things in her sleep!

Her tics were totally unpredictable, and they seemed to become increasingly bizarre. She would occasionally have a few tic-free weeks, but these mini periods of remission were often followed by *intense* new tics that gave new meaning to our understanding of the words "unnerving" and "disruptive." Throughout the next seven years, we would see such a potpourri of tics, that we couldn't imagine that there was anything "new" left for her to do!

I wasn't doing very well with all these strange manifestations coming from my sweet little daughter. The simple motor and vocal tics would have been easy enough to disguise, but Trista wasn't concerned about disguising them. She was just Trista – innocent and nice – and very immature, hyperactive and distractible.

School was very difficult for our little girl. She seemed bright enough, but she just couldn't seem to "get it all together." Organized learning had been a challenge to Trista from her very first school days. I always felt sorry for the teachers when I would drop her off for even a few hours at preschool; I *knew* her teachers really earned their pay, with the challenges that Trista presented!

After her rather non-productive first year in grade school, we made the very difficult decision to disregard the counsel of the well-meaning West Park Elementary School staff. We chose to have Trista repeat the year. They argued that Trista was a Christmas baby; she was, therefore, *already* almost a year older than most of her classmates. They warned that having her repeat her first grade might do more harm than good. She would catch up sooner or later, they reassured us.

We weren't very experienced parents but we *were* the parents. We knew that we had to do what we felt was best, and Dave and I had no misgivings about this decision. We arranged for Trista to repeat first grade, at the school across town where Dave was the physical education teacher. Trista had a delightful repeat year with Miss Bonnie House's first graders at Sunset Elementary School. In spite of all her problems, she loved going to school in those early years! At the end of her second year in first grade, we wished we could hold her back yet *another* year. That seemingly *would* have been impractical.

While all this was happening, Tia had been receiving physical therapy for her cerebral palsy through our county's Education Service District. Those sessions were held year-around at the neighborhood elementary school, and since I had to take Tia there frequently, we decided to enroll Trista in a special summer reading program that was designed to help slow readers. Under the tender guidance of John Sipp, in just two short months Trista transformed from a non-reader into an *outstanding* reader and speller! It was incredible to watch Trista catch up so fast in this one area, and that rapid progress gave us great hope. We re-enrolled her in West Park School for her second grade, and we procured extra help for her from anyone that showed an interest in meeting her special needs. Sadly, school remained incredibly difficult for Trista.

Although she was now almost *two* years older than her classmates, throughout the rest of her school career she would be immature, hyperactive, compulsive, and highly distractible.

Tia was now just one grade behind Trista, but the younger sister was beginning to assume the role of the "protective older sister." Together, we sheltered Trista from everything we could. We were embarrassed *for* her, but it is also painfully accurate to say we were embarrassed *about* her and *by* her. We begged Trista to stop doing those weird things and making those annoying sounds. We bribed, we chided, we punished. Nothing worked. Tics came, stayed awhile, and went away. New tics came, stayed awhile, and went away. We never knew what to expect next. I got to the point that I was afraid to pray for the tics to go away because they *would* go away – but a worse tic would almost always come in its place. Sometimes it seemed best to just leave well enough alone.

We couldn't *imagine* what was wrong with Trista. No one had a clue. I had never seen anyone do anything like what Trista was doing, *except* for one group of people in our church. They were a large extended family who had all sorts of similar strange movements and gestures. But those people were extremely talented and otherwise poised, and it was as though none of them even noticed that they all had such strange manifestations. And of course, I would never have dared to ask them if they knew *why* they did those strange movements and sounds. [Many of the family members were later diagnosed with the same affliction as Trista.]

One lazy summer day, the radio was playing in the background as was cleaning house. I heard, but didn't *really* hear, the tail-end of a Public Service Announcement (PSA) on the radio. The PSA was talking about symptoms similar to Trista's. By the time I mentally tuned in to the message, all I could write on a scrap of paper were the words "tour," and "New York." Although I was not even certain what I had heard, I knew it was something important about Trista's queer manifestations. I kept thinking I would hear the announcement once more. For weeks, I listened intently for that advertisement but I never heard it again. In 1980, I did not know where to begin to trace a PSA, in spite of the fact that I had worked for a radio station nine years earlier. (I did not realize that radio stations were required to keep a log of every PSA that was aired.)

Two months had passed since I scribbled those three unrelated words, and I couldn't get them off my mind. One day I visited with the school psychologist from our Educational Service District. He had a good reputation, and both he and his wife were well-known among our educator friends. I mentioned the PSA and showed him my notes on the scrap of paper. He said he had heard about a disorder called "Tourette," but he was *certain* that was not what Trista had. I have always been very trusting of people who are supposed to know more than me, and I let this man's Ph.D. intimidate and detour me. We would wait four more years for an accurate diagnosis.

I believe God was earnestly trying to help us because we came so close once again, two years later. But just like with the PSA incident, we would miss the mark again. Trista's fourth grade teacher, Audney Cosand, inquired if we had ever heard about "Tourette Syndrome." I told her that I *had* made inquiry about this to the school psychologist, and that he was quite certain that Trista did *not* have Tourette. I dismissed Audney's suggestion as casually as I would turn down liver and onions.

Mrs. Cosand was a good teacher, a neighbor and a friend, and her daughter, Willow, [20] was one of our family's favorite babysitters. I was grateful that Audney made extensive references in Trista's school record, with regard to the challenges her student was experiencing because of her tics. We would later find those records invaluable for documenting Trista's long-standing problems. [21]

In 1983, our family participated in a Fulbright Teacher Exchange to Haverhill, in Suffolk county, England. We lived on quaint-sounding Windmill Rise, in the nearby village of Hundon, for one year. We felt their British transition would be smoother if the girls could attend the same school where their father was teaching, so it was arranged for the girls to attend Parkway Middle School, in Haverhill. In those days, English schools did not hold "slow" children back. A child was enrolled in school when he turned a certain age, and if he needed special attention, the child could be placed on a waiting list for one of the special schools for severely handicapped children. The philosophy was that the "Bell curve" ability-range is always present, even in schoolrooms, and the British educators concluded it was neither prudent to hold slow children back, nor to allow bright children to skip ahead.

We protested Parkway's plans to enroll Trista in the *fourth year* of middle school, along with other 12 year-old children her age. Because of her late Oregon school entry and two years in first grade, she really should have been placed in the *second-year* class in the English school system. That proposition was totally unacceptable to the headmaster. We reached a compromise, with placement in the *third-year* class. It was too much. She struggled academically and socially the entire year. Trista simply was not ready to play catch-up in a foreign school environment.

It was in England that we began to suspect that stress made Trista's tics worse. The more challenges she met in school, the worse her tics became. She had a wonderfully kind and sensitive teacher, but young Mr. Fillingham was being stretched with Trista in his third-year class. He had never been taught to work with special-needs children, and he had little exposure to the kinds of adaptive teaching we Americans had become accustomed to. The entire English school system seemed rigid and geared towards achievement. There was just not much provision in their neighborhood schools to accommodate low-achievers and students with multiple challenges. Although the *philosophy* was to serve all students equally, there was no money allocated to give wings to good intentions. It was the familiar budget crunch issue: schools with limited finances must place their funds where they reap the "biggest bang for the buck." Special programs which serve exclusive student populations are usually very expensive, and the way this played out in England was that the special needs of handicapped students were, of necessity, virtually disregarded in their neighborhood schools.

It was also our first-month observation that British parents were unaccustomed to the level of school involvement that most

American parents take for granted. I dare-say that we felt British parents were *not* particularly *welcome* to be active participants at their children's schools. When we arrived, we also discovered that Americans were viewed with suspicion and distrust in *this* particular locality because there were several American military bases nearby, and the cruise-missile controversy was at its peak. Inasmuch as we were also the "new kids on the block" *and* guests of the British school system, it was not appropriate for me to attempt to work with the teachers in the same manner that I had been doing in Hermiston.

But God brought Trista to the attention of one very special teacher in that English middle school. Mrs. Jean Perry was a French teacher, and she became our on-site savior-advocate for Trista at Parkway Middle School. Jean was a tenderhearted, compassionate grandmother who observed our older daughter's plight. She volunteered to came alongside Trista, and she supported her in countless ways. Jean helped Trista but, more importantly, she provided a safe haven for our child. All of Trista's problems did not disappear after she met Mrs. Perry. But at least Trista had *one* true friend in the school. We eventually convinced the headmaster that the year was probably going to be written off as a waste for Trista, and the school authorities accepted that we were not going to hold their system accountable for how well (or how poorly) Trista performed. After that milestone, she spent as much time as was feasible with Mrs. Perry. Trista didn't learn any French but she was far removed from the very structured British classroom atmosphere.

Our other daughter's disability, on the other hand, had never been a problem in our American school environment. Tia was always such a good student that her cerebral palsy problems were very much in the background. Her doctors always stressed that her own activity would be her best therapy, and she did all the things doctors said she probably would *not* do: she swung and skipped and compensated beautifully. Her left hand was significantly paralyzed and much smaller than her right, and the characteristic spasticity caused her arm to be carried close to her chest whenever she was physically active. Her left leg was a little short, and she walked with a mild limp, and ran with a definite limp, with her left arm elevated awkwardly. Nonetheless, Tia always had a smile on her face, and she was so considerate and charismatic that casual observers frequently did not realize she even *had* a disability.

Tia's handicap *did*, however, present some challenges in the British school system. Although the teachers were empathic and supportive, they just couldn't bend the rules to accommodate her special needs. To cite one example of their rigidity, part of her curriculum included swimming lessons at the municipal pool. During the final examination, the students donned pajamas over their "swimming costume." They were to jump into the pool, remove their pajamas, swim across the pool, and climb out on the other side, unassisted by a ladder or human help. Although we used Velcro instead of buttons so she could remove her pajamas, it was physically impossible for her to climb, unassisted, out of the pool because she only had the use of her right side. Tia was an excellent swimmer but she failed the performance examination. She was the only child in her class who did not receive the certificate of achievement for swimming. Ten year-old Tia was bewildered, embarrassed, and deeply hurt.

Tia was fortunate to have many nice friends in England, and other than some periodic glitches due to lack of accommodation for her paralysis, she had a fantastic year. Trista, on the other hand, had no school-age friends, and she was frequently the victim of insensitive children *and* adults. Trista's tics were severe that year in England – the worst that we had yet experienced. Her tics increased proportionately with school stress. I *lived* for school "holidays," so that we could get our 12 year-old daughter out of her stressful environment. In hindsight, I am reminded that we need to count our blessings even on this unsettling experience because the Parkway School staff did all they knew how to do for Trista, and they became our family-away-from-home. What her British deputy-headmaster (vice-principal) said is true: "Trista was a bit more cotton-wooled [coddled] at Parkway, than she ever would have ever been at [any of the other neighborhood schools]." [22] Blessings come in a variety of wrappers.

In those later years of grade school, when it seemed that Trista should have been more aware of (and therefore, in more control of) the amazing things her body was doing, her tics seemed to be more intense, more noticeable, and more disruptive. And it was becoming fairly apparent that she was *unable* to control them. I was so consumed with Trista's problems that I was in a constant state of anxiety, dismay, frustration, and depression. My moods paralleled Trista. When she was up, I was up; when she was down, I was down. For a family who had children with some special needs, the decision to participate in a foreign teacher exchange was probably not the wisest. It was a very long year for me in England!

Seven years had passed since Trista's first tics began. We had no explanation for what they were, nor for what was causing them. Only three things were fairly certain: There was nothing *we* could do to make her stop her tics, *Trista* could not stop her tics, and *stress* seemed to make them worse. I could not wait to get Trista back home to America.

~ ~ ~

TOURETTE SYNDROME

It is there night and day.
It will never go away.
I feel trapped in a pit, but
I've learned to live with it.

Kids make fun of me,
but they just can't see
that deep inside,
a beautiful person hides.

Life is more difficult,
but I know it's not my fault.
God made me this way
even before my birthday.

If there's ever a cure,
you can be very sure
I will be there
no matter where.

But until I'm cured,
be assured
I will patiently wait
for that wonderful date.

by Michelle Macconi [23]
(age 12)

A Correct Diagnosis, At Last!

My parents picked us up at the Seattle Airport when we returned from our year abroad. During the drive home, Mom mentioned that she had sent away for something that she thought might interest me. She had left a white packet on my kitchen counter, and she suggested that perhaps I would like to read it when I had time.

That struck me as an unusual request. My Mom has never been intrusive. After I married and moved away from their home, she rarely asked anything of me.

It was a busy time for our little family, settling back into being Americans after living overseas for the '83 – '84 school year. We exchanged homes and cars with our British counterpart, and the swap proved less than satisfactory. My attentions were scattered among a year's worth of repairs, replacements and readjustments. It was the first part of August, and it seemed that everything inside *and* outside the house needed attention. I pushed the white packet aside until a more convenient time.

One of the hardest things about traveling abroad is adjusting one's body clock to the new time zone. I'm a night person anyway, so my body clock was completely upside down when we returned to America. One late night in mid-August, I was still unable to sleep. I wandered about the house, looking for something to do. I noticed the white packet of materials that Mom had left for me to read. It was more out of a sense of obligation to my mother, than out of personal desire, that I read the materials inside the packet. Should Mom ask me if I had looked at them, I wanted to be able to say, "Yes."

I made a cup of hot tea, curled up in my favorite blue rocker, and opened the white envelope. What I read in the next few minutes changed our lives forever.

I had only looked at the first page of the first pamphlet when I *knew* we had a correct diagnosis for Trista! Described in those brochures and articles were *exact* illustrations and examples of Trista's problems. I felt as though Trista's biography was written on every piece of paper in that packet! It was incomprehensible to me that my daughter's symptoms could be so completely described in those materials, and yet an accurate diagnosis for Trista had been elusive to even the most skilled professionals.

I read the materials again and again that night, highlighting the important points in every article. And then I penned a short note to Dr. Henneberg, asking him to review the materials in the white packet. I explained that I would be requesting an appointment, during which time I would like to have him observe Trista with respect to this possible diagnosis. I placed my note in the packet of highlighted materials, and I was waiting with the packet at the Medical Center door when they opened at 7:30 a.m. I was so excited! I don't think I had slept a wink that night. When I returned from my errand, Dave was home from his morning run. With animation, I told Dave about the materials, but since I had already deposited them at the Medical Center, I had nothing to show my husband. All he could do was listen to me babble that "we had a correct diagnosis for Trista – I was *absolutely positive!*"

Dave left for his first day of teacher in-service, and I waited with anticipation for our afternoon doctor's appointment. Dr. Henneberg had just completed looking through the materials when we arrived. He agreed that Trista's symptoms mirrored the information in the white packet. He *had* heard about Tourette Syndrome. But the young doctor had never actually seen anyone with Tourette Syndrome, and he wanted Trista to visit a specialist. We were given a September 5 appointment in the Neurology Department at the University of Oregon Medical School. Waiting for that first appointment was the longest week of my life!

Dr. Isom was the head Pediatric Neurologist at the Medical School. He did a brief examination of Trista and reviewed her chart. Then we were rather offhandedly presented with the official diagnosis: **Trista, age 12-and-one-half, had a classic case of Tourette Syndrome with associated disorders.**

We *knew* she had the associated disorder of minimal brain dysfunction, which was then being called hyperactivity, poor attention span, and learning disabilities. But we had *not* known what was causing those *tics*. She had lived with that bizarre malady since she was five-and-a-half. One brief appointment in Portland solved the mystery of *seven years* of "ticking!" The doctor unceremoniously wrote a prescription for Haldol[24] and promptly dismissed us.

The diagnosis was bittersweet. On one hand, we finally had a conclusive diagnosis that appeared to be absolutely correct. The affliction was treatable. The medication had a good track record for controlling Tourette tics, and it was reported to have few side effects. The long-term prognosis was not so encouraging. Trista had a very severe case of Tourette's, and her tics could easily be a lifelong problem for her. But Dave and I felt relief and hope because even though her future might be dim, at least we *knew* what we were dealing with. To our absolute amazement, there appeared to be a plentiful supply of information available on this rare neurological disorder called Tourette Syndrome (TS).

The Tourette Syndrome Association calls Tourette "the world's most common unknown disorder," and the majority of initial diagnoses of TS are actually *self*-diagnoses. As it was with our family, someone reads or hears about the malady, recognizes the unusual symptomology, and goes to a doctor for "official" confirmation. Tourette-awareness advertising has been very beneficial.

The irony of all this was that we were *so close* to a diagnosis four years earlier. The Public Service Announcement that I heard in 1980 described Trista's symptoms. It was sponsored by the Tourette Syndrome Association (TSA) in Bayside, New York. I heard the words "tour" and "New York," and I couldn't piece the information together. The school psychologist *knew instantly* what I was referring to, even though *I* did not! But he offhandedly ruled out the possibility of Tourette Syndrome, based on reasoning that was less than clinical. Why I didn't press in for more accountability, I will never understand. I was wrong to have not questioned the school psychologist's spontaneous judgment. Trista's fourth grade teacher was right all along!

It is my mother who was the *real* hero in this story. She also heard a PSA by the Tourette Syndrome Association, [25] but it was on *her* radio in 1983. I had never mentioned to her about hearing an advertisement in 1980, because it seemed so insignificant. But Mom listens better than I do, and she also takes shorthand. She heard the entire PSA, and *she wrote down the information, with the complete address*. It turned out that my mother had requested the material from the Tourette Syndrome Association around Christmas of 1983. I asked her why she didn't send it to me in England, or insist that I read it immediately when I got home in July. Mom answered that she didn't want to meddle. She wasn't really sure if it was a "match," and she didn't want us to get our hopes up unjustifiably, only to then have them bashed if the information proved irrelevant.

Our awareness of our children's disabilities has emerged stage-by-stage, but we have known from almost the very beginning that both of our children were challenged in unusual ways. In all our years with our children's problems, my parents have stood quietly behind us, supporting us and encouraging us. It is painful to watch your children and grandchildren struggle. But I think it is even more painful to feel so *helpless*. My parents have never pushed, they have never meddled, and they have never condemned nor manipulated. I am grateful to have such wonderful parents. My mother's timing was just right! I dare not think how many more years might have passed before someone finally recognized, *and* had the courage to suggest to us, that Trista's bizarre behaviors *might* be Tourette Syndrome.

~ ~ ~

Editor's note: A GLOSSARY and INDEX are provided for the reader's convenience, as well as an extensive chapter which presents a thorough introduction to Tourette Syndrome and related topics.
See APPENDIX – TELL ME ABOUT TOURETTE SYNDROME

JUNIOR HIGH JOURNEY

Trista was entering sixth grade when we returned from our year in England. It was to be a refreshing time of new beginnings. We had a conclusive *and* a correct diagnosis for what was causing Trista's tics. She was starting to take Haldol, and the medication seemed to provide significant tic suppression. Trista was not particularly bothered by her tics. Nonetheless, they were extremely disruptive in a classroom setting, so the benefits of the medication must have been a welcome relief for her peers *and* her teachers.

We felt fortunate that Trista was in Miss Cheryl Bouchard's classroom. The young teacher was wonderfully sensitive, new to the district, and eager to work with us in creating a safe, supportive school environment.

Miss Bouchard arranged many special opportunities for Trista to experience success. She proved to have a compassionate heart for children with disabilities, and her classroom was a welcome respite for them. (A few years later, Miss Bouchard left the mainstream classroom to became a full-time special education teacher.) After the tumultuous, and generally wasted, year in the English School, Trista enjoyed a delightful sixth grade at West Park Elementary School, thanks to one of the best teachers of her school career.

One of the most helpful things we discovered was the value of teaching Trista's peers about Tourette Syndrome (TS). When we became sufficiently armed with a good understanding of her disorder, we launched an information campaign at Trista's school. We showed Tourette videos. We handed out Tourette brochures. We staged classroom discussions about Tourette. *Everything* helped! **We discovered that the degree of tolerance and compassion demonstrated by both students and teachers was directly proportional to their understanding of the disorder – the more people learned about TS, the easier the situation was for everyone!**

The Tourette Syndrome Association (TSA) even offered a novel brochure, written especially for elementary school children. *MATTHEW AND THE TICS* explained Tourette Syndrome in simple language, and it proved to be a wonderful tool for student education.

As she "outgrew" that TSA brochure, we developed a postcard-size flyer for our daughter to hand out. Our first efforts were rather clumsy, and we have refined it over the years. Even today, she always carries a few cards with her in her purse, and she continues to distribute them freely to friends and strangers. The idea is not unique. The example shown below appeared in a recent Tourette Syndrome Association newsletter – we thought it was special. [26]

AN OPEN LETTER TO NEW FRIENDS ON HER FIRST DAY OF SCHOOL:

Hi! I'm Shelly!

I have something called TOURETTE SYNDROME. Before we get started, I just want to tell you that I'm still a normal kid! Tourette's is not contagious or anything. It's kind of like a disease and I can never get rid of it. I still have a normal kid's life.

It's just that I do stuff that are like bad habits that I'll never be able to get rid of. Sometimes you'll see me rolling my eyes or making a little noise, but that's just part of Tourette's. I can't help what I do, but I can still do the same stuff you can.

I was diagnosed with it when I was 8 years old. I started out with blinking my eyes, always shrugging my shoulders like when you say, "I don't know," stretching my chin and mouth and rolling my head. These actions are called tics. Later in the year I started being afraid to leave the house or go to school. That's when I started taking a new medicine.

I see a special doctor, and sometimes I see Gloria, my nurse. Tics aren't anything you can die from, but they make you uncomfortable sometimes. I hope some of you won't be afraid to be my friend.

Trista slipped into Junior High rather unceremoniously. Mrs. Mary Bousquet staged our first formal Individual Education Plan (IEP) meeting. The IEP is the legal formality required for schools to provide special services to disabled students. IEP forms had been completed by Trista's special education teachers every year since she was in second grade, and we were always called in to sign them at the beginning of every new school year. It just seemed like "paperwork to get services," and I never paid much attention to any of it. I remember thinking that some computer program must have cranked out all this new IEP paperwork for Mrs. Bousquet: although it was wonderfully professional, and appeared to be extremely thorough, it was terribly impersonal and mostly irrelevant. It didn't really matter to us, however, because Mary was very caring and committed to her special-needs students. She created a junior high learning environment that made Trista feel safe and unthreatened. Trista was in the "learning center" part of the day, and this special education atmosphere allowed her to receive extra help whenever she needed it. Mary and her efforts for special children were tremendous blessings.

We thought everything was okay in the seventh grade, until we received her third quarter grades. Trista was struggling in all her classes, and she was behind in *every* one! We requested weekly progress reports, and we got her caught up in all her classes. And then five weeks later, at midterm, she was "going under" again. We requested conferences with all her regular teachers, and we tried to encourage each instructor to consider Trista as a special-needs student in a mainstream atmosphere. Her tics were on the upswing again, and we wished the school year would end more quickly.

The summer of '86 gave us a much needed reprieve. Unfortunately, summer vacations always end. We always dreaded the beginning of new school years, and although Trista still had the protective environment with Mrs. Bousquet, her school mainstream problems *started sooner* and *got worse*. Trista was almost 15.

She suddenly seemed to be especially sensitive to the effect that her tics had on others. She was being ridiculed and chided by her peers, and it became a constant strain for us to keep her spirits up.

One day during a film in science class, Trista's tics were very noisy and especially bothersome. At the evening dinner table, Trista told us about the day's problems. The teacher evidently "got on Trista's case" about the disruption she was causing. Todd Spike, a classmate who had been her friend since preschool, came to her defense and rebuked the teacher by saying, "Trista can't help what she is doing." What a virtuous act that was for a junior-high student!

That her peers were on her case was nothing new. But having a teacher ridicule her was inexcusable. We were incensed! I hand delivered one of my "nasty-grams" to Blaine Downey, who was an excellent new counselor at our junior high school. [27]

Blaine:

For some unknown reason, Trista's tics are much worse lately. She has expressed concern that she is being a bother to students *and* teachers in her classes.

We are wondering if a note from you to all her teachers might be in order – reminding them of

    (1) the involuntary nature of Tourette; and

    (2) the way it waxes and wanes for no apparent reason; but

    (3) stress makes it worse.

Her tics were really bad today during a film (science, I believe), and it was disruptive to the teacher. But Trista was afraid to dismiss herself because she would have missed the material being covered.

It's really a tough dilemma but we believe it will get better again. It always has before.

An extra measure of endurance and understanding from the teachers during this time will be greatly appreciated.

Thanks for your help.

Jean Conklin

Over the course of the next four years, I would write many such crisis notes to various teachers, counselors and administrators (not to mention other people in much higher places . . . and yes, I kept a copy of them all). [28] The lesson we learned from this early encounter was that we needed to **talk individually with *all* of her teachers *every* year** (or every term, as appropriate). Our mission was to introduce the teachers to (or remind them about) Tourette Syndrome and the related disorders (TS+) which were a problem for Trista, and then to outline Trista's specific special educational needs. The longer we lived with Trista's school problems, the more *we* became the experts on her educational needs. We would re-invent the "educate the teacher about Tourette wheel" every time our daughter would get a new teacher, but the essence of our battle cry to her teachers was always to solicit their applied compassion and understanding.

At first I was very uncomfortable about presenting myself as the resident expert on Trista's educational needs, with regard to her Tourette Syndrome. But I was always pleasantly surprised how very receptive the teachers were in those meetings! They seemed to appreciate being told *in advance* about impending problems. Tourette Syndrome was totally new to most of the teachers in our school district, so almost all of her teachers were intrigued and challenged by our presentations. **I learned very early that a professional presentation for teachers, in a nonthreatening atmosphere, was a great battle plan** (and it usually prevented major wars later on).

The educators called those special meetings "staffings." We would hold scores of staffings with countless Hermiston teachers throughout the next several years. Without exception every meeting was a positive experience, and I attribute much of that fruitfulness to having unknowingly followed some personal "ground rules." My suggestions for successful parent-staff meetings are listed on the following page.

Jean's "Ground Rules for School Meetings"

1. The parent should request the meeting. Our schools are not accustomed to parents requesting meetings *before* a crisis. This almost always will give the parent advocate the advantage.

2. Ask the school counselor to schedule the meeting with the teachers. The request appears to come from a "behavioral domain," and it seems to remove the meeting from the "academic" setting (and consequently, the teachers are less prone to be threatened by a parent requesting to teach the teacher).

3. Request group meetings with the teachers. It is less intimidating for them.

4. Arrive at the meeting early, childless, not chewing gum, and professionally dressed (a skirted suit is recommended), with a briefcase (even if it is empty).

5. Have a *few* simple visuals about your child's disability, along with some very focused additional information from your "personal library," for the teachers to borrow from you if they are interested.

6. Give them at least one (concise, professionally worded, professionally arranged) *one-page* handout that pertains specifically to your child's needs, with respect to his disability.

7. Stick to your outline.

8. Keep the meeting short (30 minutes maximum).

9. Allow time for questions after the presentation, and make yourself available to stay late if any staff member wishes extra time with you.

10. Smile a lot, and don't act scared.

11. Remove yourself from the parent role and become *the professional* for the meeting. Treat the teachers as your peers, in a very normal day – they are neither superior nor subservient to you!

I always felt blessed that my husband, Dave, was a respected teacher in our school district. It gave *me* credibility. And even though many of Trista's teachers did not know that I was a former teacher in our school district, I always assumed the attitude that the people with whom I was meeting were my peers, professionally.

I also am grateful that I am gifted with organizational skills. It used to "drive me nuts" to watch my Dad prepare to do even the most simple project: he had to think about it, plan it, make a list and / or a drawing, and then execute the plan fastidiously. But I learned from the master organizer, and following his example always enabled me to give effective presentations! ((Thanks, Dad!))

I have frequently been told that I intimidate people. It's the way I carry myself, the way I dress, the way I'm slow to speak (because it takes me awhile to mentally process things), and the way I like to use "just the right word." Whenever I needed to attend a meeting for Trista, I was *happy* that my demeanor intimidates people because we *needed* the upper hand to get Trista through!

I think most people dread confrontation. I certainly do! My good friend, Shirley Parsons, taught me something she had learned from her supervisor training meetings at US Bank: *"Care enough to confront."* Although she was learning leadership skills, the principle definitely applies to advocating for others. We fought for Trista because we cared very deeply for her. We were often reminded of this truth: **caring means we must *also* confront.**

Another kind of confrontation was also happening within our family circle. Tia's cerebral palsy was becoming a source of embarrassment to her because her left hand was always in a tight little fist, with her thumb permanently tucked inside. Areas of the body affected by CP have a problem with "spasticity," i.e. the muscles contract spontaneously. She had worn various models of splints for years. They did help to keep her hand supple, and they made her arm more functional. But the devices were not sufficient. With the splint removed, she could uncurl her paralyzed left fingers with her right hand, but as soon as she would engage in another activity, the left hand would become tightly fisted again. Young

Tia was poised and very motivated, and it was no surprise to us when she wanted to have the doctors release the tendons in her paralyzed hand. She wanted her fingers to be more functional and her hand to look more normal. Tia had two orthopedic reconstructions of her paralyzed hand during the period that we were basking in a correct diagnosis for Trista. As with any orthopedic surgery, there was considerable discomfort and months of rehabilitation. Tia was a model patient, and the surgeries were extremely fruitful. We occasionally had to modify Tia's routines, and Tia, herself, learned how to be sweetly confrontive to people who did not understand *her* limitations. We learned when she was very young that Tia was astute, extremely conscientious and sensitive, and that she worked very hard to overcome her disability.

When we learned that freestyle was the *worst* swim-therapy she could be doing for her type of CP, it was *Tia* who told the swim-team coach that *she should practice only the breaststroke.* When she couldn't play left-hand chords using traditional piano technique, it was *Tia* who taught the piano teacher how she *could* play them. When she couldn't use the two-hand fingering system to learn to type, it was *Tia* who devised another fingering layout and informed the typing teacher that *she must use another keyboarding pattern.* Some of these adaptations were outwardly admired by her superiors. Unfortunately, some were regarded with selfish indignation by professionals who should have known better. Education takes time, even for some educators!

Self-advocacy is probably always the option of choice, but it is not always a practical choice. Though Tia was highly motivated, self confident and mature, we frequently came alongside her to uphold her, or to defend her in times of crisis or conflict. She learned many lessons as she observed our battles for Trista. It was always a sweet reward to see Tia putting into practice for herself the principles that we learned along the journey of advocating for her sister. **Life with a differently-abled person is a continual education – and *everyone* in the family learns from it!**

~ ~ ~

COPE, PAVE & OTHER ACRONYMS

One spring day in 1989, we received a yellow tri-fold brochure in our mailbox. The return address was of a young local woman I did not know.

DOES YOUR YOUTH'S IEP NEED A BOOSTER SHOT?

Do you get a **headache** thinking of school programs?

Are you **weak-kneed** about your parent rights?

Let **Dr. COPE** Write a Prescription for Your "Ills"

at a Parent Meeting!

March 8 – 7:30 p.m.

The flyer explained that there would be an open forum for parents of junior and senior high school youths with handicaps. It was sponsored by Coalition in Oregon for Parents in Education (COPE). The regional representative, Julie Farnam, would be there. I didn't know any of these people but I was curious.

We attended. I was amazed to learn that there was an experienced group of Oregon parents whose mission was to assist parents of special-needs children, helping and teaching them to advocate for their children. They had joined together to secure federal grant money to form a statewide coalition. It was not just in Oregon that this was happening. Similar organizations were forming all across the nation because parents of special-needs children needed help to procure the services that were mandated by law for the benefit of their handicapped children.

"Before they call I will answer"

Isaiah 65:24

It was no accident that we received this information at this particular time in our life. Immediately ahead of us were many new problems with the school district. We needed assistance from people who knew a lot more about human rights than we did!

COPE was the instrument that God used to raise my level of advocacy awareness. We had been fighting our own personal battle without a clue about what was going on in the rest of the world of special-needs advocacy. Julie informed me of many services that we could be accessing. She taught me about rights and privileges that could help Trista. I knew that this information was not going to be received graciously by our school authorities. But life was *so* hard for Trista – she *needed* a break. Dr. COPE came to her rescue!

Without the help of COPE, and many organizations like it, I don't think I could have endured the battles we had ahead of us! I had a lot of spunk and determination but we needed *facts* about our *rights*. COPE put us in touch with more resources than my mind could comprehend! COPE workers were a model for us: they were parent advocates who were well-disciplined and well-trained. At first they led me by the hand. Then they walked with me. And as I "grew up" in my parent advocacy, I only needed their wise counsel now and then. I learned from the best in the field!

Several years later, it was my privilege to meet the Client Advocate for the Spokane Department of Vocational Rehabilitation. Jeanne Burke was to me like Aaron and Hur were to Moses in the Bible [29] – Jeanne held up my arms and made them steady when it became too difficult to stand alone. During a very important hearing, Jeanne searched for a test report in one (of the many) huge "Trista Notebooks" that I had compiled over the years. [30] Jeanne said to me, "You must be a PAVE parent – you've saved *everything*!" (PAVE is a parent advocacy organization in Washington state.) Like they say in our cowboy country, "That did me right proud!"

Many years and countless encounters have passed since that golden bulletin arrived in our mailbox. We have won every bureaucratic battle so far. COPE, and thousands of similar parent coalition groups across the nation, have paved the way for weak-kneed parents to learn to stand tall, boldly and with strength on the human rights battlefield. As is true of the mother bear with her cub in the woods, parent advocates have proven that **it should be considered hazardous to come between an advocate-mother and her handicapped child!** Like my friend, Shirley, used to say, "Don't mess with my kids!"

Most of the people who have pioneered parent advocacy for special-needs children did their innovative work because of a personal need. "Necessity *is* the mother of invention." I know the cost has been great for every parent-pioneer, and I thank them all. Experience is still a very good teacher!

Reed Martin is a nationally recognized attorney, an authority on special education law, and a parent of a young adult with disabilities. Through writing, litigation, speaking and consulting for more than 20 years, Martin knows how to survive the challenges of parenting children with disabilities. Based upon his personal and professional experience, he shares the importance of parental corroboration.

> "I ask my clients if they belong to the organization that focuses on their child's disability," said Martin. "I tell parents, 'You need to work though an organization. You have a problem now: there will be others later. In disability organizations, you can work with people who have had 20 years' experience in dealing with similar situations. Why not go to the group that has done it again and again?' " [31]

One of the most useful benefits of belonging to groups like COPE is their newsletters. I don't always have the time nor the energy to read books and study manuals but I do draw great strength from the little tips and treasures that show up in such newsletters. The zeal to keep pressing on as a parent advocate has come partially through the wisdom from parents and professionals who have previously forged similar territory, and who have been brave enough to share their insights with others.

~ ~ ~

LISTEN TO THE MUSTN'TS

Listen to the MUSTN'TS, child

Listen to the DON'TS –

Listen to the SHOULDN'TS,

the IMPOSSIBLE, the WON'TS –

Listen to the NEVER HAVES –

Then listen close to me:

Anything can happen, child –

Anything can be.

author unknown [32]

It is not naturally easy for a parent to switch roles and become her child's "professional advocate." It often becomes *necessary* to wear two hats – that of the mother, and that of the parent advocate. The following page offers some proven techniques for being an effective parent advocate.

~ ~ ~

THE PROFESSIONAL PARENT –
MAINTAINING YOUR POSITION

THE DOS IN WORKING WITH PROFESSIONALS:

Pick up on cues

Be real

Act like they act

Look like they look

Anticipate problems and discuss them up front

Try to include other parents in your professional world

Find your own supports

Be pleasant and kind and sincere and honest

Treat others as you would like to be treated

Be outgoing and assertive

Serve as a positive role model

Negotiate flexibility in schedules to balance demands of job and family

THE DON'TS IN WORKING WITH PROFESSIONALS:

Pretend you're an expert in every subject

Stretch yourself too thin

Burn your bridges

Overcommit yourself

Try to do it all

Alienate your co-workers

Lose sight of your parenthood

Feel like you always have to prove yourself

Be defensive about your role

Let people "use" you

Be withdrawn or aggressive

Think of yourself as "just a parent"

by Beverly McConnell and Beth Stewart [33]

Parents of special-needs children have a unique set of demands on their lives. It has been said, "The world looks brighter from behind a smile." **Our station in life can be viewed as a tremendous blessing – or a curse. It is our choice!**

~ ~ ~

It isn't the load that weighs us down –
it's the way we carry it.

~~

A pessimist sees
a calamity in every opportunity;

An optimist sees
an opportunity in every calamity.

~~

The difference between
stumbling blocks
and stepping stones
is the way a man uses them.

~~

Optimism is the determination
to see more in something
than there is.

~~

Life is 10% what you make it
and 90% how you take it.

34

PUBLIC LAW 94-142 AND IDEA

What an incredible time to be alive! Progress is all around us, in *every* arena. I don't have to think back very far to admire some incredible advances in *my* lifetime in America: credit-card size calculators, digital oral thermometers, orphan drugs, copy machines (remember carbon paper?), cordless and cellular phones, "automatic teller" cash machines, sugar and salt substitutes, fat-free mayonnaise, and my favorites, laptop computers and E-mail . . . the list goes on and on.

But to families with handicapped children, there is one hallmark of progress that outshines all others: **Public Law 94-142**, The Education for All Handicapped Children Act of 1975, commonly referred to as PL 94-142, or EHA. Present-day legislation for special needs students actually began to emerge in the sixties.

PL 89-10 – The Elementary and Secondary Education Act of 1965 (ESEA). The statutory basis upon which early special education legislation was drafted; there were three subsequent amendments in 1965, 1966, and 1968.

PL 91-230 – ESEA Amendments of 1970. Included Part B, the Education of the Handicapped Act.

PL 93-280 – The Education Amendments of 1974. Included Title VI, which was the Education of the Handicapped Act Amendments of 1974. An appropriate education for all children with disabilities was mentioned for the first time.

PL 94-142 – The Education for All Handicapped Children Act of 1975. Mandated a Free Appropriate Public Education (FAPE) for all children with disabilities, ensured due process rights, mandated Individual Education Plans (IEPs) and Least Restrictive Environment (LRE), and became the core of federal funding for special education.

Amendments to the EHA, in 1983, 1986 (which established the Part H program), 1990 (which renamed the law IDEA), and 1992.

PL 105-17 – The Individuals with Disabilities Education Act Amendments of 1997. The current law.

In 1990, President George Bush signed into law the Americans with Disabilities Act (ADA). An important part of ADA is IDEA, the Individuals with Disabilities Education Act. The current legislation, the IDEA Amendments of 1997, are the fifth set of amendments to the Education for All Handicapped Children Act.

Before the Education of the Handicapped Act became law, children with disabilities were all-too-often *not* served in the public schools. When they *were* allowed to attend, the education they received was often not appropriate to their unique needs, or they were removed from the regular public school classroom and educated separately, frequently in entirely separate schools.

Responding to this inequity, Congress passed Public Law 94-142, the Education of the Handicapped Act (EHA), which through a series of amendments has become known as **Individuals with Disabilities Education Act** (IDEA). IDEA is comprised of six principles that provide the framework around which special education services are designed and provided for students with disabilities. These principles are:

- **free appropriate public education** (FAPE)
- **appropriate evaluation**
- **individualized education program** (IEP)
- **least restrictive environment** (LRE)
- **parent and student participation in decision making**
- **procedural safeguards**

Alone, and together, these six principles work to guarantee that children with disabilities can go to school every day, learn what other children learn, and have their individual educational needs determined and addressed. [35]

In 1974-75, when PL 94-142 went into effect, few people understood how one piece of legislation would impact so many lives. In fact, most of us didn't even realize we *needed* PL 94-142. Many of our handicapped children weren't even born!

In 1975, I providentially attended the first educators' conference in Oregon that specifically addressed PL 94-142. During much of

---

the meeting, I wondered why I was there because I was no longer teaching. I took a few notes and brought home some pamphlets. I read most of them and filed all of them. But generally, I just chalked it up as an enriching experience and a relaxing weekend away from home.

Something was birthed in me at that conference. I became a *consumer* of a new product for my girls: *equal rights for handicapped children.* Our children were born during the years that this legislation was being enacted. They have benefited greatly from it. This legislation has given them *somewhat* equal access to the public education that most "normal" students take for granted.

Recent statistics illustrate that progress in this realm has been dramatic: [36]

- On December 1, 1994, the number of infants and toddlers receiving early intervention services was 165,253.

- In the 1994-95 school year, over 4.9 million children (ages 6-21) received special education services under IDEA.

- In the 1993-94 school year, 43.4% of these children were in the regular education classroom with non-disabled children. Placement varied considerably according to the disability of the child; for example, 87.5% of students with speech and language impairments were served in the regular classroom. Children with mental retardation or autism were much less likely to be served in the regular classroom (8.6% and 9.6% respectively.) These children tended to be served in separate classes; 57% of children with mental retardation and 54.5% of children with autism received services in a separate class.

Prior generations have not been so fortunate. Closet children are still a reality – in your community and in mine. They are 40 and 50 and 60 years old. They are severely disabled. They have been sheltered in their parents' homes for their entire lives because the *only* alternative was institutionalization. I know many of these children's mothers. Their lives have been incredibly difficult! The parents have fought their battles, alone . . . losing most of them. They didn't have PL 94-142 or ADA. The legislation didn't exist.

When we lived in England in the mid-'80s, we were surprised to see the contrast between the two countries, in the realm of inclusion. A percentage of the severely disabled students were shuttled off in private cabs to special schools on a daily or weekly dormitory basis, depending on how far they lived from the special school. The remainder of the disabled students were placed in the neighborhood schools, but there could not be much accommodation made for them. Britain very simply does not spend as much money on public education as America does, so she does not have the extra money to spend on *special* education. Our daughters *did* attend the English public school where my husband was an exchange teacher. Though it was a superb school with excellent and sensitive staff, the British teachers clearly struggled to adapt to our two handicapped children. We did as much as we could to help those teachers assimilate and accommodate our children because we had the benefit of nine years of experience with PL 94-142 in America. They had none.

PL 94-142 and ADA are, for today's moment in history, unique to America. Sweeping legislation forces a paradigm shift. The shift takes time but it can, and does, happen. "America's mission was and still is to take diversity and mold it into a cohesive and coherent whole that would espouse virtues and values essential to the maintenance of civil order. There is nothing easy about that mission. But it is not Mission Impossible." [37] One entire generation of Americans has been served, in varying degrees, by this legislation. The law of our land has *forced us* to attend to the special needs of our special kids. In our theater of education for disabled children, the paradigm shift is almost complete. That truth is evidenced by my observation that most young special-needs parents today are not even aware that it was ever any other way.

Worldwide, many foreign nations are still playing ostrich, ignoring diversity by genuinely regarding inclusion in schools as Mission Impossible. That will work for a time, until progress touches their public-school conscience, as happened in America. I was pleased to read the following excerpt in a British newspaper, following a recent row among the bobbies over discrimination.

> "Being insensitive [and] thoughtless is one idea,
> but throwing aside the idea that 'treating everyone
> exactly the same is enough' will be harder for the
> [police] troops. They are proud to say, 'We treat
> everyone as equals.' Now that won't do. It needs
> more – it needs people to be treated as *individuals*,
> all with different backgrounds, different views." [38]

Subsequent to our year of living in England, we have been privileged to work behind the former iron curtain. Our focus since 1992 has been various humanitarian projects in Central Romania. [39] Communism sought to remove the "undesirables" from communities by placing handicapped people in institutions. After Romania's dictatorship was overthrown in 1989, the institution mentality was so deeply ingrained that it continues, even today. A much-too-large portion of Romania's disabled population is sequestered in unsavory mental institutions, where handicapped people are treated more like animals than very needy special children and adults.

I remember how pleased we were for the three mildly handicapped children that we met in the girls' orphanage in the village of Orlat. One little girl had crossed eyes, one had petit-mal seizures, and one had some learning disabilities. The little girls had somehow slipped through the cracks. Instead of being singled out to spend their lifetime in psychiatric wards because they were "defective," these girls were, at least, allowed to live with the "normal" children in the orphanage. Those three handicapped Romanian children were the fortunate ones among their kind. They have the opportunity to lead a *somewhat* humane life, if one can call Romanian orphanages humane. (I cannot.)

But we recently discovered one charming little girl who was not so fortunate. Sweet little Daniela was five when she was moved to the girls' orphanage in Orlat. She was as "cute as a bug's ear," and we all adored her. One can imagine our dismay when, during our 1999 visit to one of the dreaded handicapped institutions, smiling petite Dana said shyly, "Hi, Dave!" She is 12 years old now, and the reason Dana has been doomed to that awful place is that "she was a little slow," i.e. school was difficult for her.

It is unlikely that Dana will be transferred out of that hell-hole, and she will most certainly become society's castoff because of her childhood placement in that institution. Sadly, there are *many* unfortunate almost-normal Romanian children with a fate similar to Dana's, and our hearts grieve for them. Romania is generations away from the freedom that Americans take for granted.

America – where public education is guaranteed, free, appropriate, and sensitive to our "special" children's special needs. I'm so thankful my children were born in this generation! I am grateful that parents and concerned individuals before me fought the good fight to adopt PL 94-142. It is, for our generation, what penicillin was decades ago. PL 94-142 (and now IDEA) has meant the opportunity for *quality of life* for our handicapped children. The Equal Education for All Handicapped Children Act of 1975 set the stage for special-needs children to access a rich, full life. Such opportunities would have been denied our daughters in any other generation, in almost any other country. I am proud to be an American parent of two very *special* American children!

~ ~ ~

"Human Progress
is neither automatic
nor inevitable.
Even a superficial look at history
reveals that no social advance
rolls in on the wheels of inevitability.
Every step toward the goal of justice requires
sacrifice,
suffering, and
struggle,
the tireless exertions
and passionate concerns
of dedicated individuals."

Dr. Martin Luther King, Jr.

THANK YOU . . . BUT

I need no more from you
beyond the basic good manners
set down in any society:
unwritten guidelines concerning
how one human being treats another . . .

I AM NOT RARE –
any more than your nephew
or a redheaded teacher
or a skinny cheerleader . . .

I AM SORRY LAWS WERE NECESSARY
to mainstream me
. . . such a humorous gesture . . .
like mainstreaming a colt in a pasture.

I WAS BAPTIZED IN THE STREAM OF LIFE
the day I was born.

I AM A PART OF THE EARTH
like the leaves on that tree,
the fingers on your hand,
the stones and mountains
of various shapes and hues.

I AM SIMPLY A CHILD
to whom you are responsible
to teach, to guide, to discipline

and

DEPENDING ON YOUR SIZE AS A PERSON,

TO LOVE . . .

author unknown

The Conklins – 1976
Jean, Dave, Trista (4 ½ years), Tia (2 years)

photo by Oz Halling

The Longest Concert

Without a doubt, the two most offensive statements that school employees made to us were spoken by people who should have known better! During an intense meeting in the school district conference room, a top administrator said to us, "We believe in inclusion, that mainstreaming is the least restrictive environment for *all* handicapped students." And in a question-answer time during one of our parent-led Tourette Syndrome staffings for teachers, an experienced teacher who has been advisor to the honor society proclaimed, "All my students will be treated the same; I'm not going to be treating any students any differently than I do right now."

Today I can chalk both statements up to ignorance and insensitivity, but I have a difficult time understanding how any school employee could vocalize such statements when the Education for All Handicapped Children Act of 1975 had already been in effect for more than a decade! My husband was an active teachers' union member during his entire teaching career, having served several appointments to the Oregon Education Association legal-defense team. Dave's comment about these kinds of overstatements was, "Our union ends up having to defend teachers like those people!"

Those educators' words may have been ignorant and insensitive, but to *practice* those philosophies in public schools was as **illegal** then as it is today! Public Law 94-142 guarantees that every handicapped student be provided a free and appropriate public education in the least restrictive environment. The law made it extremely foolhardy for educators to express broad statements such as the two examples listed above.

In her sophomore year, Trista was 17. The primary classification on her IEP was "Other Health Impaired." In addition to multiple, involuntary physical movements and uncontrollable vocalizations, she also had these problems:

√   IQ 80-86 (10-year testing range)

√   Attention Deficit Disorder

√   Obsessive Compulsive Disorder

       (obsessive thoughts / compulsive actions)

√   Mild Speech Disorder

√   Gross and Fine Motor Skills Deficiency

√   Impulsivity

√   Hyperactivity

√   Social Skills Deficit

√   Academic Functioning Deficit

Addressed individually, none of her problems seemed too profound. But the sum of the related parts was a totally different picture. It was no wonder, then, that we had a child who has had, and would continue to have, great difficulty coping in a "normal" world. Said another way, several minor problems equalled *one* major problem, which served to create *many major problems* in Trista's life.

She was a sophomore, struggling along in a regular curriculum with an IEP. She was being mainstreamed in five of seven classes. One day, we experienced the amazing realization that we basically had two years to get her ready for independent living! We hit the panic button. We immediately launched an investigation to attempt to find what on earth we were going to do to get her "all put together" in such a short time.

In March of '89, we initiated a search – to discover some alternatives, additions and changes to the current school approaches which had not proven particularly productive for Trista.

In the next two months, we understood that **very large, immediate changes** were in order for:

a) Trista's IEP,

b) her school curriculum, and

c) her vocational training.

Through extensive research, I made some *profound* discoveries. The following guidelines were being widely circulated in special education circles:

- Section 504 of the Rehabilitation Act of 1973 (The Carl Perkins Act) recommended that Vocational Training for handicapped students should begin by age 14.

- Arc recommended that parents address vocational training issues for their child as early as age 12, or by age 14, at the very latest.

- The Parent Graduation Alliance (PGA) recommended that vocational planning should begin as soon as the student enters high school.

The appropriate terms for what all these agencies were referring to is a "Transition Plan," involving the use of a "Functional Curriculum." Over a period of two months, we discovered, and then began to understand, the relevancy of these terms and concepts. At age 17 $^1/_2$, Trista had not yet even had a vocational assessment! *Where had our specialists been?*

We were what I would call the "typical parents of an IEP student in Hermiston Schools." Each year, the format for Trista's IEP meeting was neatly executed by the professionals:

- The parents arrived at a meaningless, formal meeting with the special education teacher, where they were asked to ratify a brief typewritten plan rather than to participate in the *development* of the ideas.

- Line by line, the experts introduced a few new approaches. Some unfamiliar terms, concepts and programs were mentioned.

- The parents were asked if they had any questions or additions.

- And finally, the parents were invited to sign on the dotted line.

- The meeting was dismissed.

  - Intimidated parents walked away in a fog, feeling everything was in order.

But in spite of Trista's eloquent IEPs, we would soon discover that things were *not* okay – it seemed there were *always* problems at school! If there wasn't one at the moment, there *would* be one soon. We tried to resolve the problems through her counselor and special education teacher. Even though it was our last resort, we occasionally ended up having to clash head-on with teachers, on Trista's behalf. We kept trying to resolve problems as they arose but the *same* fundamental problems just kept surfacing from time to time, with different teachers in different situations. And we kept trying to figure out what *we* were doing wrong.

And so it went. Year after year, we kept leaving IEP meetings thinking, "this year looks like it will be better." But we kept going around the same mountain time and time again, with the same basic problems never getting resolved. Meanwhile, our student was getting older, and we were making very little progress in preparing her for the **real world.** We kept suggesting the need for modifications in her curriculum so she could be prepared to function independently, with appropriate job skills and living skills. But we were repeatedly and emphatically reminded that everything would work out satisfactorily, and we were admonished that "above all, she needs a regular diploma."

For too many years we were lulled to sleep with the school's assurance that everything would be all right for Trista as she plodded along towards graduation. She had no concept of the future, she failed a class here and there, she generally hated school, she was desperate for friends but was lagging farther behind socially, and she resented the pressure we had to exert at home to keep her passing her classes. We feared that she faced a dismal future of continued failure because her school program was not preparing her to function in the real adult world!

In the final analysis, the excellence of her program would not be determined by analyzing the schools' plans, procedures, or good intentions. Rather, excellence would be determined by the quality of our child's preparation to leave school and enter into the adult world, armed with skills for success. If a program does not provide handicapped students with the knowledge and tools they need, then the program is not valuable, and may even be counter-productive. **If the outcome of all this "special education" for Trista did not improve her quality of life, then it was *not very special*!**

We concluded that it was the school's responsibility, more specifically the special education teachers' responsibility, to provide the framework within which the student would (a) prepare to function in the adult community among adults, and (b) make an effective transition to that community. The closer we looked at the school district's responsibilities to Public Law 94-142, the more disappointed we became over Hermiston schools' failure to provide our handicapped daughter with the education she needed for her future.

When I began to look around at what *could* be available for our daughter, I knew we had been short-changed!

• *No one* suggested we address the problem from a present **"need,"** rather than from a "category" of classification.

• *No one* enlightened us about an **alternative "functional curriculum"** to prepare Trista for a productive independent adult life, with the emphasis on living skills and work experience rather than on grades and credits.

• *No one* advised us to **modify and individualize Trista's curriculum** to build and preserve her self-esteem so she could pass on competency, in lieu of a "Bell curve" grade and / or course requirements, in which a handicapped child was being measured against a non-handicapped child's yardstick.

• *No one* had informed us that she could **postpone graduation and opt for continued education and training through the age of 21**, utilizing appropriate services available through our local community college.

• *No one* arranged or even suggested a **vocational assessment**, even though our district had outstanding testing equipment and one of the most qualified experts on vocational assessment in the state!

- *No one* advised **utilizing community-based training during the regular school day,** to introduce her to different types of jobs; offering to train her on the job, and then support her on the job.

- *No one* offered **information on federally funded "parent information and advocacy programs"** (such as Coalition in Oregon for Parents in Education and Parent Graduation Alliance) as valuable resources for assistance in planning our daughter's special-needs curriculum, even though this information had been routinely made available to *all* Oregon public schools to share with parents of special-needs children.

We decided it was time to share our concerns with anyone and everyone who would listen. We had already gone through the proper line of authority: first to the teachers, then to the counselors, and finally to the specialists. We were getting *nowhere*. The proverbial buck kept being passed, and we were becoming frustrated by detours and stall tactics. We needed to go above all these people's heads, and we *had* paid our dues to exercise this privilege.

Dave and I scheduled a meeting with his former principal, who was at the time an assistant superintendent of the Hermiston School District. The man listened politely to our concerns and our requests for more services but we were not met with enthusiasm. The meeting was nonproductive, and the administrator suggested that we were being unreasonable. He closed the meeting with the statement, "I guess our next meeting will be with our attorneys present." Dave's reply: "I guess you are right."

While the administration was probably considering their course of action, we decided to take them to task in a less conventional manner. We didn't *want* a lawsuit. We didn't even want any *lawyers*! My husband is an expert peacemaker. We *knew* we were right! The local "system" was wrong, and it was time to let the bureaucracy work *for* us.

So – we communicated in the manner we knew best: On May 22, 1989, Dave and I composed a letter to our greatly respected friend of 19 years, who was also Hermiston's Superintendent of

Schools. The (much too long) three page, single-spaced letter included almost everything you have just read in this chapter, plus these closing paragraphs:

> We are sharing these concerns with you because we feel we have been let down by the system. The nation's schools were not asked to integrate PL 94-142 as soon as they could afford it, nor when they were best able to work it into the curriculum. Congress told them in 1975 to do the job *immediately*: **to give each handicapped child in America the educational opportunity that is the birthright of every American.** What we are really looking at is Hermiston School District's effectiveness in lifting handicapped children above the barriers they confront in the regular classroom. We are looking for this school district's extra margin of individual attention that should enable handicapped children to keep up with others in their grade level, and to not become discouraged. Hermiston Senior High School has had 13 years to rise to the challenge to give handicapped students a fair break, and we are finding that it is still in the starting blocks!
>
> We don't know how far the accountability buck will be passed, and we really don't care. We do not have time to fight the system – we need cooperation quickly. One girl's life is passing us by. While we wait, every day she is one day closer to failure in the **real world** unless we get some help. **Our goal for Trista's few remaining school years is to build a framework which will allow her to experience success, in a program which is relevant to the realities and expectations of adult life.**
>
> We have initiated contacts with COPE, PGA, Arc, the ESD, and the State Department of Education. Each contact has produced essentially the same response: Our requests are not unreasonable. We are somewhat out of our domain in addressing many of these issues, and it is slow-going as we, basically unassisted, find our way. We need any appropriate help you can offer, to enhance Trista's

opportunity to receive the education she needs for her future. We believe it is time to tip the balance toward **excellence** in Trista's education.

We are only one family, fairly well educated and fairly aggressive at this point to salvage one girl's adolescence. It is our observation that we have many problems in our district within this segment of our school program. We need help, and we need it fast! Our school system is irresponsibly wasting many handicapped students' potential by effectively limiting their access to a brighter future. If you fail to improve the system, you have shortchanged our handicapped students. **How will you help?**

Professionally,
Dave and Jean Conklin

cc: [names have been omitted below, but it is important to mention that some of these individuals were extremely sympathetic to our cause, and a few of those individuals had already been working hard, albeit unsuccessfully, to assist us in our plight.]

Assistant Superintendent of Curriculum and Instruction, Hermiston School District
Principal, Hermiston Senior High School
Counselor, Hermiston Senior High School
Special Education Instructors (3), Senior High School
Superintendent, Umatilla County Education Service District (ESD)
Director of Special Education, Umatilla County ESD
Director of Career Education, Umatilla County ESD
Special-Needs Coordinator, Umatilla County ESD
Chairman, Hermiston School Board
Hermiston School Board – 6 Members
Superintendent, Oregon State Board of Education
Director of Special Education, Oregon State Board of Education
Oregon State Representative, Oregon District #57
Oregon State Senator, Oregon District #57
Coalition in Oregon for Parents in Education, State Office
COPE Representatives – 2 Regional Offices
Parent Graduation Alliance (PGA), University of Oregon

We assume that the combination of counsel from school district attorneys *and* the pressure of the extensive "CC list" probably did it!

On May 25, the Assistant Superintendent of Curriculum and Instruction called to set up another meeting. "We need to talk," he said. At 7:30 a.m. on May 26, 1989, we found that the administrator had done a 180-degree turn! In an amazingly short time, he had changed his position from "This is all we can do!" to "What can we do for Trista?"

In the weeks that followed, most of the bureaucratic levels that we had contacted in our extensive letter phoned and / or wrote us to see if things were getting resolved. They were, *indeed*!

On August 21, 1989, I wrote another letter to our Superintendent of Schools (and I also sent copies of this letter to the same 24 individuals referenced in the previous letter).

> As a result of our recent letter to you about our frustrations with our handicapped daughter's special education, it has been our pleasure to watch the bureaucratic wheels turn on Trista's behalf. Our goal was to build a framework which would allow our 17 year-old to experience success in an appropriate program; a program which would be relevant to the realities and expectations of her adult life.
>
> We are pleased to report to you that a promising framework, on Trista's behalf, is already under construction. The Hermiston School District has assured us that the completed framework will be in place before school starts next week. Although our efforts have focused specifically on Trista, the concepts are applicable to handicapped students in general; we are certain that the changes we are experiencing should benefit many other "special students" in our area.
>
> Here are some of the milestones we have logged:
>
> 1) The Hermiston School District formally met with us twice before school was out: first, to query specifically what they could do to help us; and second, to discuss, brainstorm, and offer help on a variety of topics we

addressed in our May 22 letter. Recently, we had an informal third meeting to begin formulating a **transition plan** for Trista.

2) The Umatilla County Educational Service District provided a comprehensive **vocational assessment** which clearly outlined Trista's vocational strengths, proficiencies, talents and interests. A **learning style test** provided information which should prove extremely valuable for Trista's teachers and job supervisors (as well as her parents).

3) The Umatilla County ESD has for Trista's use a vast array of materials which can be implemented immediately to begin a **functional curriculum.** Trista's curriculum will now begin to specifically prepare her for a productive, independent life. For Trista, Hermiston High School will begin to emphasize living skills and work experience, rather than grades and credits.

4) The need and advisability for a **modified diploma** for Trista has been acknowledged, and plans are underway to finalize that vision. Trista will "graduate with her class" with a modified diploma, and will have until the spring after her 21st birthday to complete her full diploma from HHS. Actual post-high school coursework and training will probably be pursued in an age-appropriate community college setting, which appears to offer the least restrictive and most appropriate curriculum for Trista.

5) With the acknowledgment of the need for a modified diploma, we are now able to further slow down Trista's education to make way for some modifications in her coursework requirements. Though we have been advised to pursue a full HHS diploma as one of our final goals before she turns 21, we will now have documentation which justifies teacher / course / school **modifications without penalty** to Trista.

6) Plans are in process for Trista to work two periods a day, five days a week, utilizing community based vocational opportunities during the regular school day.

Supervision, and on-the-job training and support will be made available. Job placement can change every semester so Trista will have the benefit of **exploring a variety of vocational opportunities**.

7) We have become acutely aware of our need for a **case manager** to become actively involved in Trista's life. Many individuals have been providing bits and pieces of this role, but we have begun our search to find one person to act as Trista's advocate, to wear the following hats: her *communicator* to talk with teachers, school, and employers about her specific educational problems and her IEP; her *mediator* between school and parents; her *watchdog* over her IEP and other federally mandated rights; her *specialist* to conduct regular staffings with her teachers and related school personnel; her *coordinator* to pursue services such as SSI and vocational rehabilitation; her *assistant* to help her make a smooth transition from family to independent living; and her *advisor* for difficult personal situations. We believe it is necessary for such a person to begin functioning very soon.

8) We are in the process of requesting an array of other much-needed appropriate services on Trista's behalf: **peer tutors**; **methods for increasing *Trista's* accountability / responsibility** for class requirements; **handwriting alternatives**; **modifications in her social skills class**; **changed focus for fundamental studies class**; and **lifting all time restrictions** on tests.

9) As a result of our specific frustrations with Trista's IEP and transition plan, Hermiston School District and the Umatilla County ESD staged a one-day **staff workshop,** entitled "Transition and Futures Planning for High School Students with Disabilities." Brigid Flannery (Specialized Training Project, University of Oregon), and Roz Slovic (Parent Graduation Alliance, U of O) presented information on "Functional Curriculum," "IEP Development," "Strategies in Instruction," and "Transition Planning and Issues." We (Trista, Dave and Jean) were the "guinea pigs"

for Roz's demonstration on how to conduct a "Futures Planning Session" for special-needs students. We felt this was an extremely productive workshop, and we appreciate the efforts of the ESD and our local school district to accommodate our needs.

You can see that *many* people have been very busy to assist us. Few, if any, of these wheels would have begun to turn without the free, accessible, prompt, and very professional assistance of two important parent advocate groups whose very existence is to help parents such as us who have handicapped students! We are grateful to Coalition in Oregon for Parents in Education (COPE) for the personal assistance from their Regional Consultants, and for their "PIP" (Parent Information Packet manual). We are also extremely thankful for the counseling we have received from Parent Graduation Alliance (PGA), and for their "Parent Primer" manual. These federally funded programs were created to assist and train parents to advocate for their handicapped children through the age of 21. Judging from our list of progress since May 22, you can see that these organizations know how to make things happen!

We have been working with the counsel of many individuals and organizations, and within an extremely tight time frame. We have been pleased how cooperative and helpful the Hermiston School District has been. The Assistant Superintendent has played a key role in helping us to identify our needs, and to begin planning Trista's schedule for the two years that she has left at HHS. We also appreciate all the help that we are receiving from her counselor. We know that it is this district's continued assistance and cooperation which will enable us to meet the immediate goal of fall implementation, as well as the more distant goal of effecting her orderly transition from school to community.

You can also see that our Umatilla County ESD has been extremely helpful. Our conclusion at this point is that the woman who heads the ESD Special Needs Program will be involved more significantly in our attempt to provide an appropriate education for our daughter. It appears to us that the ESD has a wealth of consortium resources that have been partially paid for by our school district. Those resources appear to be just waiting to be tapped for Trista's use.

We can say with certainty at this point that we are well on our way to securing for Trista Conklin the educational opportunity that is the birthright of every American. We are privileged to live in a country which guarantees equal education as a basic right!

Thank you for your help in our "Advocacy Adventure." We will keep you apprised of our progress.

Sincerely yours,
Dave and Jean Conklin

My understanding of the rights of handicapped students grew proportionally with the problems Trista was experiencing in school. People don't usually bother to figure out how something works until it breaks. Our school district was coasting along with the "if it ain't broke, don't fix it" philosophy in dealing with their special-needs students. But one day we removed our blinders, and we clearly saw the gravity of *our* school problems. Our daughter's future was literally in jeopardy because of school district policies, practices and philosophies.

It would be unrealistic to say that everything was perfect after this major overhaul in our school district. We still had our day-to-day problems. But we suddenly had splendid cooperation where we had previously met with incredible apathy and resistance.

I have often compared Trista's final two years in school to driving on the freeway. When we see a state police car on the road, even if it is going the opposite direction, we check our speedometer and adjust our speed so he doesn't "get us." After our encounter with the educators, there were many "patrolmen" watching the

Hermiston School District. The educators were faithful to check their agendas, and to stay well within the safe zone. Staff at Trista's school gave Dave and me a rather wide berth, but they were cordial, accommodating and very kind to Trista. That is all we asked.

The philosophy of our school district changed overnight. After our 1989 advocacy encounter,

It was no longer, "What do we want?"

Nor, "What does the district want?"

They now asked, "What is best for Trista?"

***That's the law — FAPE & LRE.* Free, Appropriate, Public Education in the Least Restrictive Environment.**

In 1991, Trista received what our family called a "modified diploma." The award was actually a certificate of attendance because she was lacking several credits to receive a full diploma. Trista's goal was to participate in the graduation ceremonies with her classmates. She did just that, which is all that really mattered.

I could entitle Trista's entire school career, "*The Longest Concert*," because those years were analogous to my childhood. My mother played first violin in the Grande Ronde Symphony for 29 years, during my entire childhood. She faithfully attended every Wednesday night practice, and *we* faithfully attended all performances. I grew to hate Wednesday nights, once my sister and I became old enough to be left alone. We fought over petty and not-so-petty issues, and whenever a neighbor girl would join forces with my older sister, they both would harass me. I would lose every time! The only way I could get justice was to *tell* on them. When concerts came, Mom would make me go with her to the dress rehearsals *and* the concerts. I didn't like them the first time, and I *loathed* them the second time! Every production seemed like the *longest* moment of my life! I was pre-assigned a seat in the front row, where Mom could keep an eye on me, and I was not allowed to leave it until the orchestra was dismissed. My only consolation was that I could curl up in the springy velvet-covered lodge seats in the beautiful auditorium, and I would languish in the respite

---

from my sister's teasing. I read and re-read the professionally printed program, making up silly words out of the names of the performers. As the years passed, I just naturally escaped the regimen of Wednesday night sister-abuse and quarterly concerts because that young stage of my life became history.

Trista's school years were a lot like those years. Every week or so it seemed like we had another "Wednesday night" battle, and it seemed that the only way I could get fair treatment for our child was to make an issue of it, occasionally having to implicate someone. Some of those advocacy "performances" were *unbearable*, and I hated attending most of them! My only solace was that occasionally I could find a "comfortable seat" where I would do something I enjoyed, far removed from the conflicts at and because of school. I did not escape the regimen of Trista's "dress rehearsals and concerts" until she graduated. And whenever I pick up an old "program," I recall those events with disdain, and I am relieved to know that Trista's school years are *all* behind me.

Although we felt isolated and alone during most of Trista's school years, there were countless other parents, nationwide, who were learning *their* own lessons in advocating for their disabled children. Parent groups were being formed; grant applications were being written and federal dollars were awarded; and information to assist parents such as us began to circulate. We joined many state and national advocacy groups for parents of special-needs children, and we subscribed to newsletters of other similar groups. The array of disabilities represented transcended medical journals but the members had one thing in common: disabled children. On the following pages are two excerpts that appeared in the stack of monthly newsletters we received.

~ ~ ~

Effective Parent-Professional Collaboration

(OR HOW PARENTS & PROFESSIONALS CAN WORK TOGETHER) [40]

For Parents

- Believe that parents are equal partners with professionals, and accept responsibility for solving problems and planning

- See the professional as a person who is working for the well-being of the child

- See the mutual understanding of a problem as *the goal* for interactions with professionals

- Maintain a file of important documents and correspondence of services provided

- Express the needs of the family in an assertive manner to professionals

- Accept that a professional often has responsibility for service coordination and communication with many families

- Communicate quickly with professionals when there are significant changes, or when notable situations occur

- Encourage the professionals to communicate with each other and keep the parents informed

- Maintain realistic expectations, knowing that complete and definitive answers are unlikely when emotional and physical conditions of children are concerned

(continued)

- Mentally reverse roles with the parents, to consider how they would feel

- See the child in more than one dimension, looking beyond the diagnosis or disability

- Keep in mind that the child is a person whom the parent loves

- Believe that parents are equal, and they are the experts on their child

- Value the comments and insights of parents, and make use of their knowledge

- Judge the child in terms of progress, and communicate hope to the parents

- Consider the child as part of a family, and discover other's attitudes and reactions which affect the child

- Distinguish between fact and opinion when discussing problems and potentials

- Make every effort to steer parents toward solutions and resources, providing written and oral evaluations about potential services, other supportive arrangements, and financial aid

- Establish the mutual understanding of a problem as the goal for interactions with parents

- Involve the parents in the establishment of a plan of action or treatment, and in the review, evaluation, and revisions

- Make appointments and provide services at convenient times

- Obtain and share information from other appropriate professionals, to ensure that services are not duplicated and families do not expend unnecessary energy searching for providers and services

COMMUNICATION STRATEGIES PLEDGE

by Sandy DeGraff [41]

parent of a child with multiple handicaps

If I make a promise, I keep it.

I am willing to think, and sometimes I realize that the other point of view makes sense.

I share information, plans, strategies, concerns, personal experiences.

I learn about my community's resources, and I don't assume the other party already knows about them.

I meet face-to-face, if at all possible.

I try to use a variety of appropriate settings for meetings: home, school, coffee shop, office.

I am on time for meetings. If I know in advance that I will be late, I let the others also know.

I try to stick to the topic.

If more information is needed, I admit it and develop a plan on how to obtain it.

I establish deadlines, then I work to meet them.

I follow through – I don't assume someone else will take care of everything for me.

I ask questions before making demands.

I ask questions if I don't understand, and I keep asking until I do.

I thank people for their help.

PRETTY **P**EOPLE

Welcome to Holland

by Carol Turkington [42]

When you're going to have a baby, it's like you are planning a vacation to Italy. You're all excited. You get a whole bunch of guidebooks, you learn a few phrases so you can get around, and then it comes time to pack your bags and head for the airport.

Only, when you land, the stewardess says, "Welcome to Holland."

You look at one another in disbelief and shock, saying "Holland? What are you talking about? I signed up for Italy."

But they explain that there's been a change of plan, that you've landed in Holland, and there you must stay.

"But I don't know anything about Holland," you say. "I don't want to stay."

But stay you do. You go out and buy some new guidebooks, you learn some new phrases, and you meet people you never knew existed. The important thing is that you are not in a slum full of pestilence and famine. You're simply in a different place than you had planned. It's slower paced than Italy, less flashy than Italy, but after you've been here a little while and you have a chance to catch your breath, you begin to discover that Holland has windmills. Holland has tulips. Holland has Rembrandts.

But everyone else you know is busy coming and going from Italy. They're all bragging about what a great time they had there, and for the rest of your life, you'll say, "Yes, that's what **I** had planned."

The pain of that will never go away. You have to accept that pain because the loss of that dream, the loss of that plan, is a very, very significant loss. But if you spend your life mourning the fact that you didn't go to Italy, you will never be free to enjoy the very special, the very lovely things about Holland.

It has taken me a terribly long time to enjoy *Holland*! Those early years of our "detour" were probably the hardest. It would be dishonest of me to say that I have not had my own emotional battles throughout our years of parenting a severely disabled child, while "everyone else [we knew was] busy coming and going from Italy."

When I was able to be completely honest with myself, I could admit that it was *envy* that rose up within me when I considered my peers. Rich or poor, privileged or common, it *seemed* that all our peers were destined for success: a promising law or medical practice; a showcase home with everything in perfect order; adept, successful children in spotless, trendy clothing. Everything these people set their hands to seemed to be automatic; raising their children seemed effortless; and the current of their lifestyle seemed to be propelling them toward even more ease, honors and success. In my times of extreme jealousy, I privately referred to them as the "Pretty People." I could not relate to their finely dressed, perfectly groomed children with their array of tap and ballet awards, cheerleading and football trophies, prom dress decisions, homecoming queen photos, and sorority rushes and ivy-league scholarships.

But as I've gotten older, I have realized that my jealousy and envy could have kept me from enjoying the very special things about the journey *we* were appointed to travel. "They're all bragging about what a great time they had [in Italy], and for the rest of your life, you'll say, 'Yes, that's what I had planned.'" Yes, I *had* planned to go to *Italy*. But I didn't *get* to go to Italy! And because of that, I don't have a lot in common with those who did. It is difficult for me to visit for very long with those who journeyed on because wearing the correct name-brand clothing, winning the ballet contest trophy, discussing the success of the prom decorations, the appointment to the "winningest" college football team, and college sorority pledging don't have much to do with the territory we've been forging. The kinds of decisions that our family pour over must seem quite unremarkable, in contrast to their dinner-table conversations.

I thought it was just my imagination that we have become so different from the pretty people. Lots of things make people different. How could I categorize these people so glibly? I've had a quarter-century to ponder these things, to observe the lives of people who seem to have everything going their way. I have come to understand that *we* are the fortunate ones because we have had to fight so hard. Our battle scars may have left us beat up on the outside, but we must be gorgeous on the inside!

My good friend, Anna Wilde, was inquiring recently about details on our children's disabilities. As we E-mailed back and forth, she emulated my unspoken thoughts about our lifetime of challenges with this comment: "People who have a lot of adversity in their life seem to be stronger people, with more 'fiber' to their being." I jokingly replied that I have dieted a lot in my lifetime, and I've learned to become quite fond of fiber!

I like the illustration in the Bible of how trials "refine" us.[43] I can relate to how the goldsmith turns up the heat and "simmers" the molten liquid a very long time to draw out the impurities from the gold. Anyone who has spent time simmering in the fires of life understands how it feels when the heat is being turned up. These struggles aren't about Tourette Syndrome, or cerebral palsy, or depression, or any other malady. These struggles are about *building character*. We have been chosen – called out – to be refined. I don't know why. Maybe we were so awful that God had to work extra hard on us to make us usable. *Or* – maybe we have been called to a higher calling, a higher purpose. I believe that God does not just turn up the heat to watch us squirm! He has a *plan* for our lives. He has a *purpose* for us. We are the clay on the potter's wheel, and God is molding us into the people He needs us to be. He has chosen our children's disabilities and our own personal weaknesses to be the impetus to keep us soft and pliable, so that He can mold us, and change us, and use us for the purpose He designed for us. And in doing that, God makes us who He wants us to be.

I have been guilty of introspection. When I get my eyes off of myself, I see that many of those pretty people have *also* had a few detours as *they* traveled here and there. Tragedy strikes families in different ways: an athletic husband stuck with a disabling disease, a son in prison, a daughter in a mental institution, a young wife with incurable cancer, a granddaughter with AIDS. Are any of their lives any easier than ours? I don't think so.

A friend of ours (who really does live in Holland) shared a well-known Dutch proverb: [44]

"Ieder huisje heeft zijn kruisje"

Translation:
"Every little home has its own little cross to bear"

Literal Translation:
Every Home Has Its Problems

I was wrong to be jealous and envious of the pretty people. For certain, there *are* those people who, remarkably, have known very little adversity in their lives. And I probably won't ever have much in common with them. But I think that we generally don't know what most other people must deal with. People handle their problems in different ways, and most people do not publicize their woes (much less write books about them). It is not our responsibility to say who has struggled the most or the least. The only one who really knows the weight of the Cross is the one who must carry it!

Recently, Trista was having outbursts of coprolalia (involuntary utterances of obscene or inappropriate statements or words), my mother was diagnosed with cancer of the bladder, and my father had a severe stroke. My pastor commented to me that I was having more than my share of problems lately.

I was surprised with the response that came from my mouth: "It makes me strong." Actually, it makes me lots of things. But most of all, it makes me grateful that I am the daughter of two extremely wise parents, the wife of one incredibly dedicated husband, and the mother of two very special children. Without the trials that my daughters' individual handicaps have brought into my life, I could not appreciate the fact that **disabilities are a very special gift**. My children's handicaps have taught me a quality of life that is only learned through pain and suffering. If I had not fought so hard for help and fair treatment for my children, I could not understand how hard my children have had to fight in *their* daily lives. Living with a handicap is a tall order. I wouldn't wish it on anyone. Handicaps happened, not just once but twice in our family, and we are all stronger because of them.

~ ~ ~

I T IS NOT THE CRITIC WHO COUNTS: NOR THE MAN WHO POINTS OUT HOW THE STRONG MAN STUMBLES, OR WHERE THE DOER OF DEEDS COULD HAVE DONE THEM BETTER. THE CREDIT BELONGS TO THE MAN WHO IS ACTUALLY IN THE ARENA, WHOSE FACE IS MARRED BY DUST AND SWEAT AND BLOOD; WHO STRIVES VALIANTLY; WHO ERRS, AND COMES SHORT AGAIN AND AGAIN; BECAUSE THERE IS NOT EFFORT WITHOUT ERROR AND SHORTCOMINGS; BUT WHO DOES ACTUALLY STRIVE TO DO THE DEEDS; WHO KNOWS THE GREAT ENTHUSIASMS, THE GREAT DEVOTIONS; WHO SPENDS HIMSELF IN A WORTHY CAUSE, WHO AT BEST KNOWS IN THE END THE TRIUMPHS OF HIGH ACHIEVEMENT AND WHO AT THE WORST IF HE FAILS, AT LEAST FAILS WHILE DARING GREATLY, SO THAT HIS PLACE SHALL NEVER BE WITH THOSE COLD AND TIMID SOULS WHO KNOW NEITHER VICTORY NOR DEFEAT.

Theodore Roosevelt

THE AUTHOR'S PARENTS
ANITA AND "ROBY" PIPES

Special Gifts and Special Education

It is a paradox that programs for exceptional children have been so popular in school districts across the nation, while at the same time parents of handicapped children continue, nationwide, to beg and battle for much-needed extra help for their children.

Special programs for exceptional children were funded with generous portions of federal dollars. Many of our friends had children in the Talented and Gifted (TAG) program. Those children were educationally advantaged because they were smart, and zealous in school. I was baffled when I discovered that our schools further reinforced their privileged status by providing some incredible opportunities, resources and intellectual environments for a select few extra-bright students. And meanwhile, there were numerous handicapped students left out in the cold in the midst of that very rich learning environment at school, unable to access services and the extra help they *desperately* needed. The hours I spent fighting for services for our disabled child sometimes exceeded the hours that child spent in school! Parents of handicapped children are already overwhelmed and overburdened with the grave responsibilities of raising their very needy children. When those same parents must fight for services to get their children through school, I perceive it is nothing short of a slap in the face to see an already privileged student sector being served up generous *extra* helpings.

Allow me, if you will, to regress for a moment to talk about "the good old days," before such special programs.

I was a very bright student in the '50s and '60s, accustomed to earning special privileges and perks in all the schools I attended in La Grande. We "smart kids" used to be called "brown-nosers" and "teachers' pets" because we were easy to teach, anxious to learn, and we often spent our extra time helping the teachers and other students. I had ample time and opportunities along the way to help many other students.

My most memorable in-class opportunity was being a high school tutor for a classmate who was "retarded." I learned a lot, helping Jane. Students didn't always like having "those kids" in classes – many of them were smelly, loud, and ill-mannered. Certainly it was probably more comfortable (for everyone) to keep them pushed aside, off in their own special rooms. They didn't call it "inclusion" then, but I thought it was more than fair that the special education kids could and should come to class with us whenever possible. I was probably equally as advantaged as Jane was disadvantaged. It never occurred to me to feel deprived because Jane got more assistance than I did. By comparison, it was *me* who was sovereignly advantaged, and Jane *deserved* all the extra help she received because she *needed* all the help she could get! I was going to succeed *with or without* assistance. Jane, by contrast, would most certainly fail without lots of help.

In the '80s, a real push came in our region for the TAG programs. The logic seemed to run something like this: if the "retarded kids" were getting extra help, shouldn't the "smart kids" also get an equal portion of extra attention? It seemed so strange to me that we were fighting so hard just to obtain the adaptive education that Trista seemed to need more with each passing year; and meanwhile, TAG programs were offering second helpings to those students who had already been given their dessert. While handfuls of "talented" and "gifted" children were being placed in a special curriculum to challenge the untapped areas of their already brilliant minds, we were always struggling to seize some crumbs of special education for Trista. We were just trying to get the schools to *work with us*, to help our daughter experience success, and to get her through the academic "adventure."

I remember the day that our eighth grader, Tia, was invited to join the junior high TAG program. I think it is significant that Tia was aware of the inequity of the programs: while her handicapped sister's needs were being poorly met in the same school, Tia's selection for TAG was a bittersweet complement. Tia felt she would be uncomfortable with the TAG label. How could she face Trista? The contrast between the two was already painful enough, without rubbing Trista's face in it. Our younger daughter declined the invitation, on principle alone. It was a tough stance for a 13 year-old but the decision was made entirely on her own, and it was the *right* one because it was the *righteous* one.

TAG is not a new program. The Association for the Gifted, also known as TAG, was organized as a division of The Council for Exceptional Children in 1958. I don't intend to throw the baby out with the bath water as I address this issue. TAG has played a major part in helping both professionals and parents deal more effectively with one of our most precious resources – the gifted child. Everyone likes excellence, and everyone likes to be on a winning team.

But in all fairness, it is an uphill climb to keep people interested in special education. Special-needs students don't raise a school's Scholastic Aptitude Test (SAT) scores, nor a school's ranking in other comparative tests; handicapped kids rarely win the prestigious contests or gain placement in strategic academies; special education students don't receive the kinds of strokes that embellish the local schools and flatter the administrators. It is not nearly so glamorous to provide basic services to the differently-abled, to students who will probably always be underachievers. School districts receive federal funding for special education, not because it is an attractive grant program but because it is *mandated*.

The pendulum in education swings. Recent school reform efforts now emphasize improving teacher quality and ensuring accountability for results. The Educational Excellence for All Children Act of 1999 is President Clinton's proposal for reauthorizing the Elementary and Secondary Education Act (ESEA). TAG-type budgets have been drying up.

Interestingly, there is a new wave of reform in identifying talented and gifted children. There are several variations, but the basic focus is on the concept that there are *many* kinds of gifts, of which academic intelligence is only *one*. Dr. Howard Gardner, Co-Director of Project Zero and Professor of Education at Harvard University, has recently defined the Theory of Multiple Intelligences. As a result of years of research on the development of human cognitive capacities, he has essentially redefined our concept of intelligence, revealing a wider family of human intelligence than was previously recognized. Because of Dr. Gardner, "smartness" has taken on a whole new meaning.

The introduction to one of the new books on this subject is intriguing:

> In what ways are your students smart? Do you have some who can create beautiful pieces of visual art? Are others gifted in sports, making complex series of physical movements appear graceful and effortless? Some may play a musical instrument so well that listening touches chords within. A few may thrill to the challenge of mathematical precision. Others may love writing and have already learned the excitement of seeing their own stories or poems in print. Several may be natural leaders offering positive role models and trusted guidance to their classmates. And a few may possess penetrating personal insights about who they are and what they stand for, while pursuing important life goals. Among the students mentioned, who would be the most intelligent? The question is impossible to answer because each of the examples represents students who have developed different intelligences. Each student is unique and all in individual ways offer valuable contributions to human culture.
>
> Many students who fail to demonstrate the traditional academic intelligences are held in low esteem, and their strengths may remain unrealized and lost to both the school and society at large. [45]

Most special-needs students fail to demonstrate the traditional academic intelligences. But many special-needs students *are* gifted in nontraditional areas. Most special-needs students are held in low esteem. And I dare say, most of the strengths of special-needs students do remain unrealized and lost to both the school and society at large.

It is a probable truth that if special education were not a mandated program, our special-needs student population *would not be* well served. Though it may look like it to the casual observer, school is *not* fun-and-games for special-needs students. Our personal advocacy efforts when Trista was a child were focused entirely on getting Trista through school. Sometimes I jokingly say that it took our entire family to earn every credit Trista received in school. Wouldn't it have been refreshing to have also been a part of a special program that *blessed* Trista, instead of *stressed* her?

When we are pretty good at something, we generally *like* to do it. What a joy it would be to see our special-needs student population getting some second helpings of things they liked to do. "Smart" kids aren't the only ones who have gifts! The only thing special about special education is that it makes the difference between success and failure to *some* disadvantaged students. If we want to do something really special for our special-needs student population, let's bring them, right along with those easy-to-teach students, to the banqueting table that is full of things in which they might excel. Let's allow our special-needs student population to dip in for as many helpings as their plate will hold! Let us start dedicating ourselves to discovering the gifts in *every* child!

I realize it is risky for a former public school teacher (and the wife of a retired public school teacher) to write such a treatise as this. It is no secret that our advocacy efforts have *forced* us to jump through some of the traditional, politically correct hoops. We have *also* taken many potentially suicidal detours, and we've forged through leagues of dangerous territory. It has not always been pleasant. We made many mistakes that we wish we could undo. Sometimes we came away from those encounters with a very bad taste in our mouths. But in retrospect, **our advocacy efforts were always productive – and they were always worth the risks we took and the price we paid.**

> *"An investment in righteousness*
> *pays off for generations."*
>
> Joey Duff [46]

~ ~ ~

A Parent Speaks to Special Educators

A FEW THOUGHTS ON BEHALF OF THE PARENTS OF YOUR STUDENTS

Please be frank and honest with us. We need the information you have to share, and we respect your professional advice and expertise. It may be painful for us to listen to what you have to say, but inside we feel relief just hearing something. Our path has been, and always will be, long – but knowing you are there helps.

Please respect us, our children and our families. Above all, respect the feelings and thoughts that we share with you. You may believe we're unrealistic, opinionated, guilty or ignoring the obvious. Please listen though; those are our feelings, and they are important.

"They laugh so as not to cry!" Such true words! Tears come easily and frequently, and they are as much a surprise to us as they are to you. Don't be embarrassed or feel guilty when we cry. Take it as a sign of our humanness and feelings of safety that we react so when we are with you. Many people in the outside world understand neither our laughter nor our tears.

The same is true when we lash out or act defensive. Anger comes with pain. That anger has no focal point, so you may bear its brunt very undeservedly. For that we apologize. Do try to understand that it is usually not directed at you personally, but rather at a situation which makes us feel very helpless and, often, very alone. Lashing out might be our reaction to feeling we can't change the things that need to be changed.

Your work and continuing efforts on behalf of our disabled children mean more to us than we can ever explain. Teachers and others who support our children achieve a sense of self-worth, academic and physical successes and societal acceptance. Without your support our families face more upheaval and stress. Please try to understand that our lives are different from the average; we have learned to take life one day, sometimes one hour-at-a-time. We try to be aware and appreciative of the smallest steps while still maintaining our sense of humor and balance.

We are part of this vast thing called life, and you are a most important and integral part of our lives. Thank you for being there and helping us establish and maintain a quality of life appropriate to all members of our family!

by Peggy Roland [47]

mother of a 12 year-old daughter with educational difficulties

Natural Rights

WE HOLD THESE TRUTHS TO BE SELF-EVIDENT, THAT ALL MEN ARE CREATED EQUAL, THAT THEY ARE ENDOWED BY THEIR CREATOR WITH CERTAIN UNALIENABLE RIGHTS, THAT AMONG THESE ARE LIFE, LIBERTY, AND THE PURSUIT OF HAPPINESS. THAT TO SECURE THESE RIGHTS, GOVERNMENTS ARE INSTITUTED AMONG MEN, DERIVING THEIR JUST POWERS FROM THE CONSENT OF THE GOVERNED.

Declaration of Independence ~ 1776

Most Americans are familiar with this portion of the Declaration of Independence. Fewer Americans could tell us that the document is also known as "The Document of Natural Rights."

One of the men who signed that great document is Trista's great-great-great - - - paternal grandfather John Hart, of Hopewell, New Jersey. (We think it is also interesting to note that my father, Taylor Roby Pipes, is a direct descendant of the twelfth President of the United States, " 'Ol Rough and Ready" Zachariah Taylor.)

I have become intensely patriotic as a result of living abroad. I'm proud to be an American! Nonetheless, at the risk of sounding unpatriotic, I am not certain I agree that all men are created equal. It took an act of Congress to "secure these rights." The American Disabilities Act (ADA) provided the handicapped population their "certain unalienable Rights, that among these are Life, Liberty, and the pursuit of Happiness." But that, unfortunately, can never make disabled people equal to the *non*-disabled population.

When I survey the disabled population, I perceive that the way they were created has caused some of them to endure unimaginable hardships. I have wondered if those signers, in their silken shirts and feathered hats, didn't get a little too fancy with their English.

I'd be much more comfortable if it said, "that all men are endowed by their Creator," and just leave off the "created equal" phrase. There's *nothing* equal about the struggles and hardships a disabled person must endure for a *lifetime*!

One thing I do know is that each one of these special people has been created in the image of God, [48] and it is God who has given them the right to an abundant life. John 10:10 is my favorite scripture, where Jesus says:

> *"The thief [Satan] comes not, but for to*
> *steal, and to kill, and to destroy: I [Jesus]*
> *am come that [you] might have life, and that*
> *[you] might have it more abundantly."*
>
> John 10:10 (KJV)

I hate what the enemy has done to our Trista. I loathe what she must endure because of Tourette Syndrome and all her developmental disabilities. I ache so deeply because of the sacrifice that Trista has paid, due to her disabilities. I despise the way her multiple handicaps have generally ravaged our family. There have been times in my life when I thought my heart would *actually break* from the grief and pain that I felt. That anguish was caused by what her developmental disabilities have done to each one of us.

But I'm so thankful that God's design was for Trista to be part of *our* family. We have always been determined to help provide the best life available for Trista. She is an adult now but she is still our child. Trista was not created equal. But she was created in God's image. And she was born with the inalienable right to life, liberty, and the pursuit of happiness. That is truth, not only because she is an American but because she is our child, and because she is *God's very special child*. There is no higher privilege for parents than to secure the right of life, liberty, and the pursuit of happiness for their child. It also must not be overlooked that the *family* of special-needs children also have those rights for themselves. Every family member is part of the whole, but every family member is also an individual.

~ ~ ~

 Natural Rights

Parents' Declaration of Independence and Bill of Rights [49]

The following rights allow parents to determine if they are doing right by themselves; whether they are doing the right thing. The first four rights constitute the basic Declaration of Independence. Once these are realized, or at least are in process, the remaining rights become possible.

1. The right not to be blamed.

How devastating when a teacher or professional or anybody suggests that the reason why your child is in trouble is because of your guilt, or your inadequacy, or your psychological problems. Of course, in some cases there is an element, however small, of truth in some of the accusations, but rarely is it the main problem, and rarely is the criticism helpful. The right also applies to not being intimidated by professionals simply because of their presumed superior knowledge or status.

2. The right to understand what's going on.

No parent should leave a conference with school personnel, mental health professionals or physicians without a complete understanding of what they are talking about. If they use abbreviations for tests, or give a medical diagnosis in jargon you do not understand, it is always appropriate to ask for an explanation in language that you *do* understand thoroughly.

3. The right to not be exploited.

It is hard enough having to cope with the daily tasks and troubles of parenting. Imagine having to pay exorbitant rates for help from insensitive staff, and not getting your money's worth.

4. The right to accept help without apology.

If any friend or relative asks you if there is anything they can do for you, always say yes. You may lose 90 percent of your friends and relatives that way, but those who stick by you, you can count on. There is usually something somebody can do for you: babysit for an hour or two, take your child to the movies or ball game, run an errand for you. You must, however, expect in advance that most people's offers to help are not genuine.

5. The right to make decisions.

Parents are invariably under pressure to accept the decisions of experts. It is your child and your responsibility. It is up to you to make the decisions, even if you disagree with any combination of experts.

(continued)

6. The right to be angry.

Most of the progress that has been made in the field of the care and management of children with disabilities has resulted from the work of angry parents. Rarely can you count on professionals to take the initiative for progressive innovations in your child's best interest. It does occur in the realm of political advocacy, but rarely when it comes to the daily management of children with severe disabilities.

7. The right to a normal family life.

Having a child with a disability should not exclude anyone from family celebrations, parties or the whole range of what constitutes the joys and travails of family life. This is not to suggest that everybody or anybody will feel comfortable interacting with your child. The failure to appreciate the high level of discomfort that the average person has relating to people with disabilities certainly inhibits their acceptance in society. Talk about the discomfort. It is not a plea for pity; it is simply an introduction to eventual integration.

8. The right to live a part of your life that does not include your child.

There is a powerful need for parents to be on their own, to get away from everything, to go away on vacations without their children. No healthy, mature family functions well in a posture of togetherness all the time. Sisters and brothers may resent the need to play with and relate to the child with a disability to the exclusion of their own special needs.

9. The right to fake it from time to time.

From time to time it is perfectly all right to present the image that everything's OK, especially with people you do not care that much about.

Just as it is appropriate to express anger at times, it is also OK to squelch it. Recent evidence suggests that unexpressed anger is not necessarily harmful and is sometimes even beneficial. Just because we are angry does not mean that the other person is ready and able to receive our anger.

William James suggests that "Wisdom is learning what to overlook." And sometimes faking it creates the best possible conditions for improvement of really grim situations.

10. The right to expect miracles.

It is a right not to give up, not to operate on the assumption that our current scope of knowledge is a verdict of doom. It is incredible how many people have survived "death sentences." Look at the progress that is being made today with the help of computers. It is OK to expect miracles!

Mothers From ~~Hell~~ *Heaven*

If you are a parent of a special-needs child, the very fact that you are reading this book sets you apart as a parent. You are involved in your disabled child's life to a greater degree than the *majority* of parents of handicapped children.

I have observed through my work with Special Olympics (and also through my time spent in and around special education classrooms in my town) that *most* of those children's parents have not been active figures in the chronicles of their special-needs children. Special education professionals confirm my observation: relatively few parents of disabled children don the "advocacy hat" for their special-needs children.

That concept always seems strange to me. How could parents *not* fight for their special-needs children when, just by their birthright, those children have already gotten the "short end of the stick?" Parenting normal children is certainly no picnic, but parents of a disabled child know that extra commitment which is required because of their child's station in life. Parents who risc to that challenge really are "special parents!"

"The Parent Trap" is an old Disney movie from my teenage years. The title seemed funny then. But in real life, the "parent trap" is not so funny. Parents of handicapped children have *special insight* into that trapped feeling!

I hear parents of "normal" children expressing feelings about being trapped. Sometimes I think to myself, " . . . if you only knew!" I used to wonder what parents of normal children did all the time because sometimes it seemed that *all I did* was advocate for my special kids. Sometimes that *is* all we do! But the tide always turns – and we get to back off for awhile, to regroup for the next crisis.

Many parents have not been able to deal with all of those special challenges. I would not pretend to understand *why* marriages fracture, but I have observed that most special-needs children have parents who have experienced one or more divorces.

I recall our first involvement with the Oregon Tourette Association in the mid-'80s. Of the 20-or-so families represented at a state meeting, only two couples had marriages intact! Half of all children today will witness the breakup of a parent's marriage. Of these, close to half will also see the breakup of a parent's second marriage. [50] And that explains why 28 percent of all children under 18 years of age live with one parent. [51] My observation, though perhaps not so profound in light of those statistics, is that marriages become severely at-risk after the birth of a child with severe disabilities. This premise has proven fairly predictable over the years that I have been pondering this problem. Most of the time, for reasons totally unknown to me, I observed that the fathers of handicapped children sought greener pastures, and the mother was left with full responsibility for the child who had more needs than even *two* parents could realistically meet! It is also my observation that it is *usually* the mother who is left with the responsibility of raising and advocating for the disabled child.

The fact that my husband, Dave, and I are still together is only because of the sovereign Lord that we both love and live for. The Bible says, "God hates divorce." [52] The wisdom of God is wonderfully practical! When I look at all the additional problems that divorce creates in families, I think I understand why God speaks so strongly about this topic. *Every* marriage has some problems and we have not been exempt. Fortunately, Dave and I have never experienced any threatening division over managing our momentary battles on behalf of our children. The mere thought of raising our children alone probably put sufficient fear in each of us that we became terribly dependent on the other for strength and support. Neither one of us would have considered going "solo" in trying to raise our special-needs children, and that weakness has proven to be a very strong glue in our marriage. (And I suspect that it was rather intimidating for the professionals who knew they faced the certainty of taking on *both* of us whenever there was a conflict.)

When a child's disability becomes a dimension of family dynamics, new problems can ambush from every side. Parents are too often guilty of trusting professionals *before* they trust themselves, and they are frequently guilty of trusting the professionals *more than* they trust themselves. When the parent

     MOTHERS FROM ~~HELL~~ *HEAVEN*

advocate does become a viable force, the specialists do take note. Almost every time we attended yet another appointment on behalf of our disabled children, it seemed that a professional made reference to the "tenacity" that we demonstrated in our advocacy efforts for our daughters. From my perspective that always seemed to be an overstatement. Although it is the sad truth that *a very small percentage* of parents of special-needs children are in there fighting for their children who cannot fight for themselves, **I think it is *more normal than abnormal* for parents to be the primary advocates for their disabled children. The parent always knows the child best. And the parent is *always* the parent.** There is an inherent notable advantage in that status!

Parents of special-needs children belong to a tightly knit fraternity, penetrable and fully understood only by those who have paid the price. Parent advocates are often called "special parents." Perhaps that recognition, in itself, is just reward!

Sometimes we become so involved in our childen's problems that we tend to lose our own identity. If you are an advocating parent, the point I hope you catch here is that because of your extra parental involvement on behalf of your special child, you have already set yourself apart from the crowd! It is time for you to acknowledge that fact because *you* are special!

> *"To light a candle is better than*
> *to curse the darkness."*
>
> Eleanor Roosevelt

We have covered what feels like light-years' worth of territory on behalf of our disabled children. Sometimes it seems that our advocacy battles will *never* end. Perhaps they won't. "Once a parent, always a parent" is a trustworthy saying. Ask any older parent, and you will find that catchy phrase speaks truth to every generation (and I seriously doubt that the person who coined that phrase spoke from the perspective of the parent of a disabled child).

In hindsight, some of our momentary crises and battles don't seem all that significant. Others have been life-changing. But each "issue" (that's a buzz-word coined by mental-health professionals, which means "problem") required our total focus; and each issue had its own set of challenges. I would not pretend to have all the answers for you. Perhaps I don't have *any* answers for you because *each advocacy effort is unique.* Every advocacy challenge must be handled as individually as your own child.

I have not always been proud of the way I have executed my advocacy efforts. I am certain that sometimes the recipient of my advocacy efforts thought *she*, instead of the plan, was the one being executed! We have *all* learned in the course of this difficult journey, and I confess my mistakes and inappropriate efforts with embarrassment and a degree of sadness. My fledgling efforts sometimes hurt people. And, sometimes those clumsy efforts alienated us from the very people we needed "on our side."

> *Parents of exceptional children are like teabags –*
> *at their strongest when in hot water.* [53]

Having said that, I must stress that I have no remorse for any of the advocacy we have done for our daughters. The battles *had to be fought*, and most times we were the only ones who would enlist. I never won any school awards for being the nicest mom, the favorite mom, the most helpful mom, or parent of the year. There are times I felt fortunate to have not been *thrown out* of meetings at school, or permanently *banned* from school property! To this day there are educators who, as a result of former advocacy conflicts, do not regard me with great admiration nor enthusiasm. Some speak cordially with me only if they must; a few look the other way.

Nonetheless, when I lay my head down on my pillow at night, I can affirm beyond a shadow of a doubt that I have always given our children's advocacy my very best shot. And in so doing, I know that, like thousands of other parent advocates, generations to follow will reap the harvest of the energies we invested for our own children.

> *"People who believe in a cause*
> *aren't discouraged by opposition."*
>
> Milton Freidman [54]

 MOTHERS FROM ~~HELL~~ *HEAVEN*

My father often quoted this little poem to me during my childhood. I would guess that he did not realize the influence that his philosophy and his lifestyle would have on my life. Dad's motto and his model have been my greatest sources of inspiration and motivation throughout my career as a parent advocate.

> **IF YOU HAVE TRIED AND HAVE NOT WON,**
>
> **NEVER STOP FOR CRYING,**
>
> **FOR ALL THE GREAT AND GOOD THAT'S DONE**
>
> **IS JUST BY PATIENT TRYING.**
>
> [anonymous]
> Quoted by Taylor Roby Pipes

Are you feeling the pressure of the parent advocacy trap? "Don't stop for crying!" Start kicking the ends out of your trap. Keep trying. Patient trying! You'll do much great and good for your child! *You* **are the best advocate your child will ever have:** *You* **are his** *parent*!

The results that we have reaped on behalf of our children are our reward. The results for other people's benefit are pure bonus – bountiful gleaning is there for whomever shall harvest! It is small wonder that I have heard advocates for special-needs children called "Mothers from Hell!" I'd be proud to have that label – because I know in my heart that we mothers who fight so hard are a *special gift* for our children. To the opposition, we may *seem* like mothers from hell, but I think we're probably really from **heaven**!

~ ~ ~

Our deepest fear is not that we are inadequate.

Our deepest fear is that we are
powerful
beyond
measure.

It is our light, not our darkness, that most frightens us.

We ask ourselves, who am I to be brilliant, gorgeous,
talented and fabulous?

Actually, who are you "not" to be?

You are a child of God.

Your playing small doesn't serve the world.

There's nothing enlightened about shrinking
so that other people won't feel insecure around you.

We were born to make manifest
the glory of God that is within us.

It's not just in some of us; it's in everyone.

And as we let our own light shine,
we unconsciously give other people
permission to do the same.

As we are liberated from our own fear,
our presence automatically liberates others.

Nelson Mandela
1994 Inaugural Speech

VOCATIONAL REHABILITATION

My parents were always learning, and they always seemed to enjoy playing *and* working! My father was a railroader, a World War II veteran, and a captain in the U.S. Army Reserve. I was in grade school when Dad completed his Graduation Equivalency Diploma (GED). In those days, that was quite a remarkable endeavor for a family man in his '40s who had a stable job and a solid future. The GED was something he needed to do for himself. We had spelling bees at home, and Dad loaned his business mathematics book to me when I became bored in the fifth grade. I have vivid memories of walking in the door after school, greeted by the smell of fresh baked bread, and seeing my mother absorbed in a copy of *Reader's Digest*. After television came to La Grande, Oregon, I watched TV shows like *National Geographic*, *Animal Kingdom* and travelogues. Whenever our family went on vacations, we toured factories and points of historic interest. My most memorable trips were in Oregon, where we sampled cheeses at the Tillamook Cheese factory in Tillamook, tasted freshly cooked tuna in the Bumble Bee cannery in Astoria, nibbled on fresh-baked cookies at the Nabisco factory in Portland, and handled the beautiful wool threads, fabrics and blankets as we toured the Pendleton Woolen Mills in Pendleton.

I was raised by plain, moral parents who had a strong work ethic. Mom and Dad bought rental properties with hopes of paying them off quickly so that the rents could put my sister and I through college. Our family lived frugally because of that goal. Although college professors were among their tenants, my father always said that he would rather rent to blue-collar workers because they usually took better care of the properties, and he had more in common with them. He had books about plumbing and wiring and auto mechanics because he *needed* them to solve his most recent maintenance problem. I enjoyed helping my father on the rentals, and I learned wonderfully useful things as I worked with him as his young "sidekick." I was getting a vocational education, and I didn't even know it.

Vocational-technical colleges were in their infancy when I was preparing to leave high school. I felt those schools carried somewhat of a stigma. My reasoning was biased. I *erroneously* assumed that people pursued a two-year "vo-tech" degree only if they could not handle the challenge of the more traditional four-year college program. In those days, salaries were generally proportional to the number of years of college training, and my parents supported their daughters' pursuit of Bachelor's degrees. My sister and I graduated with the same degree from Oregon State University, and our major in Home Economics Education was about as "vocational" as any four-year university degree could be! We are both extremely handy, creative, and resourceful in ways that most housewives are not. Part of that was "absorbed" from our parents during our childhood, but we both received fantastic vocational-technical training as Home Economists.

So with that kind of background, one might understand why I was eager for both our young daughters to get some kind of vocational training. Most of Dave's family had been fortunate to have good blue-collar jobs without a college education, so he, too, was always supportive of vocational education for our girls. Tia was a very good student, and we knew she would succeed at whatever she chose. But we felt that Trista needed all the help she could get, and vocational training could prove to be a precious commodity in her life.

As with so many other significant events in her life, Trista was fortunate to be the recipient of Job Training Partnership Act (JTPA) services when the program was in its infancy. An outgrowth of the Education for All Handicapped Children Act of 1975 (PL 94-142), JTPA began to be implemented in Oregon during Trista's senior high years. The program created significant statewide partnerships between counties, the local employment and training system, and education institutions. Its objective was to meet the difficult challenges of providing professional development opportunities to special-needs students, to assist young adults in making informed career choices, and to pursue skill training in order to achieve employment.

During one of our brainstorming sessions with some regional and state resource people, it was suggested that we contact Jackie Raw at her JTPA Office in Pendleton. Through Jackie's able facilitation, Trista was the fortunate beneficiary of a substantial amount of services to assist her employment quest. Services from JTPA included vocational guidance, as well as financial assistance for school-related expenses and training-related services and referrals.

Under JTPA, Trista worked one school vacation as a summer recreation aide at a day care center. During her junior year, she was employed on a school-release work program as a dining room aide at a local rest home. And then the following summer she was an aide for the migrant program at a local elementary school. During her senior year, she had another school-release work program, but this time it was as a Title I reading aide at a local elementary school. She later "faced shelves" in a grocery store, tidying up displays and moving products to the fronts of shelves. After she finished high school, she worked with other disabled workers on a cleaning crew at the Umatilla Army Depot.

It seemed there was always a work-related problem of one kind or another. Although the personalities of the problems were as unique as the jobs themselves, they could always be categorized as having to do with either her Tourette tics, her obsessive compulsive disorder (OCD), or her attention deficit hyperactive disorder (ADHD). It was (and still is) difficult to separate the *problem* from the *person*. We frequently found ourselves extremely frustrated with Trista as she *appeared* to sabotage yet another wonderful employment opportunity.

Although Trista was eligible for our region's JTPA funding until she was 21, she became connected with Mr. Al Obrist, of the regional Vocational Rehabilitation Division (VRD), and JTPA was phased out of Trista's life. It was with some relief that we waved good-bye to JTPA: it had become an embarrassment to us that Mrs. Raw worked so diligently to provide new JTPA placement opportunities for Trista, only to have Trista fail, for one reason or another, at every job.

As we became acquainted with VRD, we learned that their rehabilitation services include vocational counseling, evaluation, physical restoration, skills training, job placement and preparation for independent living. In Oregon, VRD's services are provided in collaboration with other businesses, state agencies, community rehabilitation programs and independent living service providers.

Mr. Obrist had the resources to provide more basic-skills evaluation and training for Trista. We had all concluded that Trista needed more support in her employment – someone to shadow her and keep her on task. Her obsessions and attention deficit always became problematic when Trista began to get bored with her work. And lacking specific skills, Trista became easily bored at *all* menial work.

So VRD reasoned that Trista would probably benefit from being *trained* for more challenging work, and they set out trying to establish exactly *what kind* of work would best suit her. After she finished high school, VRD sent Trista to the Columbia Gorge Training Center in The Dalles, Oregon, for several weeks of skills evaluation. The quest was to discover what Trista was capable of, and what she had propensity toward. They kept running into the same thing that we discovered through her JTPA jobs: she had significant work-related problems that were interwoven with her Tourette tics, her OCD, or her ADHD; and *possibly* some of those problems were also related to lack of motivation and / or desire to work. But the Columbia Gorge Center felt they could help Trista with some of these issues, and they offered to keep her employed for an extended period of training, for which we were most grateful. Through VDR funding, Trista worked and continued to be trained at the Center for another year. It was an admirable effort on the part of the Center and VRD. Truly, Trista was, and still is, an employment challenge.

About a year later, Trista moved to Washington with the same caregiver that we first used while she was being evaluated at the Center in The Dalles. She was a nice lady, and Trista matured with this caregiver in ways that were not possible in our home. In Spokane, we were introduced to Washington's Division of Vocational Rehabilitation (DVR). As we had experienced with their sister-agency in Oregon, DVR was extremely helpful in providing more vocational training and resources. Her first Washington placement was doing piecework assembly in a rather high-functioning sheltered workshop setting. Then she moved to Spokane's Goodwill stores for more challenging employment, where she worked at a variety of different jobs in two separate employment attempts.

Trista *always* ultimately became apathetic about her employment. What followed was her either quitting or being released. In all fairness, the indifference was probably interrelated to her multiple disability issues. But we have been reticent to put the full burden of blame for her job failures on her disabilities alone. It is a "chicken and egg" issue – we have never been really sure which comes first.

One day I visited several worksites with Ron Kurtz, the associate director of Spokane's Arc. I saw some fascinating workplace models, where their disabled clients were rotated from job to job to keep them from being bored. After we concluded the tour, I was reminded of what we surmised from her high school work experiences. If we could somehow create a workplace environment where Trista had consistent shadowing-type supervision to keep her on task, and where she could be systematically rotated every few weeks to a new workcenter (so that she did not become bored with her work), perhaps Trista *could* succeed at long-term employment. Unfortunately, such employment opportunities are very rare, and the finances needed to provide such a shadow-mentor could probably only be met through long-term public disability funding. No one in the private sector could be expected to hire two people to do one person's job!

When we presented DVR with this new challenge, they had already spent a small fortune on Trista, pursuing and developing evaluation, training and employment options. I practically begged for services because I was convinced that we finally had the solution for her successful employment. Ultimately, DVR consented to help her one last time, and Arc's employment representative proceeded to identify suitable placement options for Trista.

When the day came that Trista had an opportunity to select from her palette of job choices, she announced that she really didn't want to work after all. We were devastated. And mortified.

I love to learn. I love to work. And I am a people pleaser. There is not a fiber in me that relates to Trista's decision to not want to work. But the bottom line was that she is an adult, and we had to respect her decision because we could not stand over her with a whip and insist that she worked! It has been a huge embarrassment to us that Trista has had such wonderful employment and training opportunities, and yet she continues to be unemployable. This dilemma is *not* because many concerned people did not care enough, nor because they did not try hard enough. Trista has always had 100 percent support to help her overcome her disabilities. But we met our match on this one! You can lead a horse to water . . .

We have high praise and gratitude for all the employers and employment facilitators who have worked throughout the years with Trista. Our hats are off to *every one* of them. I am especially impressed with the various arms of vocational rehabilitation agencies. The two states with which we have worked have terrific programs and accomplished people administering those programs; real people who are client-centered, who have a dream and a vision for their clients; employees who make things happen.

We have often told Trista what Dr. Jack Shore, of the Shoreline School District in the Seattle area says, "Ya Gotta Wanna." Finding the missing ingredient which will provide sufficient motivation for Trista to become employable may well be the one mystery that we will never solve. It is not normal for someone, who has the *capabilities* that Trista *does have,* to be unemployable. But *her disabilities are not normal* – they are very complex, and some of them are very severe. I dream of the day that Trista is able to conquer her various disabilities to the point that she has some kind of long-lasting purposeful employment because I believe in this quote:

"Working is more than a way of earning a livelihood.

It is a way of keeping one's self respect." [55]

We earnestly desire for Trista to discover the value of being productive. I almost titled this book *Hope Dies Last* because there are still some areas of Trista's life with which I have not yet come to grips. I rejected that title but it *is* a good motto for Dave and I!

     VOCATIONAL REHABILITATION

In his 1998 President's Message to the Tourette Syndrome Association, Paul Devore echoed our sentiments.

> "I would like Tourette Syndrome Association to take the leadership role in helping people rise above the adversity of Tourette Syndrome, and challenge them to realize and achieve their full potential. People with TS can live worthwhile and productive lives, with TS as **an** issue with which to deal, but not as **the** issue preventing them from striving for excellence and living a fruitful, productive and enjoyable life."[56]

Having said all this, I need to close this subject by emphasizing that we *don't know* whether Trista sabotaged all those jobs. She has proven herself as being incapable of holding a job, but we still *don't know* whether this is caused by her disabilities *or* her lack of motivation to work, or whether her lack of motivation to work *is* also her disability. She seems content to just exist, without what *we* consider to be fruitful, productive activity; she is satisfied to fill her days listening to music, playing on her computer, talking on the phone, and sleeping excessively. Trista functions at *such* a high level in so many *other* areas of her life, it is *almost incomprehensible* that disabilities are the cause of this employment dilemma. Yet, our welfare system is a good indicator that there are *many* people who are content to be unemployed, and who seem to have *no* apparent disabilities. So perhaps this issue isn't a mortal sin for Trista. And perhaps our attentions need to be focused, instead, on her happiness and the things that *are* important to her. Prior to her diagnosis of Tourette Syndrome, we were never sure whether she could or could not control her tics. Academically, we never knew for sure which problems were attributable to learning disabilities and which were not. We are at that same place with employment. We don't know Trista's full potential, and we may, therefore, *never know* if she is capable of realizing and achieving it. This topic requires an extra measure of understanding and tolerance on our part, lest we repeat the kinds of mistakes we made previously. Our expectations for her may just be too high.

Parenting *really is* a difficult job!

~ ~ ~

A man was putting up a sign, ***Puppies for Sale***, and before he had driven the last nail, there was a small boy standing at his side. That kind of sign seems to attract small boys. The youngster wanted to know how much the puppies were going to cost. The man told him they were very good dogs and that he didn't expect to let any of them go for less than thirty five or fifty dollars. There was a look of disappointment, and then a question: "I've got $2.37. Could I look at them?"

The man whistled and called, "Lady!" – and out of the kennel and down the runway came Lady, followed by four or five little balls of fur, with one lagging considerably behind. The boy spotted the laggard and, pointing, asked, "What's wrong with him?" The reply was that the veterinarian had said that there was no hip socket in the right hip, and that the dog would always be lame. The boy's immediate rejoinder was, "That's the one I want to buy. I'll give you $2.37 down and fifty cents a month 'til I get him paid for." The man smiled and shook his head. "That's not the dog you want. That dog will never be able to run and jump and play with you."

The boy, very matter-of-factly, pulled up his little trouser leg and revealed a brace running down both sides of his badly twisted right leg and under the foot, with a leather cap over the knee. "I don't run so well myself," he said, "and he'll need somebody that understands him."

Yes, just a boy and a dog, but they stand for a great truth of our time. What we need desperately is the desire and the concern to understand.

Matthew Hill, Judge

Supreme Court, State of Washington [57]

SSI and Other Mazes

I did not understand why Supplemental Security Income (SSI) was important for Trista. Some parents remarked how wonderful it was to receive the generous SSI monthly benefit, but that never computed with me. Trista's disabilities were not creating a financial hardship on us; it was no more expensive to raise Trista than Tia. When someone would query me about why we hadn't sought SSI for Trista, I always replied, "We don't need it."

Nonetheless, I would occasionally wonder if I was missing something. I made many inquiries all over the northwest, to check out possible housing and training options for Trista. The *first* question was *always*, "Has Trista qualified for Developmental Disability (DD) services?" I would answer that she did, indeed, have Oregon DD eligibility. And *then* they would ask, "Does Trista get SSI?" When I would explain that we felt she didn't need SSI, I would then be told that their particular program could not serve her without SSI eligibility. It didn't make sense to me. She was clearly disabled, and she was qualified in every other way for their services. But the lack of one classification kept them from even considering her. After hearing that story too many times, I determined we would try to fit the mold. SSI eligibility appeared to be *essential* for Trista.

SSI eligibility meant two things: (1) Trista's ability to be considered for various programs and services, and (2) a monthly allotment. I decided we would just apply for the eligibility, and decline the monthly dollars.

SSI told me that was impossible because the SSI eligibility classification came *with* the monthly benefit. What a system – only in America would we have to accept money when we only really needed services! I decided to pursue SSI because *we needed that eligibility classification.*

The cordial Social Security employee assisted us with the initial application for Supplemental Security Income on August 21, 1991, right there in the Pendleton branch office. When I visited with the office worker, I was told that SSI applicants could not have resources worth more than $2,000. We had a problem. We had methodically saved for Trista's college from the time she was just an infant. It was now obvious that she would never need all that money for college, but the funds had been left in her name because the "kiddie tax" on her interest was lower than for our tax bracket. I knew her SSI application would be denied *until* we liquidated her resources. The "Notice of Disapproved Claim" was dated September 17, 1991.

The disqualifying factor on her letter of denial was *resources*: "Resources are the things that you own such as cash, stocks, bank accounts, certain types of life insurance, buildings, and land on which you do not live. We do not include as resources the home in which you live, one car used for necessary activities, and some other things." The Social Security worker had informed us there were two ways to make her qualify. Trista could (1) make a gift of her college savings to us. However, this would invoke SSA's 24-month disposal rule, whereby she would not fully qualify for SSI services for two years. Or she could (2) convert the cash (a liquid, countable resource) into another type of resource (non-liquid) that they could exclude (i.e. a home to live in), and be fully eligible for all SSI benefits. We were, in fact, in the process of purchasing the house directly across the street from our family home. We had coveted it as our future retirement home, and when the elderly Mr. and Mrs. Rehm died and their house went into estate, we seized the opportunity to purchase it. Our intent was to just rent it out for a few years until we retired, at which time we would sell our house, and move across the street to a house and lot that was half as large.

Liquidating Trista's resources was suddenly very simple! There was no reason why Trista could not purchase the Rehm house, and then just live across the street from us.

I had also just received a call from a very special friend who had been displaced from her home. She wondered if we happened to know of an inexpensive place where she could live for an extended period of time.

Within a few hours, we had the solution for liquidating Trista's resources, *and* we had a responsible live-in roommate (because we were not convinced that Trista was capable of living alone).

I called the estate attorney, and informed him that the name of the purchaser for the Rehm house needed to be changed to "Trista Conklin." Then I called my friend and offered her free rent if she would not mind living in Trista's house with her.

And then it was time to get down to business. The *easy* part of the SSI application had been completed at our local Social Security office. I was given the eight page Disability Report to complete at home.

I always try to do a little research before I pursue something important. I don't like surprises. And I don't like redoing things because I did them wrong the first time. During my time of gathering information on SSI, I discovered that a business acquaintance had a good deal of experience with SSI appeals. [58] Attorney Richard McNerney [59] gave me some coffee-cup advice for filling in the SSI Disability Report: **Don't leave any blanks on the application, and give detailed supporting documentation for everything you can.**

When I reviewed the instructions on the SSI Disability Report, one phrase stood out in the first paragraph:

COMPLETE ANSWERS WILL AID IN PROCESSING THE CLAIM.

I had just heard that same advice from Attorney McNerney. I took it seriously.

There are several sections in the SSI Disability Report:

- Information About Your Disabling Condition
- Information About Your Medical Records
    (in-depth information on doctors you have seen
    since your condition began)
- Information About Your Activities
    (dates, names, addresses)
- Information About Your Education
- Information About the Work You Did
    (list and describe all jobs in the last 15 years,
    with addresses, dates, etc.)
- Remarks [*three inches* of space for additional input]

I had most of the information at my fingertips because in the previous month, I had completed the application and appeal process for Trista to be classified Developmentally Disabled in Oregon. I discovered that I was missing some of her medical reports prior to age five (the years before her first diagnosis at the Crippled Children's Division). So I sent Trista's signed and dated Authorization to Release Medical Records [60] to every doctor and hospital that I could think of that might have treatment records for Trista under the age of five. I even procured my complete obstetrical file and hospital delivery records. The new information was *most* enlightening, and it answered many questions I had pondered for years (and it also raised many more questions . . .).

As I analyzed the SSI Disability Report, I could see that we needed *something* which would clarify Trista's very confusing malady and punctuate its impact on her life. Dave suggested that some testimonials from significant players in Trista's life might be worthwhile – letters from credible people who could attest to the severity of her disability.

I mailed an urgent request to ten people who knew Trista quite well. I asked them to write, with "no regard to hurting our feelings," any information they could supply which would illustrate the gravity of Trista's disability issues. Teachers, social workers, medical professionals, a pastor and a camp counselor returned thoughtful letters describing their perceptions of Trista and her future needs.

I typed the Social Security disability report, including *several* extra pages that listed additional information wherever the pre-printed form did not provide sufficient space. Moreover, to give an accounting for her recent house purchase to liquidate her resources, I attached an addendum which spelled out the chronology of that process. Copies of bank statements showing zero balances were also attached, along with her new real estate deed and closing reports documenting her recent purchase of the Rehm house.

Trista's house closed on October 31, 1991. She and her new roommate had already moved in. I completed the SSI Disability Report on the same day, and asked Attorney McNerney to review

                    SSI AND OTHER MAZES

the entire application packet. He gave me a nominal invoice for his services, an approving handshake and a nod of complete approval, with the comment, "No additional suggestions. Good Luck!"

I composed the following cover letter:

RE: SSI Application

Trista Conklin

Social Security Number xxx-xx-xxxx

DOB 12-28-1971

Attached you will find the SSI Disability Report for Trista Conklin. I have attached several additional items of information and documentation which should prove helpful to you in your review.

Thank you.

(*signature*)

Jean Conklin (Trista's Mom)

Using typed category index tabs to separate the sections, the following items were assembled in a new black report portfolio:

- Cover letter

- The SSI Disability Report

- Several pages of additional documentation that would not fit in the space provided on the forms

- 10 letters from professionals, describing Trista's disabilities and her long-term prognosis

- Trista's most recent bank account statements, showing no resources

- Real estate deed and closing report for Trista's new house

The SSI Disability Report, et. al. was *hand delivered* to the Social Security Branch Office in Pendleton on Friday, November 1, 1991. (I had to laugh: they asked if I wanted them to photocopy the materials so I could keep the originals. They had never received such a polished application.)

Evidently we had the right combination of documentation, accuracy and thoroughness, along with an extra measure of prayer and God's blessing. A short three weeks later, Trista received a document, dated November 20, 1991, which proclaimed,

"You meet the medical requirement to receive SSI payments."

We have never talked to *anyone* who has had their SSI application approved so quickly.

Our victory was short lived. In spite of the fact that our daughter was living directly across the street from our house, the arrangement was *not* working. Although we had accomplished everything on our agenda, we continued to be too involved in crisis intervention. Her actions were putting her, and her roommate, at risk. Because of some inappropriate behaviors that threatened her safety, Trista was ultimately placed in a lock-up ward for 10 days in a Portland psychiatric hospital. The behavioral psychologist's recommendation at discharge was that our daughter needed 24-hour supervision.

She had been back in her home for less than one week, with even tighter supervision, when we discovered she had cycled back up to her pre-lock-up behavior. The revelation put me over the edge: I thought I actually was losing my sanity, and the local child protective officer heartily agreed. Realizing that I was becoming unhinged from reality, I packed my bag and tearfully attempted to check myself into the stress center at our area psychiatric hospital. The counselor asked if I was suicidal. I replied, "Not at this precise moment." I guess I should have been more graphic because they said they couldn't admit me if I was not suicidal (and it was too late to revise my statement). Feeling thwarted, I drove back to Hermiston. Once at home, I summoned Trista to our house. We sat down together and had a heart-to-heart talk. I explained to her that things *had* to change. I presented her with two options: to either go back to the Portland lock-up situation for an indefinite period of time, or to agree to move back home with us, where she would be supervised every minute of every hour of every day. Trista chose to move back home with us. We hired a caregiver to be with her whenever Dave or I could not be there. I went back on antidepressants. And we installed a security alarm system, so we would know whenever a door or a window was opened by someone other than Tia, Dave, the caregiver, or me.

I called our Social Security worker and asked what we should do because Trista's house was no longer an exempt resource if she was not actually *living in* her house. If Trista were to sell her house, then she would be right back where she was before she bought her house, with excess countable resources. The SSA representative expressed her sadness over our dilemma, and she suggested we consider liquidating her assets anyway, to get through the 24-month window so we could reapply. I thanked her for her help, and we decided to take the representative's advice. Then an amazing thing happened: the SSI representative called back several days later, saying that she had discussed the issue with her supervisor, who had researched the situation. They discovered that because Trista had been living in her exempt resource, she could *gift the house to us,* and her SSI eligibility would continue uninterrupted:

> ". . . the valid transfer of a resource at less than fair
> market value does not affect SSI eligibility." [61]

And that is exactly what she did. Using a document which indicated that Trista was gifting the property to us, we had a new deed recorded in our name, and we submitted a photocopy of the documents to Social Security. Trista's SSI eligibility was never interrupted. I have the highest praise for Social Security employees. They have always treated me with respect, and I have found them to be extremely helpful and willing to go the extra mile for their clients.

I do not like to reflect on those chaotic months, back in 1991. Some days it seemed like there was a horrible rock band in my head, playing the most awful non-music, with their whiny steel guitars screeching unending electronic discordances at a frequency and intensity that was unbearable. Sometimes I felt as though I was drugged, with my life spinning out of control around me, while I was hopelessly attempting to find something to hold onto so that I might have just one moment of stability. On a few rare occasions, I would find how to switch over to a more pleasant "channel," where everything would seem predictable, and where I could hear the "elevator music" in my head. But the tranquility was elusive, and very soon it would seem that some horrible interference would overtake the good connection, and that rock band in my head would apprehend me, steal my peace, and propel me toward my dark hole with the lie that by withdrawing from reality, I might escape its furor.

My biggest heartache was what our black times were doing to Tia. I felt so sorry for her, having to be a part of all those problems. She couldn't escape them because she was part of our family – in one way or another, what happens to one person in a family happens to them all. I know it was such an embarrassment to Tia because other students knew what was going on. And it must have been painful beyond words, watching, helplessly, as her mother dissolved into the grips of mental trauma and then despondency. We tried to shield our younger daughter from everything we could, but ultimately I became so delicate that my only focus was just getting through the current day. But life does go on, and situations get resolved. The rock band went away, and the orchestra came back. We have enjoyed much more pleasant music since those hellish months became history. And Tia has written a few of her own very enjoyable sonatas. Had Tia not been made of such strong fiber, perhaps she would have been a casualty of the chaos. We only have God to thank – He has taken *very* good care of us all!

As the months passed and life got back to normal in the Conklin house, we needed to confront an *ethical* issue that had to do with Trista's vacant house across the street. Dave and I did not feel right about simply having Trista gift her house to us in order to qualify for SSI. It was now technically ours but we purged our social conscience by arranging a way for her to be reimbursed for the "purchase" of the house. By specifying in our wills the value of her house purchase plus accrued interest, that sum will flow directly to Trista's Special Needs Trust whenever we die.

We could have funded Trista's special needs trust at that time because the legal paperwork was all in place but we have repeatedly been advised against it. There evidently remain some gray areas in SSI and DD regulations; there have been situations where special needs trust assets have been regarded as a client's ineligible resources. We would not put at risk Trista's SSI eligibility.

(Editor's Note: *See* Appendix – What Will Become of My Child?)

Throughout the process, I have been Trista's Representative Payee, which means I am responsible to receive, disburse, and account for Trista's SSI benefits. The representative payee has some annual reporting responsibilities, and I have learned how to arrange my bookkeeping to simplify that chore. I always photocopy the completed annual report before I send it in, so that I can refer to previous year's forms as I begin to fill in the current year's forms.

(Editor's Note: *See* Appendix – Creating Your Advocacy File)

One might wonder if Trista has ever benefited, other than financially, from her SSI eligibility? The answer is a resounding **yes!** Not having SSI was a huge stumbling block. Almost every opportunity for our adult daughter was linked to SSI and DD eligibility. Once she qualified for both, many doors to special assistance opened with ease. We were never greatly inconvenienced for not having pursued SSI sooner but we could not have waited too much longer. Plus it was definitely to our advantage, and to hers, that she was over 18 when she applied. As an adult, she was viewed as her own legal entity, and our household resources were not an issue.

In a way, I am glad that we did not know to apply for SSI any sooner. My conscience simply would not have allowed Trista to give us that money to "keep" her, when she was already our responsibility as a minor. She caused us no extraordinary expenses, and I see no point in taking advantage of the system just because it doesn't know better. I emphatically disagree with today's very broad policy which encourages the parents of every student who is eligible for an IEP to submit an application for SSI. While there are many deserving families whose children who are not yet being served by SSI, there are those who seem to have their hand out the fastest and the farthest, and who abuse the system the worst. I know of too many children whose SSI benefits are blatantly used to feather the parents' nests. Because of such abuses, our country still has a way to go to achieve funding efficiency.

Trista lived with us two months after she moved back home. We spent all her SSI benefits on caregivers, since I refused to become a prisoner in my own home during those chaotic times. Trista needed very tight boundaries and was content to have round-the-clock supervision. The SSI benefit provided much-needed respite services for one battle weary mother. Several months later, in the spring of 1992, Trista moved to the city of The Dalles, Oregon, for some vocational rehabilitation. From that time until the present, her SSI benefit check has always been spent entirely on her room and board at various care providers.

Although initially we said we didn't need the SSI money for Trista, it has proven to be a valuable commodity to pay for her adult foster care, particularly in view of the fact that she is basically unemployable and requires the types of tenant support that are extremely expensive.

~ ~ ~

Editor's Note: Extensive technical information on
SSI is provided in this volume.

See APPENDIX – THE BASICS OF SSI

THE "S" WORD

There is probably no easy way to talk about sterilization for developmentally disabled adults. I find that if people have considered the topic at all, they are quite polarized in their opinions. In one camp are the human rights people who say all people have the right to experience everything that they choose to experience, and it is society's responsibility to "be there" for them and their offspring. In another camp are the religious rights people who say that childbearing is a God-given right, and if God didn't want disabled people to have children, he would have made them sterile. In yet another camp are the medical professionals who are afraid of malpractice suits based on ethics or misplaced regrets, and they don't want to risk being involved. There is the camp who believe that sterilization should occur as a social responsibility; they may or may not have an agenda that includes some of the theology that radicals like Hitler preached and practiced. And in an almost totally concealed camp are some already very involved parents of severely disabled children, who are mostly reluctant to talk about the very difficult, quiet decisions they either face or have already made with their adult children.

I was terribly naïve about the vehement polarization against sterilization for severely disabled adults. As the years ticked by, we began to realize we had far greater problems than we ever dreamed possible. We had a sexually active teenager who was incapable of being responsible for her actions. And she was being abused by anyone who was able to entice her with a play of affection. We were heartsick over her poor choices, angry at those who were using and abusing her, and afraid for her with respect to sexually transmitted diseases, not to mention our fears of a pregnancy.

To further complicate matters, we had become alarmed years earlier when we saw how cruel she could be to our baby kittens. The way she antagonized them it seemed like she was, at times, almost possessed – squeezing them too hard, dropping them angrily but with a smirk, or playing with them fiercely. We began to notice that she could demonstrate this behavior, without provocation, with *any* small animal. We stopped allowing her to babysit or to work with little children, in even the most casual sense. We reasoned, if she could be this mean-spirited with baby kittens, what might she do with a *human* child? She admitted to me once that she didn't like it when she heard babies cry too long, and she sometimes felt that she could not bear for them to *not* be quiet. We took our cue and provided situational restrictions to safeguard her, the best we could, from potential problems whenever little children were around.

And then there were those genetic concerns. A person with TS has about a 50 percent chance of passing the gene to one of his / her children with each separate pregnancy. It is also known that a higher than normal incidence of milder tic disorders and obsessive compulsive behaviors occurs in the families of TS patients. [62]

It was becoming more clear to us that Trista could not effectively raise even herself. She was almost an adult, but she was functioning six to eight years behind her peers in basic life skills. We asked ourselves, if Trista became pregnant, how in the world would she be able to raise a child, especially considering the added risk that her child could easily end up with Tourette?

As the gravity of specific sexual problems unfolded over a period of several years, we also frequently discussed with her the potential consequences of her unwise choices. Before Trista turned 18, she and I visited with our local family physician. Trista asked him to sterilize her. He declined, and explained that he could not do that procedure for a minor, but he invited her to come back when she turned 18.

After Trista reached the age of majority, she asked me to accompany her on a visit to our family doctor; her purpose was to once again request sterilization. Evidently the doctor had given her prior request more serious consideration, and he declined to help her. He muttered something about ethics and liabilities, and suggested she visit a specialist – out of town.

The more problems we had with Trista and her young male "friends," the more we became alarmed that we could easily be forced to deal with a pregnancy. We were increasingly aware that there was no way that Trista could responsibly parent a child, now nor probably ever. Trista was severely challenged, and her prognosis was not good. As she was getting older, she also seemed to be *more* disabled. Her body was continuing to mature, but her judgment and function levels were at a standstill.

A pregnancy was always a possibility. We could not put our head in the sand and hope the problem would pass. If there were a pregnancy, abortion was simply not an option of consideration because of our personal convictions. Adoption was unrealistic. Trista was a legal entity, and we had *no guarantees* that she would chose this option if she did become pregnant.

We decided to take a more diplomatic approach. I spoke to Trista's neurologist in Walla Walla, Washington, and we requested his assistance with genetic risk considerations. He was basically unimpressed, but he agreed to order a genetic inquiry for us. What followed with the geneticist was a mundane encounter. The expert in genetics was clearly prejudiced before she began. During our lengthy appointments, she gathered data from us. Then the geneticist explained that statistics were just that, and the reality of Trista's ability to successfully parent a Tourette child was not an absolute – it was an issue we might never confront, and perhaps we did not need to deal with our perceived problem, nor with our genetic concerns. The Tourette Syndrome research that I had in my briefcase was more current than her references. We were incensed, offended, and amazed how cold and calculating was her flawed statistical approach. She clearly had not yet tried on the Indian's proverbial moccasins!

Following that benign detour, Trista was even more eager to have the sterilization matter behind her. We had experienced other rather scary encounters that further reinforced the potential danger of her being fully responsible for a child. There was significant risk involved in the consequences of her actions of a sexual nature, and Trista understood.

Therefore in 1991, Trista and I visited with a gynecologist in our region. The female specialist knew our family situation fairly well, and she was extremely sympathetic to our problem. However, the specialist had to decline to do the surgery because the religious hospital where she practiced forbade sterilization. However . . . she offered to put us in touch with *another* sensitive female doctor in another region – one who *would* have the necessary hospital freedoms to consider such a procedure.

We moved with ease through the medical maze from that point on. Trista had two very thorough independent evaluations with the recommended gynecologist. The doctor requested a host of additional documentation. By this time, Trista had qualified for SSI and Oregon Developmental Disability benefits, and her disability was well-documented in the public domain. The physician's energetic investigation clearly confirmed Trista's carefully considered decision, her high genetic risk, her low functional IQ level, and assorted other disorders and disabilities. The specialist's conclusion: it was unwise, in her opinion, for Trista to consider parenting any children. Trista was an adult, she was requesting sterilization, and that request was granted by a very professional specialist.

Several months earlier, I had attempted to discuss the issue with our pastor. He made it clear that we would be stepping over his line of imposed morality, and in an attempt to stay out of the line of fire, I determined to not further discuss this subject with anyone outside our immediate family. But it was a difficult time for all of us, and I was experiencing that woman's need for an understanding female friend to "hold my hand." Right before Trista's sterilization procedure, I made the disastrous mistake of trying to solicit emotional support from a very close friend. My friend was well acquainted with our family problems, but she also had a number of bright, healthy children and grandchildren, and the very thought of my depriving myself of the option to be a grandma to Trista's children was inconceivable to this friend. All the wrath of her "religious ethics" came down upon me. I learned very quickly that the pending surgery was to be a closed and *very private* family issue.

With our encouragement, Trista had independently composed, signed and dated a detailed explanation of why she made the decision to be sterilized. If Trista, or anyone else, ever later questioned why she made that choice at age 19, her handwritten self-composed letter would be a good point of reference. To this day, the letter is in safe keeping.

The most confusing issue we have had to deal with has always been that Trista has a low-normal IQ, so she *is* capable of making rational decisions. **But her low *functional IQ* compromises her ability to live responsibly in a lifestyle that includes wise spontaneous choices for herself and others.** In culminating several years' pursuit of sterilization, Dave, Trista and I quietly slipped out of town. Trista checked herself into the hospital, signed releases which were witnessed by hospital staff, and she had her fallopian tubes cut and tied in a one-day procedure, in a large public facility, by a licensed and well-respected gynecologist. We spent the three-day weekend away, where we could be together without judgment or condemnation as she recovered from her elective surgery. The procedure was handled with dignity, and no one pointed fingers at any of us for making a difficult, controversial choice. We all grew a little closer that weekend. **When I look back on special times in our life, this is one of those weekends that we heard the sound of music in the midst of utter chaos. I cannot explain how the hardest times can also be the sweetest.** I only know that we had that familiar *"peace that passes all understanding"* – the peace that we so desperately need when we find ourselves in hard places – the peace that we have found is only available from God. [63]

As the months and years have passed, we have experienced more sexual problems that have put our daughter at-risk in other ways. At first we wrestled with her sterilization decision, fearing that the procedure had become an unspoken license for her to be even more sexually active and irresponsible. But we have come to realize that Trista's choices in these matters have no relationship to imagined or real consequences, and her well-considered decision for sterilization, made over a period of years, was appropriate and responsible.

Throughout Trista's life, we have had many choices. Some were easier than others. And sometimes we have, individually or collectively, been wrong. But on this particular decision, we will not look back with regrets. Voluntary sterilization was appropriate for our severely disabled daughter, and she readily acknowledges the fact that she could not be a responsible parent to a child.

"Experience is not what happens to you;
it is what you do
with what happens to you."

Huxley

~ ~ ~

Not to Drive or Not to Bike –
That is the Question

Trista was our accident waiting to happen. We were on a first name basis with the emergency room staff in our local hospital. It seemed that Trista was always "crashing and burning." I remember the snowy day when she torpedoed under our neighbor's car on a sled. She was laying in the prone position, and we were relieved that the metal bar on the front of the sled didn't slice off her lower lip (but all those stitches inside her mouth couldn't have felt very good). In spite of yet another trauma, we were grateful that she was not decapitated!

And then there was the time she tried cliff-jumping. We were at a church picnic on the Columbia River, near Hermiston, and the teenagers were swimming. She had not been gone very long when someone came running to get us. Trista was hurt. It seems that she was watching the older teens cliff-jump into the river far below. Evidently, Trista was visibly intrigued by the sport and someone dared her to try it. So she did! Fortunately she hit the water instead of the bank but it must have stunned her, because when she got out of the water, she passed out, fell backward and hit her head on the rocks, making a nasty split in her scalp. I guess it could be said that she has Zorro on her mind now – Trista has a Z-shaped scar on the back of her head.

Cycling also proved hazardous to Trista's health. When she was a tricyclist, she had more than her share of tricycle accidents that earned her several trips to the hospital for stitches. Through the years we spent a lot of time staring into her eyes, watching for symptoms of concussions. Once, on her way home from junior high, Trista turned her bicycle in front of an oncoming car on a main road in Hermiston. Taking a quick trip across the woman's hood, our daughter's foot went through the front windshield before she plummeted to the ground. The uninsured woman was fiercely angry that our daughter had broken her window! This accident should have been a forewarning of things to come, but we did not perceive how very dangerous a bicycle could be for Trista.

All four of us Conklins were quite experienced cyclists, and we all understood the value of helmets. But a helmet would not have protected Trista's throat when she ran into the back of a parked pickup truck. She had just finished her high school cross-country practice, and she was moving at a pretty good clip down a small incline when she collided with the immovable object. She never even saw the pickup. She didn't know the man who picked her up and carried her into the Hermiston police and fire station. (It was quite convenient – the accident was directly in front of our city safety center.) She fainted in his arms, and when she came around, her throat was hurting and she was dazed. (The amazing coincidence is that the man who scooped up Trista this day was the husband of the woman who brought Trista home from her previous bike / auto mishap several years before.) There was no *visible* damage – to anything beside the bicycle. However, she was spitting up a little blood at the scene of the accident, so she was transported by ambulance to the local hospital.

She had been riding in the lower drop position on her handlebars, and she was looking down at her feet. So the impact thrust her neck into the gooseneck of the bicycle – the part that secures the handlebars. She had taken the full brunt of the impact in her cervical collar, commonly known as the "Adam's apple." After several hours of observation and non-observation, the emergency room doctor phoned a local physician and explained that Trista was having a difficult time talking but there was no *visible* damage. The local physician said, "Get her to a specialist, **now**." Trista and Dave were transported to Kennewick General Hospital, 35 miles away. The otolaryngologist was waiting for Trista when the ambulance pulled in. The specialist did a quick examination in the emergency room and could see that the damage was extensive.

I had been called out of a class in Pendleton as they were leaving for Kennewick. It took me one hour to get to Kennewick General, and just as I arrived Dave was signing a consent form for emergency surgery. The throat specialist said that Trista's air passage was being blocked by swelling. Without a tracheostomy, Trista would suffocate. The doctor explained he had been in surgery all day and his team was too fatigued to begin Trista's tedious repair surgery at such a late hour, so all he intended to do that night was to make an incision in the windpipe and insert a plastic tube to create a new airway. Dave was livid that specialists were not consulted sooner – the notion was beyond our comprehension – our daughter could have suffocated in an emergency room!

Tearful, scared and unable to breathe well or speak, 17 year-old Trista scribbled a note before she was wheeled to surgery: "Mom and Dad, I am so sorry I wasn't paying attention!" When Trista awoke from surgery that night, she was breathing through the "trach tube" and she could not speak because her vocal cords had been bypassed by the surgery. After extensive surgery the next day, the physician informed us that the shattered cartilage of the cervical collar had completely severed one vocal cord and it was irreparable. The other cord was injured. The prognosis was tenuous: If the repair to her other vocal cord was not successful, Trista might never again speak.

I wondered how long it would take us to learn sign language.

Trista spent 10 days in intensive care. Several people who came to visit fainted at the sight of her – she was hooked up to so many machines and tubes, it was visceral shock. When she came home, we continued to have to aspirate her lungs by inserting a suction tube into the tracheostomy tube and running it down into her lungs, to remove excess secretions and to prevent pneumonia. It was a horrid, scary task. Trista hated it because it literally sucked her air from her. I *always* broke out in a cold sweat during the procedure.

When the trach tube came out, Trista was able to speak, albeit softly. No sign language for this kid! She *used to have* a nice singing voice. In the years that ensued, her voice has always fatigued quickly and it is weaker than most people's. She had a number of follow-up surgeries to remove permanent stitches that have worked loose, and to remove polyps from her vocal cords. The *office examinations* are probably the worst for her now – it is just no fun to have the doctor insert a scope down her windpipe to examine her one remaining vocal cord! It has been 10 years since that accident, and Trista's throat is as healed as it will ever be. She has the familiar mark on her neck of someone who has had a tracheostomy, and she has another long horizontal neck scar at the Adam's apple, where the repair work was done.

The bike visited the bike-doctor, and we assumed this was a lesson well learned. But when she collided with another car about a year later, we got rid of her bike. She was not injured in this collision but her bicycle did not fare so well. Trista was, fortunately, no longer interested in cycling.

When her younger sister got her driver's license, 18 year-old Trista decided she wanted hers too. We always figured Trista would not be able to pass the automobile driving exam, so we were going to let the system tell her she could not have the privilege to drive. She had passed driver's education, and her instructor-father dutifully tutored her through many additional hours of road experience. To our absolute amazement, Trista *did* pass the driving exam on her first attempt! The examiner told us he thought she would become a better driver with more experience. *Wrong!* Trista could steer the car to its destination but she was *never* a good driver.

Her tics were severe during her teens, and she was also beginning to deal with obsessive compulsive issues. Stress exacerbates both Tourette tics and OCD. So whenever Trista drove, she would become focused on trying *not* do the tic that could make her jerk the steering wheel. In addition, she concentrated intently to resist the compulsion that might make her pull the car off the road. She was paying more attention to *not doing things* than she was focusing on good driving, and she knew it. It was fearsome to ride with the young driver because she was working so hard to just stay normal. One day we hesitantly allowed Trista to drive the car five miles out of town to pick up her girlfriend. Our daughter reported when she got home that a tic / compulsion made her almost pull the car off the road, into a ditch. We all concurred that her driving career should probably end. She has not driven since that day – and Trista has no desire to ever be behind the wheel again.

It was *me* who was unwilling to accept reality on this one. I encouraged her keep her driver's license valid through the next renewal period, hoping things might change. She eventually let it lapse.

Now Trista goes to the Department of Motor Vehicles, to purchase her photo ID that looks almost like a driver's license. She is more than satisfied with this denouement, and so are we.

~ ~ ~

PARENTAL PRO SÉ

When our daughter moved from Oregon to Washington with her caregiver, I just assumed her "Developmentally Disabled" classification would move with her across the state line. Logic told me it would be a simple paperwork process, transferring from Oregon to the State of Washington. Trista had become eligible for Developmental Disability (DD) services in Oregon, and she had met the federal definition for developmental disability. It seemed unquestionably straightforward.

When the State of Washington denied her August, 1993, application for Developmental Disability eligibility, I was astounded! Essentially the Developmental Disabilities Division (DDD), Division of Social and Health Services (DSHS), State of Washington, said that *Trista was not handicapped enough.* With what was later deemed "a moving target approach," the state contended that Tourette Syndrome is not a neurological condition, and they reinforced their contention with the statement that she should never have been *allowed* to even apply for DDD benefits because she was not eligible in Washington. The Spokane DSHS office asserted that Tourette Syndrome is a psychiatric condition, for which they would not award DDD eligibility! We, of course, took exception to their ruling and filed an appeal.

My philosophy has always been that the parent is the best advocate for the child, providing he or she is *able* to represent the child. So it never even occurred to me to hire an attorney for this minor variance. We had battled teachers and school districts and appealed state rulings before, and we had always won. I just gathered up my paperwork and my righteous indignation, and launched yet another battle, with winning on my mind.

"Hell hath no fury like an angry parent." [64]

In legal circles, the Latin phrase that means "representing yourself" is "pro sé" – literally, "his own person, without the benefit of an attorney." Of course I charged no fee but the cost of this particular legal battle, in terms of the toll it took on me, proved to be excessive beyond my wildest imagination!

I did my homework well. It felt like I was preparing a doctoral thesis! Over the years, I had accumulated originals, carbon copies and photocopies of almost every document from every file that ever existed on Trista. They were neatly and not-so-neatly filed in binders that were layered in large cardboard boxes. I isolated myself in my home office for several weeks, totally focusing on preparing my "case" for the appeal to Trista's eligibility denial. When I finished, I had selected 45 exhibits for the judge to review, along with a detailed 18 page outline which built my case. Together with a title page, contents and index pages, my "thesis" was complete in its new black report portfolio. I had given it everything I had!

Unfortunately, the *one* document I needed most was one which *did not exist*. I needed to cite a legal precedent, to substantiate that Tourette Syndrome is a neurological, rather than a psychological, disorder. When I called the Tourette Syndrome Association in 1994, seeking a copy of a precedent, the TSA receptionist said there was *no such ruling* yet handed down in any court of law. But she hastened to add, "When you win your case, please send us a copy of the ruling. We have attorneys all over the country asking for the first precedent." Some consolation that was!

I appeared for the appeal hearing on January 18, 1994, with the lofty impression that we would walk in and introduce ourselves, I would hand over my well-prepared materials, and we would leave. (In Oregon, our successful DD appeal amounted to one well written personal letter which asked them to reconsider their decision.) I arrived early, as did Trista and her caregiver. A local DDD supervisor was there, representing DSHS. We were introduced to a very distinguished older gentleman, Judge Clayton F. Harrington. Trista was nervous, and her tics were extremely severe. During the early part of the hearing, we played a five-minute videocassette showing some of Trista's worst tics that we had captured on film.

Trista had to excuse herself because viewing the film exacerbated her tics to the point that it became unbearable for her to stay. An hour or so later, both Trista and her caregiver were allowed to be permanently dismissed from the hearing because Trista's tics were so disruptive. We were later accused by the DDD supervisor of twice "staging" the tic performance by Trista, both on videotape and in the appeal hearing. I found this entire encounter with the mental health professionals disgusting and demeaning.

Much to my surprise, the judge did not want to examine the documents himself. He wanted *me* to present the materials, which meant that for *the next three days*, we endured the tedious process of me reading and substantiating every single word in the outline and exhibits . . . and I thought all I would have to do was hand the black notebook to the judge, to read in his private chamber!

When I had arrived at that 10:30 a.m. meeting in Spokane, I assumed I would be back home in Oregon for dinner. When the hearing concluded three days later, I was still in the same clothes that I had worn to the first meeting. I was *not* going shopping for clothes for a hearing that should have never been necessary in the first place!

I was *shattered* when the hearing concluded. There were many moments when I didn't know if I could finish. At times I had to request a recess, to leave the room. I would go out and cry a bit, get myself put back together, and come back to face the music again. The hearing was one of the most stressful situations of my lifetime. It was extremely painful, having to relive and recount to the judge all the pain and frustrations of Trista's 21 years of problems, as well as to reiterate her current status. Then I was *hit broadside* when I was cross-examined by the state. I was called a liar and all sorts of other ugly implications. Emotionally, I was raw and fragile. And I kept wondering why it was *me* that the state was putting on trial – I thought it was *Trista's eligibility* that we were contending!

When the hearing concluded, I determined that I would *never* go through such an ordeal again. Win or lose, it would be the *end* of my legal battles with the Developmental Disabilities Division of the State of Washington.

Judge Clayton F. Harrington handed down the Initial Hearing Decision (Conklin vs. DDD / June 10, 1994). We won. In the 13-page ruling, the state was ordered to make provision for Trista to retake the qualifying examination. And, Tourette Syndrome was not allowed to be a condition for denial of benefits.

On July 8, 1994, the Division of Developmental Disabilities, Department of Social and Health Services (DSHS), filed a Petition for Review, which meant the state was now *appealing the appeal-decision*. This time the state brought out their big guns. Evidently I wasn't the only person in that first hearing who resented being there! The DDD Administrator was now out of the picture, and the Attorney General's Office for the State of Washington was filing the appeal. The state had unlimited resources to jump rank and pull out all the stops. I had said I wouldn't put myself through another hearing. I didn't have time to train an attorney for our case. I had backed myself into a corner. I *had* to respond to the petition because time was of the essence, and with powerful rebuttals to every point the state protested, I was certain that the ball would be in our court when the judge reviewed my Response To The Petition.

It was "thesis time" again. I spent several days composing our five-page response to the Attorney General's flawed (and offensive) assertions. I filed my Response To The Petition For Review on August 1, 1994, to the Washington State Office of Appeals at Olympia, the state's capital. I wondered, would this case end before it reached the Supreme Court?

On September 8, 1994, the Review Decision and Order of Remand came down from Christine Stalnaker, the Review Judge in Olympia. The Initial Decision had several legal technicality problems. Judge Stalnaker ruled that the Initial Decision was "vacated" (nullified), and the case was "remanded" (sent back) to the first judge, Clayton Harrington, "to hold another hearing, to allow additional testimony and argument . . . and to correct the above referenced procedural errors." The new hearing date was scheduled October 7, 1994.

Six months previously, I had vowed that I could not go through another hearing. Now, it seemed that I had no choice. I discussed the problem over and over with Dave, and tearfully accepted his wise counsel: I had come too far to turn back. However, I simply could not position myself to be "shot at" again by the state. I didn't think I had it in me to even walk into the hearing room again – just thinking about it made me tearful and sick to my stomach.

So we put "Plan B" into action. On September 12, 1994, I filed a Petition for Reconsideration, requesting that the Initial Decision stand. I requested

(1) that the Initial Decision *not be vacated*;

(2) that the case *not be remanded* for another hearing;

(3) that there be *no additional testimony nor argument*; and

(4) that the procedural errors be corrected in *another manner.*

I don't know where I dreamed up this "legal-ese" because I never sought any legal counsel, and I have no legal training. (I had never even *been in* a courtroom for such a hearing.) It amazes me even today as I review the details of our strategy. The Bible says if you need wisdom, ask for it. I did. And I received it!

"If any of you lacks wisdom, he should ask God,
who gives generously to all"

James 1:5a

On October 6, the Washington Office of Appeals in Olympia called to inform me that they had canceled the hearing schedule for October 7. The reason: The State Office of Appeals needed to make a decision on my Petition for Reconsideration.

On October 10, 1994, the appellate court judge incorporated into her decision the conclusion that *it was not necessary to reconvene an in-person hearing.* The case was remanded to Judge Harrington in Spokane. Judge Harrington was instructed to (1) address Judge Stalnaker's concerns set out in the Review Decision, and to (2) issue another Initial Decision.

On February 1, 1995, we received notice from Judge Harrington in Spokane. He needed to reopen the hearing to address technicalities. The hearing was scheduled for March 3, 1995, and *it could take place by telephone conference.*

God knew my limitations. He spared me from having to attend another hearing in person. know the Lord could have given me the strength and courage to attend another hearing but in His great grace, God gave me a way of escape.

> *"No temptation has seized you*
> *except what is common to man.*
> *And God is faithful;*
> *he will not let you be tempted*
> *beyond what you can bear.*
> *But when you are tempted,*
> *he will also provide a way out*
> *so that you can stand up under it."*
>
> 1 Corinthians 10:13

On March 3, 1995, promptly at 1:30 p.m., the hearing convened by teleconference. Neither side had any significant additional evidence or new witnesses. The teleconference hearing lasted less than five minutes. How do you spell *r-e-l-i-e-f* ?

On May 22, 1995, Judge Clayton F. Harrington handed down the new Initial Decision. This decision was even firmer than the first Initial Decision which had been vacated and remanded. Judge Harrington's new Initial Decision had grown to 17 pages. [65] *It was a resounding victory for us on every item contended by DSHS!*

We were fairly certain that DSHS would, once more, appeal the new Initial Decision. A victory for Tourette would be far more expensive for the State of Washington than any legal expenses they might incur. If a ruling defined Tourette Syndrome as a neurological disorder in the State of Washington, there could be a flood of Touretters who could be candidates for state disability services on the basis of their Tourette Syndrome.

Washington had 21 days to file their appeal. Just as we predicted, the DSHS Petition For Review, dated June 9, 1995, arrived in our mailbox. This Petition For Review was, essentially, a rehashing of their first Petition For Review, so I just reiterated and fine-tuned *my* first Response To Petition For Review. Simple enough. Almost a year had passed since I had composed a response.

I had done a lot of thinking about the whole case. My new response to the petition was concise and powerful! My husband says there is no weapon in my arsenal quite so deadly as one of my handwritten munitions – woe be unto the recipient!

January 18, 1996, was our "V Day." Review Judge Christine Stalnaker of Olympia handed down the Review Decision and Final Order for Docket No. 1293 A 1027 (Trista Conklin, Appellant). Thirty months had passed since we made a routine application for services in the Washington State DSHS system. Twenty-four months had passed since that first appeal hearing that lasted three days. We had won every decision that was handed down, and we also won this Final Decision! History had just been written!

Judge Stalnaker set a **national precedent** in her ruling.

"The undersigned . . . agrees with the ALJ's conclusion that Tourette's Syndrome is a neurological condition." [66]

Never before had anyone succeeded in forcing a state to classify Tourette Syndrome as a neurological disorder. Insurance companies and mental health professionals *nationwide* had always prevailed with the definition that Tourette Syndrome is a psychological disorder. In many states, that "psychological disorder definition" had *always* served as an expedient and reliable basis for denying benefits to victims of Tourette Syndrome.

In this ruling, DDD was ordered to readminister the Inventory for Client and Agency Planning (ICAP), the measurement instrument by which Trista would eventually qualify for and receive DDD eligibility and benefits in the State of Washington.

The order had the usual appeal rights and notices of deadlines. The state would again have 21 days to appeal. This thing *could* go all the way to the Supreme Court! By now I was ready to fight it to the bitter end, without regard for personal cost. I waited 21 days. Nothing happened. I waited a few more weeks, just to be safe. Still no word from the State of Washington.

Was it possible that the state was not going to appeal? Had they actually taken all the licks they intended to take? *Every decision had been an overwhelming loss for the state.* After three losses in a row, had the Attorney General's Office finally seen the handwriting on the wall? Did they finally give up their losing battle? *Had we actually won the appeal?*

We were *afraid* to celebrate. We were even reluctant to accept a tentative victory because victory had been so elusive in this thirty-month legal battle. *Every* decision that was handed down had been in our favor. And every single time, the decision had been contested by the state. It seemed that the appeal process had no end!

On March 18, I apprehensively called the receptionist at the Office of Appeals in Olympia. I inquired whether the state had filed a petition to appeal the January 18 decision. The receptionist replied, "You would have received a copy of the state's petition, via certified mail, if there was an appeal. Since you have not received a copy, the state has not appealed the Final Order." I asked her to check the record, just to be certain. She obliged me, and responded with a sweet chuckle. There had been no further communication from the DSHS or the Attorney General's office regarding this case. I asked her if there was any possibility that appeal deadlines could still be waived? She assured me that was impossible at such a late date. The appeal deadline had expired more than a month earlier.

I asked her one final, tenuous question: "Does this mean that we really won?"

"Yes, of course you have won! Congratulations!" The receptionist continued, "Mrs. Conklin, this is the first time anyone has ever called to verify that they won a Final Order. You can relax now and enjoy your victory. Congratulations."

We won! Trista could now become eligible for the benefits she obviously deserved. Our victory was very important for Trista. Nationwide, it was especially valuable. **For Touretters and attorneys throughout America, we had set the *national legal precedent* !**

I faxed a brief victory announcement, along with a copy of all the legal documents, to the Tourette Syndrome Association. One can imagine how pleased we were to receive their reply:

March 27, 1996

Dear Jean,

Congratulations! I'm circulating your letter to those who need to know of this precedent-setting decision. We will try to get a short mention in our upcoming newsletter.

Thank you on behalf of all children with Tourette Syndrome, and from all of us here at TSA.

Sincerely,

Sue Levi-Pearl, Liaison
Medical and Scientific Programs
Tourette Syndrome Association, Inc.
42-40 Bell Boulevard
Bayside, NY 11361-2820
Fax: (718) 279-9596
Tel: (718) 224-2999

Sue Levi-Pearl kept her promise. Below is an excerpt from the article which appeared in the TSA Newsletter (Summer, 1996).

LEGAL DECISIONS FAVOR TS CAUSE

On the job, in school and in social services, the wall of discrimination against people with TS is steadily crumbling away. These breakthroughs do not come easily. They are the result of determined legal battles, some aided by the legislative protections of the Americans with Disabilities Act (ADA) and other laws. We have selected these examples from a number of recent cases that represent victories on three different fronts.

(continued)

Social Services

In the State of Washington, the Department of Social and Health Services denied benefits for Trista Conklin, contending that TS was not a neurological disorder. [Unwilling to hire] an attorney, her mother took up the battle. Twice she won favorable rulings, only to see the Attorney General's Office succeed in overturning them. She pursued the case all the way to the State Capital, and finally won the review decision she sought. It was a two-and-a-half year struggle. This ruling may be a precedent-setting decision that could serve as a model for cases in other states."

In the years that have passed since this item appeared nationally, we have had countless inquiries from attorneys throughout the nation. It always makes me feel so good when they marvel aloud that I represented Trista "pro sé." I always hasten to tell them that we have always believed that a child's parent is his best advocate. I explain that at the rather late stage of our advocacy career, we did not have the time, nor the desire, to train an attorney about Trista and Tourette Syndrome. They always hear me say that God gave me the ability to fight, and He won the battle for us.

I never chronicle this sequence of events without tears in my eyes. The tears are a mixture of anger and joy. I am incensed that we had to fight so hard to prove what the medical professionals knew all along: Tourette Syndrome *is* a neurological disorder. I am offended that Trista was denied benefits in Washington state for three years, while the legal battle was being waged. And I resent that the battle took such a toll on me, personally. This scripture pretty well sums it up:

"Stone is heavy and sand a burden, but

provocation by a fool is heavier than both."

Proverbs 27:3

Nonetheless, I am so very pleased that we won! I'm so thankful that I was given the ability to fight so hard, so well, and for so long. I am grateful that my husband encouraged me to persevere to the end. If Dave would have given me some slack, I might have thrown in the towel at the precise moment that I needed to press on!

The greatest thrill of all is that we penetrated bureaucracy! From almost the very beginning with Trista – our battle has been getting the "system" to work with us. Instead, we have been met by organizations which have fought us tenaciously, discounted and discredited us, and dismissed us whenever they could. Little did we realize when we began this battle that we would literally be "going for the gold." A national precedent was desperately needed, and we are so happy to have been able to blaze the trail for many to follow. For years to come, Tourette families will share our prize.

Sometimes in the symphony of our life with Trista, it has been the *professional musicians* who have created the dissonate chords. Such was the case in this chaotic opus. However, *the finale was spectacular*!

Truly, paying the price to win the precedent was *our privilege*. Serving others in this way is just an overflow of the love we feel for Trista. We would do just about anything to help our daughter. Wouldn't any parent?

~ ~ ~

IF I AM NOT FOR MYSELF,

THEN WHO AM I FOR?

BUT IF I AM ONLY FOR MYSELF,

WHAT AM I?

AND IF NOT NOW, WHEN?

Hillel [67]

Rights of Parents

The right to cry

The right to be angry

The right to not be judged

The right to know the truth

The right to make decisions

The right to be respected

The right to ask for help

The right to have hope

The right to get on with living

The right to be human

The right to laugh

The right to believe in miracles

68

RUBBER BAND RESPONSE

The best synonym I can find for Tourette Syndrome is *bizarre*. We have lived with Tourette Syndrome for 22 years. We know we will *always* have some coping challenges because of this contemptible disorder. We acknowledge that there's not too much that can surprise us about living with Tourette. We know that our daughter's "new tic" is someone else's "old tic." Although Tourette is totally *un*predictable, the erratic, uncanny nature of Tourette is *totally* predictable. Whenever we think we have seen the worst of tics, we can just wait because a worse tic is probably lurking *just* around the corner!

So it should come with little surprise that we parents of Touretters feel like there's not a whole lot more to jostle our lives. We have lived with chaotic jolts, off and on, for what seems to be far more than *one* lifetime with Tourette. I suspect that any family of *any* special-needs child probably mirrors that experience.

I have heard people say that I seem so cool and collected about everything – that nothing seems to throw me off-center. Some of that is just my personality. Some of it is an *artificial poise* that I have learned, to cover up my not knowing what to do or say. But some of that demeanor is the natural result of living with the incredible package of goods which "special" families must endure. In some ways, it seems that our child's disability has chewed us up and spit us out. But when the mill of life pulverized us the worst, most of us were re-formed into very strong people! At times, it seemed like we have had to practically take on the *world* in defense of our special-needs child. Some of the barbells with which we've done calisthenics have been extremely heavy, and we have developed some incredible grit. **It is called making music, in the *midst* of chaos.**

One of my most perplexing challenges has been the acceptance of what I call the "Rubber Band Response." After Trista left high school, it seemed that she regressed to favoring peers who were far below our perception of Trista's ability level. During her eight post-high school years, I have come to realize that all the high school stimulus of tutoring, special classes, parental intervention, and the almost exclusive contact with "normal" people served to pull her up to a level far above her comfort zone. High school was a continual war for our daughter. She never really met the grade, and we all knew it. Non-disabled peers befriended her and patronized her but those friendships were, at best, shallow and undependable. Her countenance during her high school years was at an all-time low, and her tics were horrible most of the time. After she left high school a few of her normal peers and newly-found friends used and abused her, and we became increasingly cautious about (and often suspicious of) most of her friends and acquaintances.

By contrast, Special Olympics[69] has always been a "safe haven" for Trista; she has always seemed comfortable in the midst of the other special-needs athletes. Special Olympics has proven to be a consistently nonthreatening environment for our daughter. There she has always thrived and even excelled. In the leisure arena away from Special Olympics, if she sought out someone for socialization, it was almost always a person with some degree of mental handicaps. It was very perplexing to us that her friends functioned so far below our perception of Trista's abilities. Even *we* were often fooled by her excellent verbal skills – it was *easy* to relate to her as "normal."

It is an understatement to say that we have had difficulty accepting the extent of Trista's disabilities. Slowly, we became painfully aware that her functional level is far below her verbal skills. Because Trista could interact with us on our level, at least for a time, it has been difficult for us to accept the reality that much of what was going on around her was simply not registering.

As the months turned into years, we perceived that Trista *regressed* after she left high school. Casual acquaintances could hardly comprehend our description of the challenges we were dealing with. I recall many "shopping cart conversations" with people we have known over the years. When they would ask about

   Rubber Band Response

Trista, I never knew what to say; so I would just say she was living with a caregiver in Spokane. They couldn't figure out *why* Trista would need to live in an assisted environment because most people perceived her as we mistakenly had – just a little slow, with lots of tics. They found the severity of her disabilities quite unbelievable.

As a result of these awkward encounters, I became quite skilled at explaining the scenario: All the prodding and pulling and intensive tutorial support tended to keep Trista fairly well caught-up with her high school peers. And then after she left the very focused school environment, much of the succoring ceased. No longer forced to continually rise to the demands of people who were "towing" her, she fell into her own stride, and those steps were far shorter than we aspired for her.

Nonetheless, after so many years of our intensive efforts in "getting Trista through," we were tired. We backed off primarily because of fatigue, and for our own self-preservation. We *needed* a rest. We had enlisted in many good causes for Trista's benefit. However, just because they were good causes, it did not mean that they necessarily served Trista's best interest. There were several programs in which we were heavily invested – and some of those systems proved to actually be counter-productive to her well-being later on. We enlisted because we felt we owed it to Trista to do what the skilled professionals were touting. We should have known better. The programs didn't "feel good" to us, and we validated them out of a sense of duty. God was talking but we weren't listening. Those bad choices would come back to haunt us later.

As Trista became farther removed from the structured school regimen and other people's parameters, our daughter had much more time to just *be herself*. Whenever she sought out a friend, it was always someone with significant mental disabilities.

And thus, I came to acknowledge what I term the Rubber Band Response. Given sufficient reinforcements, one can make a person *appear* to be someone he is not. It is essentially compromising the integrity of the vessel. We did that to Trista by *not* allowing her to fail in high school. She was stretched taut, being forced to continually rise to everyone's expectations. It simply was not an option to fail because someone was always there to rescue her.

The lesson we were all being taught was that Trista did not really regress after high school. *When all those props were removed, Trista became who she really was.* The rubber band was no longer being stretched unnaturally (and unmercifully, I now see). Left alone, it resumed its resilient, un-stretched size. It is still capable of stretching to accommodate demands, but left to its own nature, it will readily assume its former relaxed state. We never allowed that to happen while Trista was in school. So it should not seem strange that it has been such a difficult task for me to accept the severity of her disabilities. We simply *did not know the whole person* with whom we were working.

In her efforts to please everyone, she *almost* became everything we aspired for her. However, **Trista's personal limitations prohibited the attainment of everyone else's dream for her.** It has only been fairly recently that life has allowed Trista to seek out her *own* dream.

The Vineland Adaptive Behavior Scale in 1991 showed that Trista, then 19 years old, was functioning in life skills about **nine years behind her chronological age.** The test results were reassuring but they were also devastating. Although we were delighted to have "proof" of the depth of her disabilities, we were understandably slow to fully accept its implications. The Inventory for Client and Agency Planning (ICAP) score in 1996 concurred with the Vineland findings. Although Trista has great verbal and communication skills, her life skills are formidably compromised. Professional labels like "functionally retarded," "severely disabled" and "profoundly handicapped" have been really tough for us to accept.

Since 1984, we had just been "coping with Tourette Syndrome." Suddenly, in 1991, we found ourselves dealing with an *adult* child who was "mentally challenged." It has taken many years for me to concede to her labels without experiencing a lump in my throat. Even today, I sometimes find it difficult to swallow.

~ ~ ~

Ten Valuable Things to Remember

1. I will get better.

2. Taking time for myself and other healthy family members is just as important as therapy for the disabled person.

3. Doing my best is good enough.

4. Other people's criticisms cannot hurt me unless I allow it.

5. My situation is not "normal," so normal ways of doing things do not apply.

6. People who are critical and who make my life difficult may need to be cut out of my life.

7. I can learn a great deal from this experience; and that knowledge may help me, my family, and others.

8. A good laugh at myself or my situation is worth an hour of counseling.

9. Learning to be flexible in my expectations can save lots of anger and disappointment.

10. Other people do not always have the answer.

author unknown

Dave and Jean Conklin

Future Shock

I am always surprised when something out of the past reaches out and levels me. In 1997, I thought I had fully accepted the depth and breadth of Trista's complex developmental disability. Although I knew I had probably not seen the full scope of her problems, I thought I was sufficiently armed so that nothing could throw me too far off center.

A year had passed since we had begun to search in earnest for a more permanent housing arrangement. Trista's state Developmental Disability (DDD) eligibility qualified her to receive housing dollars from Washington. We wanted her in a licensed facility so that she could be fully served by the department that we had so tenaciously pursued. I had given up hope, for the time, at least, for creating our own private adult group home. That dream was premature, at best – unrealistic, at worst. When the state called us, informing us that there were three "beds" available in three separate homes, I left the next day for Spokane to take a look. I ruled out two of the homes without even looking at them. One rural home was even farther out of town than her current residence. The second home, although located in the center of Spokane, would position her with a single, nonverbal roommate; we knew this would not be an enriching placement for our daughter whose strength is communication.

When Trista and I visited the third site under consideration, it turned out to be a very large group home which housed 17 female clients. I met four of the residents during our morning tour of the huge old elegant Browns' Addition home, and I was significantly taken aback. I wasn't prepared for the severity of mental disability that I saw in each client. I discussed this observation with her DDD caseworker, and I was told that this level of client is fairly representative of those being served in group homes. Clients like Trista, who function at a higher level, are usually in semi-independent living situations. However, because of vulnerability issues, semi-independent living clearly was not an option for Trista.

I decided I needed to visit with the other residents and more staff to have a look at the varieties and severities of the disabilities being served in this home. We were graciously invited to the evening meal where we could meet everyone.

All the women were anxiously awaiting our arrival, and we were "group ushered" to our assigned seats at the family-style tables in the beautiful old dining room. I studied the residents during the mealtime, searching for someone who seemed to be about Trista's level. It is difficult to measure levels of functioning at a dinner setting, but I surmised that there were probably only two or three women who had social and verbal skills similar to Trista. I concluded that Trista would be the highest functioning client in the home.

Mealtime was happy and peaceful at the Browns' addition group home. Four kind and energetic female staff members drifted in and out of the huge industrial kitchen. The clients chatted with them and called each one of them "Mom." Nonetheless, the dinner was not a pleasant social event for me; conversation was difficult and strained and often one-way because many of the ladies at my table were almost nonverbal. I had raised a developmentally disabled child and worked with hundreds of handicapped children and adults in various activities and programs over the course of my lifetime. But at that moment I was confronted with the reality of Trista's disability dilemma, and my hopes and dreams for **our** child were being pulverized and flushed down life's disposal system as I sat there and reflected on the quandry of what her disabilities were doing to her housing options.

I was relieved when dinner was over and I could leave. I needed some space to sort things out. Trista was elated. She already knew several of the women: some were in Special Olympics with her; and Cindy, her favorite, was working at the same firm where Trista was currently employed.

I talked openly with Trista about my observations. I wondered if she would be happy there, where most of the clients had disabilities so much more severe than her own. She asked me when she would know if she was going to move in. I told her that I wanted that to be *her* decision. Trista said she wanted *me* to help her with the decision. I told her that my criteria for her living arrangement was: "Number one: that you are safe. Number two: that you are happy." She asked me if I thought this would be a safe place to live. I told her, "Yes, definitely." I asked *her* if she thought she would be happy there. She told me, "Yes." So what did Mom think? I told her I needed to talk with her dad . . .

This was another one of those trips that I should have been accompanied by my husband. One would think I would *learn*! I was incapable of making this decision alone but *everyone else's* decision would be solely based upon *my* input. Hoping I could discuss this with my other daughter and her husband, I stopped by Tia's home on my way back to Hermiston. They weren't home. Dave was due home a few hours after I arrived at our house. I was anxious to talk this over with him. Then he called and said he wouldn't be home until the next day. We talked some on the phone but Dave was tired and hungry, and it was obvious that we needed to talk face to face about Trista's housing.

I turned to my parents; I needed their reassurance *and* their approval. I guess we are always someone's child! I had not been alone in trying to come to grips with what I called Trista's "Rubber Band Response." My parents also experienced difficulty in accepting the reality that their granddaughter was disabled far more than they ever allowed themselves to believe. More than once, they had expressed concern over Trista's circle of friends; they were often perplexed that she seemed so comfortable with people who seemed to function at such a low level. I think it is extremely difficult for grandparents to accept their grandchildren's disabilities because parents quite naturally want the very best for their children, and grandchildren are, in a very complex way, another generation of a parent's loving concern.

By telephone, I tried to be candid with my parents about the placement option. I attempted to be unpretentious about my concerns and doubts. It was a lengthy conversation, and it was very late. When I laid my head on my pillow, I felt the reassurance of my parent's loving counsel. Later, after I had discussed the situation with both Dave and Tia, I knew I could encourage Trista to step into this new living arrangement with the full endorsement of her parents, her sister, and her grandparents. That was important to all of us.

I thought it was a "done deal." It appeared that all we had to do was give our approval, wait for the administrative shuffle to give us the thumbs up, and then move Trista into her new home.

As a courtesy, I sent my usual introductory packet of Tourette materials to the elderly lady who operated the group home. I included, on Trista's request, a video which very graphically showed one of her most severe tic routines: "chicken." (This is the same home-video that the DDD Administrator, during our appeal hearing, accused us of having staged.) During Trista's senior year, I just happened to catch on video her full-blown tic emulation of a chicken. We were eating fried chicken, and her "chicken tic" started. The video captures her frantic hopping and crowing and flapping her arms, crowned periodically with stomping her feet and a heart-piercing scream. (We used to suggest Trista go outside to vent her worst tics, but when the screaming tic began we *begged* her to stay inside, lest our neighbors turn us in for child abuse.) Trista had always sworn that video to secrecy, but *she* suggested we send it to the group home owner so the woman would better understand her tics.

It seemed like a good suggestion. I don't like people feeling deceived when they learn too much about Trista's tics, so I try to prepare them well ahead. This was a good idea, from everyone's perspective, it seemed.

I was *speechless* when I heard back from the DDD caseworker: the group home had turned Trista down! I couldn't believe it! But after I thought about it, I could understand. Although she is often in remission, **Trista's Tourette** *is* **severe**, and **her behavioral issues** *are* **severe**.

Here, all this time I was fretting over placing Trista in a situation which was not challenging enough – and that was *the precise reason* she was rejected! The group home *did not want*

　　　　　　　FUTURE SHOCK

Trista's kind of challenge! It was difficult for us to explain to Trista that she had been turned down. And although at that time it was difficult for me to say the woman made a wise choice, I do now affirm that hers was the correct decision.

I suspect this was an exercise in trust. We had worked so hard to procure DDD residential placement *and* the services of a DDD caseworker; now it was time to let the system work. After we recovered from the shock of the group home rejection, we were hopeful that the "right" placement would soon become available. The caseworker seemed optimistic, and that was enough for me. Optimists are easy to placate, and I *am* an optimist.

It wasn't long before the caseworker called to say he had another placement option for us to consider for Trista. There was an Intensive Tenant Support (ITS) "bed" available in a well-established community living project for developmentally disabled women. The project is sponsored by a corporation within a reputable religious organization, and they contract their services to the state. The group rents a block of six apartments in a large apartment complex. With an on-site manager and 24-hour-a-day roving staff, they seemed to have a good track record with the state. Dave, Trista and I toured the complex and we met all the staff and the potential roommates. The placement we were to consider would be with two other roommates in a two bedroom apartment. (Trista would share a room.) Roving staff would provide assistance in shopping, food preparation, laundry, housekeeping and other independent living skills. Dave and I had great reservations about the proposal. We felt it provided too much liberty for Trista, who was accustomed to living under very close supervision in a private caregiver's rural home.

We checked out several other housing options. We were feeling an increasing need to re-house Trista because her current living situation with an unlicensed caregiver was presenting some domestic concerns that we did not wish to address.

We also felt an urgency to seize the moment – partially because of the DDD's sudden interest in working with us, and partially because of the immediate availability of a coveted Intensive Tenant Support "slot." I was told that only way the highly-funded ITS slots become available is if a client dies, moves out of the system, or becomes ineligible for services. If we were not found to be cooperative, we feared that Trista might be wait-listed for years, on what seemed to be a very elusive internal system that we did not know how to penetrate.

Neither Dave nor I had complete peace about the apartment setup but we decided to let Trista *try* this new semi-independent living configuration.

Trista moved into the north-Spokane apartment in February, 1997. We moved her *out* of the apartment in November, 1997. By the time we rescued her from that much too independent setting, she was carrying 40 extra pounds (on her formerly 115-pound frame), she had resumed some of her previously detrimental independent-living activities, and she was entangled with a boyfriend who had a criminal record and other significant issues, the worst of which was sowing discord between Trista and Dave and me.

Not all the decisions we have made along the way have been good ones. Although two years have passed since we got her out of that living situation, we are still dealing with some of the problems created in Trista's life by that short-lived residential setting. That's life, I guess. We are human, and we are not all-knowing. But *Trista is not our guinea pig*. We try to not make bad decisions at her expense; but when we do, we try to learn from our errors. And we strive to not make the same mistake twice.

"We learn wisdom from failure
much more than from success." [70]

~ ~ ~

THE STATION

by Robert Hastings [71]

Tucked away in our subconscious is an idyllic vision. We see ourselves on a long trip that spans the continent. We are traveling by train. Out of the windows we drink in the passing scene of cars on a nearby highway, of children waving at a crossing, of cattle grazing on a distant hillside, of smoke pouring from a power plant, of mountains and rolling hillsides, of city skylines and village halls.

But uppermost in our minds in the final destination. Bands will be playing and flags waving. Once we get there our dreams will come true, and the pieces of our lives will fit together like a jigsaw puzzle. How restlessly we pace the aisles, damning the minutes for loitering – waiting, waiting, waiting for the station.

"When we reach the station, that will be it!" we cry.

"When we are done with treatment . . ."

"When the next test is over . . ."

"When we put the kids through college . . ."

"When I get a promotion . . ."

"When I retire . . ."

Sooner or later we must realize that there is no "station," no place to arrive at once and for all. The true joy of life is in the trip. The station is only a dream. It constantly out-distances us.

"Relish the moment" is a good motto, especially when coupled with Psalm 118:24 – "This is the day which the Lord has made; let us rejoice in it." It isn't the burdens of today that drive people mad. It is the regrets over yesterday, and the fear of tomorrow. Regret and fear are the twin thieves who rob us of *today*.

So stop pacing the aisles and counting the miles. Instead, climb more mountains, eat more ice cream, go barefoot more often, swim more rivers, watch more sunsets, laugh more, cry less. Life must be lived as we go along. The station will come soon enough.

The Conklins – 1992
Tia (age 18), Dave, Jean, Trista (age 20)
and Ponza

Guardianship

I began collecting information on guardianship when Trista was in junior high. I kept hoping that we would not need it. As the saga began to play out, our fears became reality. After she left high school, Trista became anyone's prey. Mean, injurious people were drawn to her. She seemed to be attracted to deleterious situations. And she was *incapable* of escaping on her own from any of those deceptive snares.

I vividly recall the time when I discovered that Trista was not spending the nights in her new apartment in Hermiston. More than once when I visited her during the daytime, I had the impression that we were not alone, that someone had just disappeared out the back door, or that she was hiding someone. Trista has always had the unfortunate "blessing" of having many family friends watching out for her. *Unbelievable* reports about our daughter began to filter through to us via those concerned individuals. Not only did I view her behavior as unacceptable, immoral, and generally dishonorable, we feared for her health and safety. One night I decided to take matters into my own hands. The city police had refused to assist me because I was not her guardian. Trista, age 19, was legally regarded as a "competent adult." At 4 a.m., I marched, unannounced, into a total stranger's house and compelled my daughter to leave the bedroom of their minor son. Not a good thing for a mother to be doing!

Later we learned that one of the minor boys she was seeing had threatened her with an aluminum baseball bat whenever she wouldn't make her tics be quiet. Evidently the teens felt it was okay to use and abuse her sexually but it was not all right for her tics to annoy them. *Dave* had threatened to do bodily harm to those particular boys if they didn't leave our daughter alone. Once again, the police told us they couldn't help us, and they warned Dave that *he* might be the one behind bars if he wasn't careful. Not a good situation for a father!

We forbade Trista to see the boys, fearing she might be slapped with statutory rape charges by the boys' parents. This situation resolved itself when the boys, who were frustrated with parental intervention from all sides, stole a car and drove it across the state line and wrecked it. The boys suddenly were involved in a federal offense, and they ended up doing prison time in Idaho. The blessing in this story is that just before they left Hermiston, Trista's tics were too offensive and the three minors reneged on their invitation to her, providentially refusing to allow her to ride along with them!

There were other incidents that caused unnecessary problems for us, such as when Trista spontaneously purchased items of significant value. In one instance, when Trista had proudly displayed a wedding ring set in a local mall, someone "tipped us off" that the motive for her purchase seemed questionable. It was an impulse purchase for her hew boyfriend. She had written a check which would soon be returned because of non-sufficient funds. After we covered the check, I tried to return the rings to the store. The problem wasn't with Trista – the problem was with the shop! I was incensed that a major jewelry store caused me to jump through all sorts of hoops (a note from Trista, proof of her signature, proof of my identity, and the actual receipt rather than a photocopy). After *months* of consumer gymnastics and ultimately a couple of "nasty-grams" to the head east coast office, I collected her refund.

We frequently encountered problems securing services for Trista, and we were sometimes even denied involvement in her appointments because she was a "competent adult." The reason we were excluded by the Washington DDD, in the initial application denial process, was that we were not Trista's guardian – we were only her "Significant Other" on the paperwork, which carried absolutely **no** legal clout.

The topic of *guardianship* frequently surfaced in our conversations. It was a chore we knew we needed to tackle. For years, I had kept telling myself that I would work on guardianship

    – right after we got Trista's school problems behind us . . .

    – right after her Oregon DD eligibility was secured . . .

    – right after she had her SSI eligibility . . .

    – right after we got her living arrangements stabilized . . .

    – right after she had adequate vocational training . . .

    – right after her Washington DDD eligibility was settled . . .

    – and on and on . . . There was always something.

There *was* always *something* more urgent to deal with. We invariably had some kind of fire to put out, or something new that we needed to advocate for. I knew that our pursuit of guardianship for Trista would be an all-consuming new endeavor, and I could only handle *one* major undertaking at a time.

After we won the Washington DDD appeal, my plate of responsibilities was clean at last, so I gathered my waning strength and tried to investigate guardianship in Washington state. All my inquiries led to dead ends. I even ordered a new revision of a guardianship packet from a parent advocacy group in Washington but it was just a lot of useless information. Someone had photocopied a stack of documents and other legal briefs and organized them creatively but I found it all rather useless. I needed a road map – step one, step two, step three.

Admittedly, I was extremely tired. Even *with* a road map, I didn't think I had the strength to fight another big battle on my own. I'd had enough of parental pro sé! Yet we *needed* to pursue Trista's guardianship. Trista was 25, and so many years had somehow slipped by that time really *was* of the essence. We decided we would hire an attorney. I inquired of several Spokane lawyers but I couldn't locate even *one* who seemed interested in taking up our cause. The fact that we were Oregon residents seeking guardianship for our daughter who lived in Washington did not help.

But like everything else that has always happened in our advocacy journey with Trista, something came across our path just as we needed it.

We have always made it a point to belong to organizations that affect the life of our daughter, such as COPE in Oregon, the Tourette Syndrome Association, Special Olympics, and various Arcs. The Arc of Washington spring newsletter featured a section called "Legal Briefs," written by an attorney.

PARENTS WASTE MONEY ON GUARDIANSHIPS

by Larry Jones, Seattle Attorney [72]

Parents frequently waste money when establishing guardianship. Unfortunately, even if they are represented by a lawyer, they are often too unaware – because many lawyers do not know – that the county will pay certain costs if the person with disabilities has less than $3,000 in assets.

There are several different kinds of costs incurred in setting up a guardianship.

If a lawyer is used, he or she will charge a fee. That fee cannot be waived, although it can and usually should be paid for out of the funds of the person with the disabilities.

Two other kinds of costs will be paid for by the county, if a parent knows enough to ask.

The first cost is the fee of $110, which the court ordinarily requires to file a guardianship.

The second cost is the fee for the guardian ad litem, which typically ranges from $300 to $1,000.

The guardian ad litem is a lawyer or other trained person whom the court will appoint to investigate whether a guardianship should be established.

In unusual circumstances, it may be necessary to retain a medical consultant to render an opinion on the condition of a person with disabilities. Counties may pay for these costs as well, if the person with disabilities has limited funds.

With the assistance of the Internet white and yellow pages, I determined *which* Larry Jones must be the Seattle attorney-author of this article. I faxed a letter of inquiry to the man, and promptly received a follow-up phone call and then his explanation of services and contract documents. I learned that Mr. Jones represents parents statewide in guardianships, special education, estate planning and trusts. So the fact that his practice was in Seattle was a non-issue.

It was significant that we had already secured SSI eligibility for Trista, and symbolic that we had her in an Intensive Tenant Support slot with the Department of Developmental Disability in Washington. The premise that we were seeking guardianship for Trista because she was "severely disabled" was now indisputable.

From time to time over the years, we had discussed with Trista the importance of guardianship and our future intentions to pursue the legal safeguard for her. We felt it was important to have family accord on this important decision so that it didn't later become an issue of contention. She always seemed to understand our concern and appreciate our caring, but Trista was fearful that we were trying to "run her life." We scheduled an appointment with Sandie Shepard at the Spokane Arc office. Sandie is a client advocate, and her wise words and compassion helped calm Trista's fears before we contracted attorney Jones.

The procedure to obtain guardianship for our adult daughter was expedient, painless, and seamless. We were in eastern Oregon; Jones was in western Washington. We communicated by phone and by fax for about a month but we only actually *met* our attorney for the first time a mere half-hour before the guardianship hearing in the Court House in Spokane. I had previously told Jones on the phone, "I'm short, I have brown hair pulled back, and I'll be wearing a navy-blue suit."

Meanwhile, Trista was being victimized in Spokane by well-meaning "friends" who rallied to her cause, scaring her with ugly threats of our evil intentions in trying to rob her of her independence. "They'll lock you up again in a psychiatric ward, and throw away the key," one influential woman warned. "They'll never let you do anything fun again – this will ruin your life!" a girlfriend admonished. Her nettlesome boyfriend arrived at the court house an hour early, to "support" her at the hearing. He brought with him a note, in Trista's handwriting but not her words, addressed to the judge. The note stated that she didn't want us to run her life, and that she didn't want us to be her guardians. Trista showed us the note and asked me if she should tear it up. I asked her if the words in the letter were really what she believed in her heart. She replied a thoughtful "no" and tore it up before we entered the hearing room. We ignored the boyfriend as we conferred privately with our attorney and waited to be called for our guardianship hearing. When we entered the courtroom we seated Trista between Dave and me, and my husband and I treated the boyfriend as though he did not exist. It was a public hearing but we were not there to be hospitable to an unwelcome antagonist.

Immediately before and during the hearing our daughter came through with remarkable common sense and trust in the parents who had always tried to do the very best for her. During the hearing the astute judge interviewed her, and he also ascertained that Trista approved of our intentions to become her guardians. We were awarded the guardianship of our 25 year-old daughter, without dispute. Trista left the courtroom smiling, relieved, and extremely happy. We three celebrated by having lunch at her favorite restaurant.

The Letter of Guardianship for Case No. 997400653-0 was issued on August 13, 1997, by the Superior Court of Washington, County of Spokane. The Order for Guardianship states "the ward was found to be in need of guardianship because she is incapacitated." Both Dave and I were appointed "guardian of the person and of the estate of the incapacitated person" for our severely disabled adult daughter.

A few days later we received the official copy of the court appointment. Per our request, Tia, who lives in Washington, was appointed the Standby Guardian (since we reside out-of-state). We requested that Tia also be appointed the Assistant Guardian because we are frequently out of the country. Trista was pleased with that decision. She greatly admires and trusts her younger sister.

As Trista's guardians, we are required to report to the court periodically. And Trista understands that if the day comes that she is able to function without a guardian, the decision can be reevaluated.

We keep the Order of Guardianship in our safe. Photocopies are kept handy in my "Trista File" [73] in my office; periodically I need to FAX or mail that documentation to some agency in Washington. I also keep a photocopy of the guardianship order in my wallet for those times when people question my right to conduct business for Trista. It is always with great relief that I am able to casually present the Order of Guardianship when well-meaning person challenges my authority!

Guardianship is just one more milestone along the road tenuously traveled by most parents of severely disabled children. The intensity and the longevity of the individual battles to win each milestone varies, and the human cost is without measure. While I was in combat on our DDD appeal battle, there were times that I thought the emotional trauma would cause me to perish on the spot (and I am not normally a weak woman). In contrast, the guardianship procurement was a "piece of cake."

In spite of the fact that the price of some victories is greater than others, no one milestone is more important than another. They are like the stone walls in the Yorkshire Dales, which separate fields and define property lines. Every stone used in the fence-like structure is a slightly different size and shape, but they are all part of the composite that makes the wall strong and unique.

I would like to bravely proclaim that guardianship was the *last of the major battles* we will need to fight on behalf of this child. There is a resolute peace in considering that prospect, and I yearn for that station. Nez Percé Indian Chief Joseph said it – "I will fight no more forever." [74] In my *head*, I can affirm that it seems to be a true statement for us too because in this journey on behalf of our disabled daughter, I don't see *any* ground that we haven't already covered!

Nevertheless, in my *heart* I know that there will *always* be some sort of challenge looming on the horizon. That's just life. Once a parent, always a parent. We're getting a little older each year, and we are more battle-weary. We *will* assault future problems because that is just the way life is when you are a parent of a special-needs child. We will be a more worthy adversary for our opponent b*ecause* of our experience gained from past conflicts. And we will be more resilient b*ecause* of our battle scars. One day we might be too old and senile to care for our adult child. Probably *only then* will we "fight no more forever." Trista's sister has been well-groomed to pick up the cause whenever that day comes. We have done everything we could do to make the way smooth for them both. We have always had sufficient help whenever we have done anything for Trista – and Tia will have that same expert assistance.

> *"Where does my help come from?*
> *My help comes from the LORD"*
>
> Psalms 121:1b-2a

~ ~ ~

Editor's note: A chapter on long-term planning is included.
See Appendix – What Will Become of My Child?

THE ROAD NOT TAKEN

by Robert Frost [75]

Two roads diverged in a yellow wood,

And sorry I could not travel both

And be one traveler, long I stood

And looked down one as far as I could

To where it bent in the undergrowth;

Then took the other, as just as fair,

And having perhaps the better claim,

Because it was grassy and wanted wear;

Though as for that, the passing there

Had worn them really about the same,

And both that morning equally lay

In leaves no step had trodden black.

Oh, I kept the first for another day!

Yet knowing how way leads on to way,

I doubted if I should ever come back.

I shall be telling this with a sigh

Somewhere ages and ages hence:

Two roads diverged in a wood, and I –

I took the one less traveled by,

And that has made all the difference.

Practice Facing East

Of all the battles we have fought, the most monumental has been *the battle of the mind.*

In the early days, we became introspective about Trista's development. She was lagging behind her toddling peers. We asked ourselves, "What weren't *we* doing right?" As a potpourri of doctors began to confirm our suspicions about various handicaps, Dave and I continually beat ourselves up with ongoing doubt and uncertainty about our parenting skills.

During the grade school years when Trista's tics got so much worse, we felt responsible for each new tic. Again we asked ourselves, "What were *we* doing that would cause this bizarre behavior?" When tics waned we breathed a sigh of relief, wondering silently what we had finally done right. When they waxed we individually used ourselves as emotional punching bags, silently incriminating ourselves and punishing ourselves for her newest tic, for we felt we *must have* had a hand in causing the new manifestation in our daughter.

After her diagnosis at age 12, a huge load of guilt was lifted off our shoulders. It took many years for us to fully validate the understanding that although stress exacerbated her tics, we were incapable of controlling her life to the degree necessary to keep her tic-free. It was impossible to structure everything to make all tics go away because not all tics have a cause-effect relationship. Like a hiccup or a sneeze or a cough, some tics just appear. There is not always any particular reason. Tics just come. And tics just go. Subscribing to a c'est la víe attitude has not been a simple modus operandi. But like so many things in life, time has a way of softening the impact of traumatic events.

It has been 22 years since Trista's tics appeared – and 15 long years have passed since she was diagnosed with Tourette Syndrome.

Detesting TS as we do, we are fairly well able to take a hands-off approach to her manifestations: her tics just *are*. Sometimes we do things that make them worse; sometimes we do things that make them better. But most of the time, her tics just do their own thing. We are most supportive to Trista when we can continuously provide love and encouragement in the good times, and then try to add an extra portion of reassurance and tenderness during the hard ones.

Julie Farnam, my COPE friend, once sent me an encouraging note which said she hoped I used a lot of "self-talk" to get me through the rough times. I remember asking her what she meant by self-talk. I can't quote her answer but I would say it is a term that psychologists and counselors use to talk yourself up from a down situation. I'm not overly fond of the term because it implies that we, in our own strength, are capable of rising above situations. Without God's help I can do nothing. But I do know that my own frame of mind has a lot to do with how *I* am doing. I have learned many "can do" Scriptures because God's Word is filled with promises for dealing with life's burdens.

I have also become fairly effective at *willing* myself to adopt the attitude that "these things too shall pass." I am an optimist, so the process has been fairly natural. However, **I practice becoming a *better* optimist!**

Many times I have felt as though I had a ticket on the "Disorient Express," zooming through unknown lands without a clue how I got there, where I was headed, nor if I would ever return. In times like those I had to remind myself that things don't always stay bad — that things *will* get better! I had to remember that even the "worst-ever" tic periods had been supplanted by junctures of total tic-remission. I had to reassure myself that *I always came through* those intense periods of depression and despondency. Most times the tough situations resolved themselves. Nonetheless, even today we are still dealing with Tourette Syndrome. Not everything goes away.

I have noticed that when the *situation* does not change, *I* do. One can't stay "between a rock and a hard spot" forever. Humanity

 PRACTICE FACING EAST

has been gifted with incredible resilience. **If circumstances do not change, then we surely will!**

The sun rises in the east every morning. The sun sets in the west every evening. That is not a particularly new revelation. But it is amazing that challenged families find that concept so elusive.

The Old Testament tells us that the Israelites faced their tents toward the east. God told them to always set up the tabernacle facing east. East was a sign of hope, of expectation, of new horizons.

The Sioux Indian tipi almost always faced east because, as Nancy Horn Cloud tells, "the cold wind blows from the north and northwest. Because warmth comes from the east they built their tipis facing east, and also [because] the wind wouldn't blow the tipi down [when it faced that direction]." [76]

No matter how dismal today's moment in history has been, tomorrow is a new day, with new hope, new expectations, and new horizons. Whether we are positioning ourselves for God's blessing or for protection from the unwelcome blasts that life hurls at us, we need to practice facing east! Sometimes we can hardly *see* the sun: some days can be dreadfully dreary; sometimes they are dark and stormy, or so very cold and foggy.

But the sun does *rise* on even the darkest of days. Begin to notice that the sun also *sets* on those days when daylight is questionable; and the sun always *rises again* the next day. Seasons come and seasons go, but the sun always rises, regardless of the day or the season.

Practice facing east!

~ ~ ~

*There is a time for everything,
and a season for every activity under heaven:*

a time to be born and a time to die,

a time to plant and a time to uproot,

a time to kill and a time to heal,

a time to tear down and a time to build,

a time to weep and a time to laugh,

a time to mourn and a time to dance,

a time to scatter stones and a time to gather them,

a time to embrace and a time to refrain,

a time to search and a time to give up,

a time to keep and a time to throw away,

a time to tear and a time to mend,

a time to be silent and a time to speak,

a time to love and a time to hate,

a time for war and a time for peace.

*I have seen the burden God has laid on men.
He has made everything beautiful in its time.*

*He has also set eternity in the hearts of men;
yet they cannot fathom what God has done
from beginning to end.*

Ecclesiastes 3:1-8, 10-11

SOUTH HILL SORORITY

Our goal for our daughters has always been for them to live a normal life. Tia has mild Left Hemiplegic Cerebral Palsy, college training, a husband and two babies. CP has presented its own set of challenges for her, but Tia has been able to overcome or adapt to her limitations and she is a stronger person because of them.

By contrast, Trista has an assortment of chronic disorders, was unable to graduate from high school, is basically unemployable, may never marry, and will never have any children. Multiple disabilities have wreaked havoc on every facet of Trista's life, and many of her challenges are impossible for her to *ever* overcome.

Life must go on for our family. I have known for a long time that Trista would not live her adult life with us. It was a decision that was being formed many years before we could have predicted the extent of her disabilities.

The initial seeds for that decision were planted when I was just a child. My parents had close friends whose daughter was brain damaged as the result of a difficult birth in 1942. Ruth lived a protected and rather isolated life in our small rural eastern Oregon community. Whenever our families got together for meals and card games, my parents set the example by giving Ruth the same respect that they gave any other person, adjusting the activities so everyone could participate. I vividly recall the day when I realized that raising a child with disabilities impacts the entire family. The Morris family was concerned about Ruth's future and, believing it was the right thing to do, they made the extremely difficult decision to have pre-teen Ruth become a ward of the state. (This meant that if anything happened to her aging parents, Ruth would be cared for by the state because she was already the state's legal responsibility. Societal philosophy has obviously changed, and public wardship was later rescinded by the state.)

Although today there might be some who would question her family's motives, in all fairness, they walked in the only light that they had in those "dark ages" of parent advocacy. Mrs. Morris was probably one of Oregon's parent-pioneers of broader horizons for disabled children. Ruth's mom invested a great deal of time and effort in pushing for help and change to brighten Ruth's future. Her energetic research took her to the other side of the state to discover the greater opportunities of metropolitan Portland. (In those years, the trip to Portland was an all-day drive on narrow, two-lane highways.) One result of their combined parent and teacher efforts is that Ruth was the first developmentally disabled employee hired by Goodwill in the Portland area. Today, almost 40 years later, Goodwill Industries is renowned for their excellence in employing and training the disabled.

Ruth's mother was the principal advocate in Ruth's life; when Mrs. Morris died, Ruth was 22. Her aging father ultimately placed Ruth in a state institution in western Oregon. In one sense, her horizons were broadened. Fairview housed over 2000 people with assorted disabilities, and Ruth had many experiences that life with her elderly father in La Grande would not have provided. She met many new male and female friends; she was trained as a physical therapy aide, and Ruth learned to work and live semi-independently. But she paid a heavy price for some of those well-meant family decisions. Today Ruth describes living at Fairview as "being locked in prison with bars." (Fairview is almost empty today, and is targeted to become history at the turn of the century.) Ruth eventually left Fairview, moving with two friends to central Oregon where she was employed in a nursing home and lived on-site.

Although life's emotional scars are still somewhat painful to her, Ruth has been an overcomer. With the help of many friends advocating for her over the years, she has had an amazing journey! Ruth has been a state and local president for "People First," a rapidly growing national self-advocacy program, and she is a trustworthy friend to her peers, often being sought for counsel and comfort. She has represented Oregon at various national conferences, and Ruth has been used as a speaker and resource person for self-advocacy projects and research. She no longer has a guardian but she does have an assortment of friends and professionals who are interested in her life. Ruth has lived in a large Oregon city with her two closest friends for 20 years. She has been informally "married" to one of her roommates, and she does all the cooking, cleaning and management for their "family" home. Ruth enjoys a rich, full, happy life, and she is respected by those who have seized the opportunity to know her.

I lost contact with Ruth when she was placed in Fairview. But when we moved to Hermiston, I frequently observed two separate families who once had similar circumstances to the Morris family. The widows each had daughters with Down's syndrome. Both families lived in our end of town, and I would see them taking their daily short walk around the neighborhood. Beyond that, they lived reclusive lives. The daughters were each in their fifties but the mothers *looked* like they were over 100 – tired and worn out! I later learned that both widows had individually decided to keep their daughters at home rather than place them in Oregon's dreaded institutions. Both daughters died in their mid-fifties, and *both* mothers died shortly thereafter. It was then that I began to ponder the question: perhaps it was not wise for parents to shelter their adult children at home, *forever*? Perhaps such an arrangement was as deleterious to the child as it seemed to be to the parents? After ruminating on those impressions, I became fairly certain that I would never allow our adult disabled daughter to be trapped in our home, nor would I allow *myself* to be a victim of such a scenario.

A few years later, the widow-mother of my good friend Mary became ill and died. Mary had an older sister, Lanetrae, who had severe OCD and mental retardation. The mother had been the sole caregiver for Lanetrae. The family had a crisis: What would become of Lanetrae? The siblings knew their own families could not shoulder such a responsibility so, after much agonizing, they placed Lanetrae in an adult family home in Eastern Oregon. Mary told me that she felt her mother died many years prematurely. The reason: the mom was literally *worn out* from being the primary caregiver for her severely handicapped daughter. But the epilogue to this family's story is a happy one. They all stood in utter amazement as their extremely dependent sister reached levels of independence that they never dreamed possible for her. In the larger group home setting Lanetrae saw more of her world, had more diversified activities, and lived a fuller life in the five years before she died than in all of her previous 50 years.

We had another neighbor who gave birth to a profoundly disabled child with Down's syndrome and other disorders. After several troublesome years, the couple acknowledged their limitations and they placed their young child in the care of a local family who had a similar-aged Down's child. The two disabled boys were raised together in a very caring and loving family atmosphere. When they reached young adulthood, both men moved into local residential group homes. The first mom confides that the second family did more for her son than she and her husband could ever have done. The second mom tells that her "boys" have matured in different ways as a result of moving out of the family home. The men are now in their mid-thirties. One year ago the second man bought his own home, where he now lives independently with a variety of community and family supports.

The Bible says it is not good for man to live alone. [77] I have also come to believe that it is not always best for adult disabled children to live with their families.

We have had several false starts in our efforts to launch our daughter for independence. A supported-living arrangement in a Hermiston apartment proved to be too much responsibility and too much independence for her.

Living with an adult roommate, in the little house across the street from our family home, had also provided too much responsibility and independence for her.

Following that, Trista lived for five years in a sufficiently restrictive private, non-licensed foster care setting. It worked pretty well most of the time but Trista was lonely for younger companionship, and we also wanted her in a licensed facility.

Then the state facilitated her transition into a semi-independent apartment arrangement with two special-needs roommates. Trista had companionship there, but we realized almost immediately that she had succumbed to the same old problems of having too much responsibility and too much independence.

For many years, I had envisioned a housing configuration where our daughter could live in a real home with two or three other young women, with on-site 24-hour staff, balanced meals, structured and scheduled residential recreation, community outings, participation in Special Olympics and other special activities, and the blessing of the involvement and support of the families of the other residents.

I had read about such places – a prototype here, a model there. I had visited a variety of unique housing concepts in several states, and I dreamed of the day we could have such a home for Trista. But we could not figure out how we could put it together on our own. We always had more questions than we had answers. Who would manage it? Who would hire and fire staff? Who would supervise staff? Where would we find the roommates? How would it be financed? . . . and on and on.

I heard about a "model" home in Spokane. When I inquired, I learned that there was an innovative Spokane mom who had a similar dream for their disabled daughter. However *that* woman worked her way through the answers to all those questions! Shari paid her dues for the task by investing many years in special-needs political advocacy in Washington state. With the help of her supportive husband and Arc of Spokane, they moved Katie and three other disabled young women into the first Arc South Hill house in 1990. The three-bedroom house proved to be too small because the girls needed their own rooms. So in 1992 they bought a bigger five-bedroom house, just down the street.

Here, in summary, is how it works. South Hill house is
    – owned by Katie's special-needs trust;
    – managed by Arc of Spokane; and
    – licensed to Arc as an Adult Family Home.

To illustrate the stability of the arrangement, the original four girls lived together for eight years! Because it appeared that there would *never* be a South Hill vacancy, we tried to interest Spokane's Arc in assisting us with replicating the South Hill house. Although we were always met with enthusiasm and encouragement, the bottom line was this: they did not have appropriate clients, with DDD funding, to place in such a *new* home. The success of the configuration seemed to depend on finding a good match in clients who were not currently being served residentially. Those clients needed to have eligibility *and* funding slots already secured, and that status could not be just pulled out of a hat! There *were* several aging parents with adult disabled children who would someday need placement outside their family homes. But none of these parents had secured DDD eligibility for their children, and we knew we wouldn't be interested in waiting for that to materialize.

But God was watching all of this. At the very moment that we were *desperate* to get Trista out of her newest apartment setting He sovereignly arranged for a vacancy at the South Hill house! We romanced the feasibility, visited the house again, visited the parents of the residents, visited Arc, visited with Trista's state DDD caseworker, and prayed fervently! Because we were selecting a long-term placement for Trista, we wanted the final decision to be hers.

She was South Hill's dinner guest several times. Interaction with the girls and staff included house visitations for several different occasions plus participation in one of their weekend outings. These activities helped her to get a fairly good feel of how the house really worked. After a handful of visits they "invited" Trista to be a part of their house. In my college days, we called that "rushing."

Remarkably, her new living arrangement *is* similar to a sorority house! The home is absolutely elegant, thanks to Shari's ongoing commitment to excellence. It is extremely well run by an on-site administrator and round-the-clock staff. Everyone is pretty happy most of the time, and it is busier than most sorority houses. One of the girls is employed at a pizza house, all of the girls take special classes at college facilities, and three of the girls are involved in day-recreation programs. The girls utilize para-transit facilities (door-to-door special-needs transport), they all have their own checking accounts, and three of the girls have participated in counseling programs to help them adapt to the stresses of community living. They all have yearly physicals, biannual dental checkups, and daily showers. And all the ladies have an amazing resource list of available boyfriends. The house is governed by state Adult Family Home (AFH) regulations which provides a myriad of safeguards and provisions for the well-being of the young women. Things like balanced meals, telephone privileges, spending money, privacy, and client choice (with responsibility) are all mandated. The home has a series of annual state audits but everyone knows that the there are *many* people watching most of the time, not the least of which are the parents. Arc's South Hill house is a model facility for four very blessed young women, and we are thrilled beyond measure to have our Trista be one of them!

To meet the large budget which is required to provide such intensive staff support for the women, the house is closed at least 45 days each year. Trista comes home about once a month, and we also have her for ten-day-vacations in the summer and at Christmas. South Hill shuttles her to and from the bus but she travels unaccompanied. She has flown alone across the nation to various events and she always enjoys traveling, with the companionship of her headphones and her laptop computer. She seems generally pleased to be at our home but she is also always ready to go back to Spokane. South Hill is her home now and she usually considers it a privilege to live there.

Although Trista lives in Spokane, she continues to be under the expert care of her Seattle neurologist, Dr. Brien Vlcek.[78] We found Dr. Vlcek in 1988 after an extensive search to replace her local neurologist who intimidated me. We consider Dr. Vlcek one of the best in his field. He has *many* Tourette patients, is client-centered, and stays on top of new Tourette research and technology. Her Social Security benefits only pay a small portion of his office exam fee. It is an arduous journey for us, traveling up to Spokane to meet Trista, and then to the other side of the state for her doctor's appointment. Nonetheless, we consider Dr. Vlcek's primary care worth our considerable expense and effort. Spokane agencies occasionally request that we "doctor locally," but this is one wheel we are not going to reinvent. "It ain't broke," and we are *not* going to fix it.

Trista's world is a happy one most of the time. We have done everything within our resources to make her life complete, safe and stimulating. She is happier and more settled than she has ever been, and she has matured in ways that were not possible under our care. She can be strong-willed and extremely resourceful and creative. Sometimes those virtues work to her disadvantage because she doesn't always have the wisdom and understanding to utilize her strengths in making wise choices. She is easily influenced, and she periodically resents some of the life-restrictions that are necessary for her health, safety and well-being. But we have logged enough travel miles in this journey to be fairly certain that the route we are traveling is our best present option. We are pleased to have it "all quiet on the western front," and we want to keep it that way. Life is extremely good for Trista, and Dave and I feel immensely blessed.

~ ~ ~

WHAT ABOUT THE SIBLINGS?

> *A family is a circle of love –*
> *growing through good times and sorrow,*
> *sharing the difficulties,*
> *the differences,*
> *the memories*
> *and the joy . . .*
>
> *We're family. That will never change. And the special things we share will always keep us close.*
>
> *I Love You Mom!*
> *From Tia*

(Tia left this on my pillow during a very painful time in our life.)

Siblings of special-needs children have a difficult station in life. They are caught in the web of incredibly complex family sagas. I have often compared siblings of disabled children to children who contract AIDS from a life-saving blood transfusion – the injustice of their burden is almost unspeakable.

From the very beginning, Tia was sweet and sensitive, and she was a joy to be around. She was a faithful friend to Trista (and frequently Trista's *only* friend) and she seemed unbelievably strong. I drew strength and inspiration from Tia even when she was very young. She could get Trista to do things that I could not get her to do, and she could also make their little playmates be nice to Trista. She always had maturity beyond her years, being helpful and obedient, and just plain nice company.

Unfortunately, I did not realize there were feelings that Tia could not share with anyone, perhaps not even with herself.

I painfully recall the holiday we were visiting my parents' home. For what appeared to be no reason at all, Tia fled the family gathering, sobbing. I found her on the guest bed, weeping pitiably. I was totally confused because I had not seen *anything* that might have provoked such a response. When Tia quit crying enough to talk, she said with embarrassment, "I just want to be the *little sister – just once!*" Those 10 words had the impact of a bulldozer on me! I just didn't *know* how hard it was for the *little* sister to have to be the *big* sister *all the time!*

Several years later our family was experiencing some almost unspeakable problems with Trista. I was walking an emotional tightrope, and I finally fell off. Sobbing uncontrollably, I thought I was alone in the kitchen. Tia walked in, put her arms around me, and we cried together. I was inconsolably sad. The moment, although tender, became doubly sad because Tia *saw* the depth of my pain. I had tried to hide it from her but families have few secrets behind closed doors, and I suspect Tia knew far more about my personal pain than I ever realized. Somewhere in her life's journey Tia became who *we* needed her to be, and who *Trista* needed her to be, and perhaps who *Tia* thought she needed to be. I don't think this is an unusual scenario for siblings of disabled children.

It is my opinion that being the sibling of a disabled child is even more difficult than being the parent! One can judge for himself: the following accounts have all been written by siblings of severely disabled children. [Some of the names have been changed.] The life stories are as individual as the people, and even within the same family, siblings lives are touched in remarkably different ways. **The seldom-heard melody that weaves through all these scripts is that siblings are deeply impacted and forever changed when disability visits the family.**

~ ~ ~

Siblings become advocates to the differently-abled at a very early age.

I was aware of, could initiate dialogues about, and defend taunts regarding my brother's Down's syndrome by the time I entered kindergarten. To my family and I, Tom's mental retardation was never "a big issue" – he was treated as his three siblings were treated. Granted, he had special needs, and those, of course, were met. But I've never really thought of Tom as being much different from other kids. Tom is quite high functioning despite a slow beginning – he was very sick as an infant and was developmentally delayed. But now he's able to read and write a little, he has a "regular" job, and a social calendar that puts mine to shame!

Fortunately for Tom and others with Down's, legislation and benefits, which protect their rights, have been established for quite a while now. (I believe Down's syndrome was one of the first recognized handicaps to receive SSA and SSI benefits.) My family, however, tries to keep abreast of any new victories or setbacks on the special-needs advocacy forefront. (My mom serves on the Arc board, and is active in Special "O" and other advocacy groups.) Your family and my family can attest to the fact that sometimes you can't rely on the physician, or the system, or the law to protect and help someone you love deeply. And as you have so aptly illustrated in this manuscript, "Ya Gotta Wanna."

Contributed by Scotty, sister of Tom. Tom, age 33, lives with his mother in Washington state.

[Editor's note: When Tom was born in 1965, the doctors told his mother to "go home, and forget you had a baby," indicating that he would never be more than a "vegetable." Tom was in the hospital almost nine months because the hospital would not release him. His mother ultimately sneaked in and kidnapped her baby, and Tom has lived with her since that day.]

~ ~ ~

MARK, MARTY'S BROTHER.

My greatest challenge in living with my developmentally disabled brother has been separating actual and perceived responsibility. I felt resentment because of this, and I allowed it to build up inside me. Although I am two years younger than Marty, I was finally able to accept the reality that with or without me, my brother was going to become an adult, with his own life to live. I then could deal with feeling responsible for him because I *wanted* to – not because he "needed me." Once I understood this, he became my brother, not just a burden.

When I was in the third grade, my brother began to be mainstreamed at my grade school. He was two years older than me. Very few people knew he was my brother at the time. A few boys my same age began harassing my brother and other disabled children in the school. It was really tearing me up inside to watch this, but since I was considered one of the "cool" people, I was too embarrassed to do anything. My parents did not know it was happening but they perceived that Marty's time at school was adversely affecting him.

One day I just couldn't take it anymore. The boys were standing in a circle around my brother, and pushing him back and forth between them. He was so confused (since all he ever wants is to just be liked), and he had started to cry. I just went ballistic. I attacked the group (which had no idea an attack was coming), and I punched any face that came into view. I finally had the "leader" pinned by his neck to the ground, and I was crying all over him, begging him to "leave my brother alone." This was very shocking for him, as well as most of the other kids. After that day, my brother was left alone. But the real conquest was that Marty, as well as the other disabled kids, began to be included at school.

It would seem that the personal victory here is to stand up for what you believe is right. But for me there were *two* victories. The first was finding out that I had the guts to get through life, accepting my brother as he was. The most important lesson, though, was something that took me far longer to realize, though its roots were planted that day. Even though my brother was harassed, scared, and alone, he never once called for me. If he would have called, I would have intervened earlier because I would have felt obligated to him. I began to understand that very day that Marty had started to live his own life, and he didn't "need" me to save him. He was figuring out how to cope all by himself – and that is what is getting him through life today.

My parents were fallible, and I know it was difficult for them, too. They are very ambitious people, and they probably spent too much time fighting the big fights and causes for disabled children, and being over-extended in their community and church responsibilities. My sister and I probably had too much responsibility caring for our brother and a foster brother who also had Down's and autism. There were many times that I felt the only reason I existed was because my brother needed someone to grow up with – someone to look out for him.

I have learned most of the important lessons in life from my brother. They were all lessons that I understood after I was in my mid-twenties. Marty taught me by his example – unconditional love, toughness, and to always strive for excellence. My brother taught me the true meaning of independence.

Contributed by Mark, brother of Marty. Mark is married and lives with his family in western Oregon. Marty is in his thirties, and lives independently in the same eastern Oregon town where his retired parents reside.

~ ~ ~

KAREN, STEVEN'S SISTER.

I have many memories of my mom being in so much turmoil and pain about the uncertainty of Steven's future. He started out being a sweet well-adjusted baby, with nothing but smiles and joy written all over him. I am 16 months older than Steven, so we grew up together, and I never saw any indication that he was mentally ill. He was a very athletic kid, never abused drugs or alcohol, and was well liked by his peers. It wasn't until he entered adolescence that we started to see anger in him – it literally came from nowhere. We later discovered that he had a chemical imbalance, which, for want of a more specific diagnosis, has been called a schizoaffective disorder. The disease progressively got worse, until everyone in our family was afraid to be around him. He could be volatile one moment, and in the next moment, he was sobbing from remorse, or from some painful thought or memory.

I had a hard time watching my mom hurting over Steven's illness. She cried out so much to God. I remember holding her one morning as she sobbed. She felt so helpless watching her "baby" go through each outburst of anger, pain and then fear. My dad had difficulties of his own. He often felt he was letting his son down. He is a doctor, and it is in his nature to research every medical means for healing of his patients. Although he doesn't consider Steven to be his patient, he spent countless hours researching, and contacting psychiatrists and other experts in the field of mental health. He monitored all the tests and medicines that his son took. I can't imagine the hurt and frustration he feels on a daily basis, with regards to Steven's prognosis.

My greatest challenges in living with my mentally disabled sibling continues to be watching my parents grieve because Steven probably will not become the man they had hoped he could be. It hurts me to watch my parents endure the pain of having their son live with his turmoil and anguish. It has been difficult seeing my brother try to maintain a normal healthy life, while his mental illness continued to overtake him. Even today, he so much wants to be "normal." He is willing to do everything it takes, and to try anything to get better.

My other challenge was remembering that Steven had no control over what he did. He would get extremely angry and, at times, violent. I worried about him harming my mom and dad because many times he didn't know what he was doing. My other brother and sister lived with my parents and Steven's mental illness longer than I did; they were robbed of one-on-one with my parents because Steven's problems became all-consuming. He got a lot of attention, both negative and positive. I saw my other siblings becoming very resentful, and at times, I was, too. My younger sister and younger brother were very close to Steven before his illness began manifesting. They all played together and were confidants. This is no longer the case, as it has been very difficult for them to accept Steven's mental illness. My brother's disorder has plundered our whole family.

I still hurt for my parents. They did all that they could humanly do. We were all living a life of "trial and error" as we discovered the nature of my brother's disease. And though I am now far removed, physically, from the situation, I have a very tender heart towards Steven and all that he has been through. I pray for my parents on a daily basis, that the hurt of the last 15 years will be removed. I still pray diligently for Steven's complete healing. All of his problems are far from being over, and my family's pain is still very fresh.

It has been my personal victory to be able to completely release Steven into God's hands, and to know that God will take care of him. I love my brother with all my heart. I hurt for him. I hate to see him in so much pain. But I hurt even more to see my parents hurting. I just keep praying for Steven's healing.

Contributed by Karen, sister of Steven. Karen lives in the northwest, where she is taking time off from her teaching career to raise her two little girls. Steven, age 33, lives in the northwest, where he works part-time and is supervised by a mental health specialist.

~ ~ ~

Being *the* oldest sibling, I use to *think* that I treated Ruth like a younger sister. My girlfriend and I liked to tease her: if we made siren sounds (Ruth was afraid of sirens for many years), she would run into the house, and leave us alone. Of course, we would get in trouble for that!

I think Mom must have had a difficult time *making me learn* that Ruth was different, and less capable – making me understand that I had to make allowances for her, to become the responsible older sister. But I did eventually learn my role very well (and even passed that responsibility on to my oldest daughter: she was admonished to look after the younger kids, even though she was only 18 months older than her sister).

My sister and I grew up in the '40s and '50s, and I don't think I was allowed to identify my feelings, let alone express them *out loud*. Handicapped people were just *becoming* "visible." They weren't as understood, nor as accepted as (hopefully) they are now. As Mom became more involved in community and school activities, advocating for the handicapped, I remember doing more with Dad. (Because of that companionship, I became a champion rifle shooter.) They also encouraged me to participate in other activities, such as scouts, band, school clubs, and church youth group. As an adult, I continued to remain the ever-responsible big sister.

During the first couple of years that we were married, I developed a severe case of contact dermatitis on my hands. I had assumed responsibility not only for Ruth, but also for my husband's youngest sister, who had come to Portland with us after her high school graduation. (She didn't live with us but she did have mental problems.) As I counseled with my pastor about my "sister situation," he was very emphatic that they were God's and the parents' responsibility – not mine! When I gave them back to God, my dermatitis cleared up, and it only comes back with self-imposed stress. Dermatitis has been my reminder to "let go, and let God!"

Time and distance have changed our relationship. We have minimal contact, now that Ruth's needs are being met by others. We phone and write infrequently, although we do exchange E-mail, now that we are both on-line. But as a cousin observed after we stopped at Ruth's house to visit a few years ago, "You really have nothing in common, do you!"

Contributed by Deanna [Morris] Hasen, sister of Ruth. Ruth, age 57, lives in western Oregon, several hours south of her older sister.

~ ~ ~

DEBBIE, MARTY'S SISTER.

I am the oldest child in our family, and the only girl. My special-needs brother, born two-and-a-half years after me, has Down's syndrome. Then two-and-a-half years later, my youngest brother was born. And after eight more years, my family became a foster family for another special-needs child.

My greatest challenge in living with a special-needs sibling is probably happening *now*. While I was growing up, we treated Marty like any other kid, and I didn't see any difference when I compared my childhood to others families. But now that we are all older, and with our parents getting older, I feel the responsibility for Marty's care and well-being. He is easily influenced, and he is a people-pleaser. Marty does not want to make anyone unhappy, even if that means making unwise choices. Since he does have this characteristic, people *do* take advantage of him. Because I am the older sister, I feel the need to protect and shelter him. Putting Marty in God's hands, and then guiding Marty in life choices, seems to be how we are overcoming those challenges.

Marty is an amazing human being. I admire his "childlikeness" in everyday living. He has a true heart for God, and he puts me to shame with his faith. I remember that when we were growing up, he would never "fight right" – you know, sibling stuff. We would try to get him to fight back, and he would always say, "I'm sorry," or "I love you," and try to give us a hug or a kiss.

My parents always involved all of us in family decisions. I felt very comfortable with our family unit. Marty was just my *brother*, and he still is. I don't remember that my parents treated him differently.

Patience, understanding and support are key ingredients to growing up with a special-needs sibling. Being able to talk-out situations with someone you can rely on has been helpful to me. Also beneficial has been learning more about the disability, and then understanding how other families have dealt with similar circumstances. Knowledge has helped take the fear out of the unknown – things like finding out what it is, how it happened, what characteristics are common, what can be expected, and what might happen. I need to be informed, and I need to be able to make wise decisions because Marty is my *brother*!

"I pray that out of his glorious riches he may strengthen you with power through his Spirit in your inner being." Ephesians 3:16.

Contributed by Debbie, sister of Marty. Debbie is a stay-at-home mom, and she resides two hours west of her special-needs brother. Marty, age 33, lives in his own home in eastern Oregon. Debbie is the older sister of Mark, whose story also appears in this chapter.

~ ~ ~

While I was growing up, I saw how Trista's life affected my parents. I think life with Trista was difficult from *day one*, but it was especially difficult for them when her Tourette's became so severe. They didn't just have problems every once in a while – it was a *daily* thing that started first thing in the morning, and it wouldn't be over until she was asleep. Their life was very difficult, and sad. Trista couldn't help what was going on (well most of it), but that didn't help Mom and Dad. It caused a lot of stress, and I felt really sorry for them.

I remember one time when I found Mom crying. She was at the end of her rope, not sure where to turn. This event showed me that they struggled tremendously with the difficulties they had with Trista. No matter how "strong" they seemed to be, there is only so much that a person can handle.

I think that the greatest challenge that I had while growing up with Trista is something that I still deal with today. I can't say exactly when it started; I just know that it became the way I did things, and even now, I haven't figured out how to do things any differently. I didn't want to cause any further problems for my parents, so I tried to be the daughter that they didn't have to worry about. For the most part, I didn't cause waves (although I may have once in a while). I got good grades, did my chores, helped out with Trista, and generally helped out around the house. I just plain tried to be a good daughter. I figured that they wouldn't have to worry about *this* child because they already had enough on their hands with Trista.

I know that my being "good" helped them out greatly but I still feel like I fit that mold, even though I am married and live away from their home. I always try to do things and say things in a manner that won't cause any waves. I try to not be the cause of more stress and hurt for Mom and Dad because, in my eyes, they have had more of that in these past 27 years than any person deserves to have in one *lifetime*.

Because of that, I don't feel like I let the real "me" out. In order to keep peace in our family, I find that I often do and say what I think my parents want to see and hear. I tend to keep my feelings inside because I feel that un-shared problems will not cause conflict.

But because of doing this for so long, I don't know how to let my true feelings out, even when it comes to my friends or acquaintances. I remember a friend telling me something that my dad said long ago: that I was very hard to get close to. Even my own father felt that he couldn't get close to me. I knew it but I couldn't change. Although all he wanted to do was get to know me, I had locked up my feelings inside me. I didn't know how to be myself.

I just wanted life to be normal for my parents. They had so many trials with Trista, I just felt they didn't deserve any more. I always knew that they would have to worry about Trista and what goes on in her life. That is why I have always felt the need to just "do the right thing" for their sake. I know that this sounds silly, but this is probably the best way that I felt I could help my parents.

I think anyone who has watched their parents go through these types of struggles understands that the hardest part for another child is to watch their parents hurt and suffer through life. No one deserves that amount of pressure: they take on the life of their disabled child as well as their own. It is hard, and rough!

Nonetheless, I have had some personal victories in dealing with my disabled sister. Trista always had a difficult time with life, in general. People didn't treat her right, school was hard for her, and she just really wanted to be "normal." I always loved Trista and felt sorry for how things went for her. But after she had a serious bicycle accident in high school, I fully realized how strongly I felt about my sister. In this accident she was critically injured but she miraculously survived. I remember going to visit her in the intensive care unit, and all I could see was another letdown in her life. She had tubes in her body, her hands were tied down to the bed, and she looked like she had been run over by a steam roller. I didn't know then if she would survive. All I remember thinking was, "Why did this have to happen to her?" She had to live with so many trials in her life, dealing with things like cruel classmates and tough classes. Why did this tragedy have to happen to her? I remember asking my mom why God couldn't have let this accident happen to *me* instead. Trista didn't need any more battles. I would have gladly traded places with her. This was when I realized how strongly I loved her and how I wished she didn't have to endure any more problems.

I don't think it is possible for outsiders to understand, or even imagine, what life is actually like with a disabled child. It is a hard and never-ending challenge. I give my parents so much applause for how they have dealt with it. Sure they made mistakes, but what parent of any child doesn't? I heard a statistic that 80 percent of parents of severely disabled children are divorced within the first five years after that child's birth – life is that rough! But my parents have been together for over 30 years, and they are the best role-models that I know for a good marriage. They gave everything over to God, and He continues to be in the driver's seat.

Contributed by Tia [Conklin] Pollick, younger sister of Trista. Tia is a stay-at-home mom, and she is the Standby Guardian and In-State Representative for her 27 year-old sister. The Pollicks live one hour north of her parents and two hours south of Trista, in Washington state.

~ ~ ~

OUR SIBLINGS SHARE THEIR "TIPS FOR SIBLINGS"

Tia says:

Love your sibling . . . treat her like you would treat anyone else. God had a reason for making her the way that she is. It is not our job to know why – just to accept it and thank God for what he has given you! God has our lives under His loving control . . . whether we realize it or not.

Mark says:

Love him first and foremost but live your own life. If you get caught in the guilt / responsibility / "have to" trap, you will end up hurting your sibling *and* yourself. You need him, just like he needs you. You are family. Help him because you want to, not because he is "different" and needs protecting. And by the same token, don't help him if you don't feel the need to do so. *You* would not want someone to be your friend out of obligation, and neither does your disabled sibling.

Karen says:

Pray, and seek God for patience and peace, and for His comfort and wisdom. He is a loving God who cares deeply about us and all our needs. Continue to love and accept your sibling. The more hope you have for him, the easier it is to encourage and support him, especially when he is despairing. Your support gives him the courage to endure the hardships that may come his way in life.

Debbie says:

Treat him like you would want to be treated, and give him extra time and attention (positive attention). Never think that he doesn't understand what you are saying – sometimes he understands way more than you think! And don't be afraid to voice your fears, concerns and embarrassments with your family or someone with whom you can talk. It's okay to feel "cheated" sometimes, and to wonder, "What if he were 'normal.' " Just don't dwell on the negative because there is always someone who has it a little bit harder than you.

MORE TIPS FOR SIBLINGS [79]

- Help siblings to develop their own identities, seeing the differences and similarities between themselves and a child with special needs, and achieving successes without guilt.

- Acknowledge the personal strengths siblings have and their ability to cope with stress successfully.

- Respect a sibling's reluctance to be with or include a child with special needs in their activities. It is not a failure on parent's part to instill proper love.

- Legitimize reasonable anger. Even children with disabilities behave badly sometimes.

- Understand that each child has different needs. Allow siblings to set their own pace for learning and involvement.

- Recognize that children mature and relationships change. No attitude endures forever. Through all the changes flows the continuity of belonging to each other.

- Maintain balance in family life through the use of professional and informal support systems.

- Do not tackle problems as a "whole." Break them into manageable parts.

- Recognize your own need for extra help and care. Accept support offered by others.

- Relay information to siblings so they feel like part of the family.

- Use family conferences to provide an open setting for siblings to ask questions and acknowledge feelings.

- Recognize and admit what is happening, expressing feelings and concerns honestly.

- Keep care routines (bed, meals) as consistent as possible.

- Prepare siblings for changes in home life before they actually occur.

- Dethrone a child who is ill or has a disability, putting him / her back in perspective and in the proper place in the family, rather than as the focus of the family around whom all else revolves.

- Weigh the cost of actions to all children against the benefit to one. It may be a mistake to devote all time and attention to one child, even one who is terminal.

- Find ways to include siblings realistically into care and treatment of the brother / sister. Seek professional help for decisions which involve consideration of other children (rooming-in, etc.).

- Recognize that lengthy explanations designed to anticipate every question work no better for illness or disability than for sex.

- Let teachers know what is happening so they can be understanding and helpful to school children.

The Pollicks – Dean, Tia, Ashton (3 years), Addison (10 days)

How High is Your Mountain?

I cannot imagine enduring the scandal of Watergate. But I think even Richard Nixon probably became a better person because of it. Perhaps I felt more compassion for the Nixons because I knew one of them. Lawrene Nixon Anfinson is President Nixon's niece. She was also my sister's college dormitory roommate at OSU in the early '60s. I don't know how they did it, but after the President's fall the entire Nixon family seemed to find the strength to dust themselves off and retrieve their dignity. Life goes on.

> " . . . THE GREATNESS COMES NOT WHEN THINGS GO ALWAYS GOOD FOR YOU, BUT THE GREATNESS COMES AND YOU ARE REALLY TESTED, WHEN YOU TAKE SOME KNOCKS, SOME DISAPPOINTMENTS, WHEN SADNESS COMES, BECAUSE ONLY IF YOU HAVE BEEN IN THE DEEPEST VALLEY CAN YOU EVER KNOW HOW MAGNIFICENT IT IS TO BE ON THE HIGHEST MOUNTAIN."
>
> Richard Nixon [80]

My friend and former neighbor, Barbara Moore Lynch, says "nothing lasts forever." Six of the major players in this woman's life have died: her father, her brother, her husband, a grandson, her mother, and most recently, her second husband. Barbara has come to the realization that one must strive to just hang on through the hard times because the tide will turn. Conversely, one must learn to savor the good times because, like the hard times, the good times won't last forever either.

I wish I could tell you that God has healed Trista of all her disabilities. He hasn't. Perhaps that day will come. I suspect, however, that our Trista is God's instrument for this appointed hour, and that hour may last the rest of our life. She has worked in us qualities that come only through extreme trials, deep suffering, and intense pain. Trista's problems have taken us through the deepest valleys *and* onto the highest mountains. I don't have to look very

far to know that Trista has been a tremendous blessing to many
people, having touched their lives with the quiet melody of sweet
and tender music. I have noticed that when people ask about Trista
their words are often spoken with a reflective aura, as though they
are savoring some sweet memory. She is deeply tender and
responsive. Those who have allowed her to share their pilgrimage
here on earth know the gift of a steadfast and caring friend.

We chose Trista's name from a character in a TV show. It was
not because the show was so special but because the name was so
beautiful and melodic. When I learned that her name in Romanic
languages means "sorrow" or "sadness," I regretted that we gave
her that name. But Trista has always had deep compassion, and
she has taught us more about mercy than we ever thought we
wanted to know!

So when people ask about her unusual name I explain that it
means "compassion," for *out of sorrow comes compassion.*
Indeed, that is Trista to me.

> *"But God chose the foolish things of the world*
> *to shame the wise;*
> *God chose the weak things of the world*
> *to shame the strong.*
> *He chose the lowly things of this world*
> *and the despised things —*
> *and the things that are not —*
> *to nullify the things that are,*
> *so that no one may boast before him.*
> *It is because of him that you are in Christ Jesus,*
> *who has become for us wisdom from God —*
> *that is, our righteousness, holiness and redemption.*
> *Therefore, as it is written:*
> *'Let him who boasts boast in the Lord.' "*
>
> 1 Corinthians 1:27-31

Did God "do a number on us" with Trista? No way! God has blessed us beyond measure with this very special child, and I shall be eternally grateful. It is because of Trista that I met Jesus Christ as my Savior. It is because of God's amazing plan that I serve the Lord today. **In the midst of all the chaos in raising this special daughter, God has created some absolutely beautiful music!**

And what about that promise that He gave me back in 1995: "Physician, heal yourself." God impressed me with the understanding that as I would write this book about Trista, He would heal me in the process. Chronicling the narrative of our family's saga has been exceedingly difficult. As I penned my thoughts I participated in every word, often reliving the pain and sorrow that I have carried for so many years. Having recounted our years with Tourette and Trista, I observe that today I *am* different because the writing was cathartic, just as God said it would be. The tearing, ripping, gnawing grief that relentlessly consumed me in 1995 is gone. Oh, I still shed a tear now and then when I ponder or speak about the challenges that Trista must endure. But I am different now. My gut-wrenching ache is gone. My countenance is changed. Sorrow and grief have vanished from my reflection in the mirror.

It would be a lie to say I am *totally* healed because I know I still have a few miles to log in that journey. However I *can* say that I am certainly *on my way*! God has promised to continue the good work in me that He has begun. [81] The Lord knows everything about me. He is in control of every circumstance in my life, and I can trust Him with His timing because he is my Father. Could anyone ask for more?

Whenever life and music have played together, they are always *replayed* in my mind together. Forty-two years have gone by since Mrs. Spear passed me on the wooden stairway at Willow Elementary School in La Grande. Whenever I think of her I feel the slick varnish on the old wooden banister, I smell the faint aroma of her wonderful cologne, and I hear the rhythm of the hand-operated spirit-mimeograph machine cranking out copies at the top of the stairway. Even today whenever someone walks by me wearing Elizabeth Arden's *Blue Grass* cologne, it evokes those remembrances of Mrs. Spear. In the same way, whenever I reflect on our advocacy journey, a portion of the life-script revisits me. The joys and the sorrows, the ecstasy and the pain, the laughter and the tears, the peace and the despondency, the celebrations and the anguish – they are all part of my life's music. The aura, the aroma and the aria will always play together as integral parts of our saga.

We are able to hear music in the midst of chaos because God loves His children with an everlasting love. [82]

> *It is no secret*
> *What God can do –*
> *What He's done for others*
> *He'll do for you.*
> *With arms wide open*
> *He'll comfort you –*
> *What He's done for others*
> *He'll do for you!* [83]

Jean Conklin

Hermiston, Oregon   November 17, 1999

Depression – My Close Companion

It is impossible for one who has never been depressed to fully understand the pain of depression. Family members involved with special-needs children are particularly susceptible to depression and despondency. Some differently-abled children are also potential victims of those black hole experiences. (The added burden of dealing with a chronic illness may predispose individuals with Tourette Syndrome for depression. Research has also shown that individuals with TS are at a slightly higher risk for depression than the general population. [84])

More people are affected by depression than one might think. Five percent of the population in the United States may have major depression at any given time. Researchers believe that between 10 and 25 percent of all people in America will experience an episode of major depression at some time in their lives. [85]

Depression strikes people of all nationalities, backgrounds and life-styles. Depressive illnesses are not due to personal weakness or a character flaw. They are biological illnesses related to imbalanced or disrupted brain chemistry. The brain is an organ of the body and it can get sick, just like the heart, liver or kidneys. Possible causes for depression are genetic (inherited) factors, various life events and stresses, and chemical imbalances in the body.

Professionals know that depression is almost always caused by a *combination* of factors in a person's life. Sometimes it may be possible to pinpoint a certain life event that may have set off a depression. Yet for other people, depression may seem to strike for no reason at all, even when life is going well.

Clinical depression (depression that requires treatment) is a common medical condition with very specific symptoms. These symptoms have a significant intensity and duration, and they can affect a person's functioning and sense of well-being in a variety of ways. Clinical depression requires treatment, as it can seriously impair a person's ability to carry on with normal life activities, work, and relationships.

Depression can affect a person's mood, his outlook on life, his behavior, and even bodily functions in a number of ways – including deep sadness, worthless and hopelessness, loss of interest in formerly pleasurable activities, troubles with sleep, appetite or fatigue, and thoughts of suicide.

Depressive illnesses are nothing to be ashamed of. In the same way that we are not embarrassed by needing to seek medical help for the treatment of other biological illnesses like heart disease or diabetes, depressive illness also may require medical intervention. We would never expect a loved one to treat her high blood pressure on her own; neither should we expect a person to treat her depression on her own.

For most people, early recognition and treatment programs seem to decrease the length and severity of depressive episodes. There are a variety of therapies for treating depression. Drug therapy, or non-drug approaches such as psychotherapy, may provide some relief. Especially encouraging is the breadth of treatments available today; if one therapy or antidepressant prescription fails to provide relief for an individual, another may be useful. (As with all drugs, antidepressants can present side effects, and medications need to be monitored carefully by the physician.)

Depression is a total-body illness that affects a person's thoughts, feelings, behavior, physical health and appearance. At home, at work, at school and socially, the black hole experience invades one's entire existence.

"Depression clouds your thinking and judgement.
Sadness is amplified.
Motivation is nonexistent.
Sleep is just a memory.
Nothing matters anymore.
Life doesn't matter.
Depression robs you of your soul,
of your very will to live."

L. A. Taylor [86]

Depression is the most common, most misdiagnosed illness in America. Of the estimated 17 million Americans who suffer from depression in any given year, 80 percent can be effectively treated but only 30 percent seek help. Of that number, slightly more than half are accurately diagnosed and receive appropriate treatment. Obtaining an accurate diagnosis and getting treatment for depression is serious business. The number one cause of suicide in America is untreated depression! [87]

The good news is that depression is a treatable illness. People can feel good again! If you know someone who is suffering from depression, tell them that *there is hope – there is help*!

~ ~ ~

DEPRESSED ???

If you or someone you care about answers yes to several of these questions (including questions #1, #2, or #3) . . . and if those symptoms have been present nearly every day for more than two weeks, you should consult a health care professional about depression. (Other explanations for these symptoms may need to be considered.)

Yes   No   _Are you or they experiencing:_

___ ___   1. a persistent sad, depressed, or empty mood?

___ ___   2. a general loss of interest in formerly pleasurable activities?

___ ___   3. feelings of hopelessness, helplessness, guilt, pessimism, or worthlessness?

___ ___   4. an unusual loss of energy, or chronic fatigue?

___ ___   5. irritability, or increased sadness or crying, or generalized anxiety, or panic attacks?

___ ___   6. withdrawal from social activities?

___ ___   7. disturbances or significant changes in eating or sleeping patterns?

___ ___   8. difficulty concentrating, remembering, or making decisions?

___ ___   9. great concern with health problems; hypochondria?

___ ___   10. persistent physical symptoms, or pains that do not respond to treatment (headaches, stomach problems, neck or back pain, joint pain, mouth pain)?

___ ___   11. drug or alcohol abuse? (often masks depression or anxiety)

___ ___   12. thoughts of suicide; suicide plans or attempts?

APPENDIX

WHAT I BELIEVE

1. I believe in one God – Father, Son and Holy Spirit.

2. I believe that the Lord Jesus Christ, the only begotten Son of God, was conceived of the Holy Spirit; born of the virgin Mary; crucified; died; buried; and resurrected. He ascended into Heaven and is now seated at the right hand of God the Father and is true God and true man.

3. I believe the Bible is the Word of God, fully inspired and written under the inspiration of the Holy Spirit; and is our rule of faith and practice.

4. I believe that all are born sinners; the Holy Spirit convicts of sin; the Lord Jesus Christ paid the price for sin by shedding his precious blood on the cross as the atonement for sin; those who refuse to accept His sacrifice for their sin are eternally lost; and those who repent of their sins and personally accept the Lord Jesus Christ as Savior receive forgiveness of sin and life everlasting.

5. I believe in the baptism in the Holy Spirit with evidence of speaking with tongues as the Spirit of God gives utterance, that all of the gifts of the Holy Spirit are valid and operative today, and that the fruit of the Holy Spirit should be increasingly evident in a Christian's life.

6. I believe that the redemptive work of the Lord Jesus Christ provides healing for our spirit, soul and body.

7. I believe that we should obey Jesus' command to preach the gospel to all the world.

8. I believe that the members of the Body of Christ are the Church and encourage women to be part of and participate in the activities of their local church.

9. I believe in and look to the personal return of the Lord Jesus Christ. [88]

My momentary struggles have been *insignificant* compared to what Christ has done for me. When my friend Shirley Crane's son, Kevin, was in a five-year coma caused by viral encephalitis, she experienced anguish and suffering that was beyond expression. Yet today Shirley says that on the scale of tragedy of suffering hers was *small*. Trista and Kevin – the aroma and the essence of God's love and kindness. How will we understand the Cross if we don't carry it? [89] Christ died so that two thousand years later we could live with life's challenges. *All* things are possible for those who believe! [90] The Lord has always provided *all* the strength and comfort that I needed to get through *all* those hard times; without Jesus Christ I might not have survived our family's saga on the human rights battlefield.

If you have not asked Jesus to become your personal friend, your Savior and your Baptizer in the Holy Spirit, don't wait a moment longer. He is just a prayer away! I know that the Lord will give you exactly what you need because He *loves* you!

Dear Lord, please forgive me
for every sin in my life.
I now believe that You died for me,
and I thank you for forgiving me of all my sins.
Please come into my life right now,
and be my personal Savior and my Lord.
Take over my life, and help me to follow You and to obey You.
And Lord, make me the kind of person You want me to be.

I do believe that You are the Baptizer in the Holy Spirit.
I ask You to baptize me in the Holy Spirit right now.
Cleanse me from all unrighteousness,
and fill me with your precious Holy Spirit.

Thank you, Lord Jesus

~ ~ ~

CREATING YOUR ADVOCACY FILE

Good record-keeping is *the* most important ingredient for successful special-needs advocacy. Better to have saved and not needed, than to have not saved and needed! The legalities of proving a child's disabilities can be so complex that the lack of essential documentation can actually result in disqualification from available services.

For example, if we would not have been able to document Trista's lifelong history with Tourette Syndrome, we would probably have never qualified her for disability services in the state of Washington. As another illustration, SSI eligibility proved to be the primary qualifying criteria for other services that we desperately needed for our daughter. The SSI application process requires thorough documentation in *many* domains. I believe the reason her application was approved in 19 days is because we submitted thorough and complete information, with photocopies of all significant documentation. When a client is unable to provide accurate, detailed documentation, the SSI application is usually denied – and sometimes the denial and appeal process continues for *years*.

Even if one were to disregard the bigger issues like eligibility for state and federal services, record-keeping is important for local advocacy concerns. A parent's request for help in some arena is usually followed by someone wanting more information. The quality and speed of services *received* is, initially, often related to the quality and speed of information and documentation *provided* by the advocate.

In the early stages of record-keeping for the disabled child, I suggest saving *everything*. When a child is first diagnosed, or whenever a parent begins to suspect the child has some type of disability, it is important to begin collecting copies of anything that could verify a history of the child's problems. It is never too soon to begin, and the longer one waits, the more difficult it becomes to document the journey.

Most parents save cute "first" school papers, report cards, school photographs and newspaper clippings. But special-needs parents need to be also be hawking copies of notes sent by *and* to teachers, journals of meetings with educators, specialists and administrators, copies of medical records, and all IEPs. Such items aren't nearly as pretty in scrapbooks but they certainly can save a lot of stress and frustration later on. My recommendation is to save everything now – and sort later!

At the end of this chapter are categories of items we have found useful – some have been indispensable and irreplaceable! (And some were totally useless and just took up space – but I was never able to discern that fate when I saved something.) Over the years, I had to ferret out some documents from other sources to resolve specific problems, but most of the stored items were routine papers that I had just saved because I thought I might someday need them.

It is a challenge to know *how* to store everything so that the items will be most useful in the years ahead. During the first few years everything I saved had sentimental value, and those items were nostalgically tossed into ordinary cardboard boxes that were labeled for each child, "Trista's Memory Box," and "Tia's Memory Box." I didn't think I would ever *need* any of those treasures. As the girls' problems began to surface, certain items which became necessary were *somewhere* in each girl's memory box, and my filing system just evolved from those cartons. The farther we traveled on each girl's special-needs saga, the more I understood what, specifically, I needed at my fingertips. Ages and stages brought about different problems, and some information migrated from the bottom of the boxes to file folders, and then to the front of my notebook filing system. (I trained myself to always file to the front, so that the most recent document is right on top.) Some information became completely outdated and was discarded after I was *absolutely certain* it would never be needed again. However, some pieces of information are so essential that they will never see the light of day during Trista's lifetime – those items are securely stowed in our fireproof safe!

Housekeeping in filing systems is a necessary chore that is usually needs-driven – it generally occurs because I *can't find something*. Before I begin sorting through files, I always ask God to show me what to *not* discard. Many times I have sensed Him

 CREATING YOUR ADVOCACY FILE

saying, "Don't throw *that* away," and I did not understand why; then a year or so later I understood the reason. If an item in my advocacy boxes was valuable enough for me to consider saving it in the first place, then I need to be mindful that it might still prove valuable to me sometime. So when I am cleaning old advocacy files and find things that look fairly benign, rather than trashing them I usually put those useless stacks of papers in old manila envelopes. Then I list on the outside of the envelopes the contents, in *very* general terms, along with a **bold** label that says, "**discard in year 20_ _.**" That date is *five years in the future from the present year*. It may seem like overkill, but if something gets discarded prematurely, one generally knows about it within five years! (This one tip has proven useful *many* times during my advocacy career.)

I have revised my filing system several times during our 25-year journey. There are ages and stages in every child's development. In parent advocacy, the *resource information that is needed* changes *with* those ages and stages. The beauty of having to periodically revise the filing system is that it is wonderfully therapeutic to move old information to the back of the file, closing chapters on challenges that have long since been resolved.

Stowed away on a high closet shelf in our house are some old "45" records from Dave's childhood. And we also have a stack of 33 ⅓ albums from our honeymoon years. Those records are just pieces of plastic in shopworn covers but, for us, they hold memories of days gone by. Though we haven't played any of them for years, we know where they are if we should ever have a use for them. Someday, someone will probably trash them and wonder *why* we saved those old things! It is the same with the girls' important files which are full of their life history. Someday, *someone else* can dispose of them and wonder *why* we saved all those old things!

On the following pages is a category framework to begin planning parent advocate files. (The list is not intended to be exhaustive, and the main topics are listed alphabetically only for organizational simplicity.) When a parent must graduate from the "just throw it all in that box" stage, the first step will probably be to file folders. Placed in a filing box, a few file folders may be an appropriate beginning for the "Parent Advocacy File."

~ ~ ~

Categories for a Parent Advocacy File

Advocacy

- Tips & suggestions
- Things to ponder
- Inspirational items
- Memories

Disability Information: Insights on my child's disability

- Disability organization newsletters (or portions of)
- Newspaper clippings
- Brochures, booklets, handouts
- Journal reprints, etc. about child's specific disability

Educational / Academic [91]

- IEPs
- Report cards, diplomas
- Progress reports
- Test results on district-wide testing, private testing
- Child's permanent school file. (Periodically request photocopy updates of the entire file. Carefully review the information to be certain it is accurate. Reasonable requests for the purging of certain items from the permanent file must be considered by the school, and *may* be granted. If serious objections persist after contacting the principal, go to the top!)
- Notes sent **to** school (*photocopies or duplicates* of *every* special-needs-related correspondence)
- Personal correspondence *(every piece)* **from** teachers, specialists, administration
- Notes taken during all advocacy meetings. (Always list at the top of page: date, time, who was there, & purpose of meeting. Include details, plus a brief summary, including who is going to do what, and by what date.)

- Questions to ask next time
- Things to ponder
    - good ideas
    - notes about things that don't "feel right"

FINANCIAL

- Wage statements (a *must save* for SSI recipients)
- Banking records for child's account
- Other financial records for child – information on stocks, bonds, savings bonds, etc.

HOUSING

- Present caregiver – all correspondence to and from caregiver
- Former caregivers (a separate file for each caregiver)
- Future caregiver ideas, possibilities
- Housing consortium samples
- Private group housing ideas
- Other housing ideas

LEGAL [92]

- Power of attorney (copy – keep original in safe) (after Trista turned 18 and before we obtained guardianship, I carried a duplicate copy of our power of attorney for Trista in my billfold)   *– or –*
- Guardianship documents (copy – keep original in safe) (carry a duplicate copy in billfold)
- Special needs trust (copy – keep original in safe)
- Letter of intent (copy – keep original in safe)
- Parents' wills (copy – keep original in safe)
- Information on legal abuse issues, parent recourse articles
- Brain bank registration (important for research on specific disabilities)

(continued)

MEDICAL

- Birth certificate (copy – keep original in safe)
- Medical records that have anything to do with the child's disability (especially the prenatal, hospital, and postnatal records, if appropriate)
- Medications – list each kind, what for, dosages

PSYCHOLOGICAL

- Doctor reports
- Psychological evaluations, test results

SERVICE VENDORS

- Applications for any type of service (keep copies of every one that has been filled out – many applications are similar; this info can simplify filling in other forms)
- Arc file – information, correspondence, etc.

STATE DEVELOPMENTAL DISABILITY INFORMATION

- DD application
- DD letter of eligibility
- DD communication (to and from)

SOCIAL SECURITY INFORMATION

- Social security card
- SSI application
- SSI letter of eligibility
- SSI communications – to and from
- SSDI letter of eligibility
- Medicaid information
- Medicare information

TRANSPORTATION

- Application (copies) for local special-needs transportation services

TRANSITION / FUTURE (S) PLANNING IDEAS

VOCATIONAL

- Journal of vocational activities (useful for job applications later on)
  - Who the child worked for
  - When (dates: month/year through month/year)
  - What he did
  - Who his supervisor was
  - How much he was paid
  - How much he worked (hours per week)
  - Why he terminated specific job
- Vocational rehabilitation – contact information, history of service, etc.

MISCELLANEOUS (when it doesn't seem to fit anywhere else . . .)

Beaten Before You Start

If you think you're beaten, you are.

If you think you dare not, you don't.

If you'd like to win but think you can't

It's almost a cinch you won't.

If you think you'll lose, you're lost;

For out in the world, you find

Success begins with a fellow's faith:

It's all in the state of mind.

Full many a race is lost,

Ere ever a step is run,

And many a coward fails

Ere ever his work's begun.

Think big and your deeds will grow.

Think small and you'll fall behind.

Believe you can, and you will:

It's all in the state of mind.

If you think you're outclassed, you are.

You've got to think high to rise.

You've got to believe in yourself before

You can ever win a prize.

Life's battles don't always go

To the stronger or faster man.

But soon or late, the one who wins

Is the one who thinks he can.

author unknown

WHEN PEOPLE ARE INSENSITIVE

Families experience different forms of rejection. Sometimes it is a neighbor who stops inviting you for coffee, or it could be a physician who refers to your child as a "case" or a "condition." Or maybe it's a grandparent who seems to ignore your child with disabilities, or a close relative who seems to favor the "normal," talented or gifted children.

Whether the failure of others to appreciate your child is subtle or obvious, *resilience is needed*. One of the protective factors contributing to the resilience of families of exceptional children is *social support* from family and loved ones, neighbors, friends, physicians and professionals. Loss of this social support can increase the strain on a family managing a child with chronic illness or a disability.

HERE IS WHAT FAMILIES IDENTIFY AS HURTFUL BEHAVIOR[93]

EXTENDED FAMILY MEMBERS:

Lack of support and understanding

Lack of contact and involvement with child and the family

Giving advice and information that is unsolicited, not helpful

Not accepting the child or the condition

FRIENDS:

Withdrawal of contact and friendship

Lack of interaction, for fear of doing or saying the wrong thing

Lack of interest and involvement

PROFESSIONAL PROVIDERS:

Lack of understanding of a family's need for support

Inadequate or incorrect information

Insensitive treatment

Condescending attitude

WORK ASSOCIATES:

Lack of understanding and concern

Unfair treatment because of family needs

STRANGERS:

Insensitive, cruel and invasive comments

Staring, cruel, rude or hurtful behaviors

~ ~ ~

HERE IS HOW SOME FAMILIES COPE WITH HURTFUL AND INSENSITIVE BEHAVIOR[93]

- **FOCUS ATTENTION ON THOSE WHO ARE SUPPORTIVE.** Sometimes families simply let go of old friends and find new ones, often among other parents who have children with disabilities. These new friendships are particularly supportive. They are able to get support and give it in return.

- **EDUCATE OTHERS ABOUT DISABILITIES.** Often, insensitivity comes from ignorance. Many people simply need to learn what is appropriate and how to be helpful. Families can serve as teachers.

- **AVOID AND IGNORE THOSE WHO ARE INSENSITIVE.** Some people can't be taught. Trying to educate them is wasted effort. For these incorrigible few, ignore them.

- **FIGHT FOR YOUR RIGHTS.** Parents can ban together to affect policy changes. Such efforts have yielded big rewards, as is evidenced by PL 94-142 (every child's right to a free and appropriate education) and the Americans with Disabilities Act.

~ ~ ~

Hurrah for Special Olympics!

We are years away from real inclusion. Gardner's Theory of Multiple Intelligences [94] will take decades to be integrated into every school's curriculum, for every student. I doubt that it will ever sweep the nation as fully as the TAG program did. It's too expensive. It's too difficult to implement. It's too big!

However, I would like to shine the spotlight for a moment on one international program which *has* already recognized multiple intelligences. It is one of our family's favorite organization: **Special Olympics**.

Founded in 1968 by President John F. Kennedy's sister, Eunice Kennedy Shriver, the first Special Olympics Games marked the beginning of a worldwide movement to demonstrate that people with mental retardation are capable of remarkable achievements in sports, education, employment and beyond. The program now provides year-round training and athletic competition for more than one million athletes in nearly 150 countries and all 50 United States.

Special Olympics offers remarkable opportunities for the special-needs population. The nonprofit program of sports training and competition for individuals with mental retardation provides local participation in both Olympic sports and nationally popular sports:

Alpine Skiing	Cycling	Rollerskating
Aquatics	Equestrian	Sailing
Athletics	Figure Skating	Softball
Badminton	Floor Hockey	Speed Skating
Basketball	Football (Soccer)	Table Tennis
Boccé	Golf	Team Handball
Bowling	Gymnastics	Tennis
Cross Country Skiing	Powerlifting	Volleyball

Eunice Kennedy was born into a political dynasty. Joseph P. Kennedy (1888-1969), an American businessman and financier who served in government commissions in Washington, D.C., and as ambassador to Great Britain, was father of U.S. President John F. Kennedy and two other sons who became notable politicians. Joseph and Rose Kennedy also parented five daughters, one of whom was Rosemary. Born in 1918, the oldest Kennedy girl was institutionalized for retardation from early adulthood after undergoing an unsuccessful lobotomy. Her condition inspired her mother to become a benefactor for the mentally handicapped. Eunice, born in 1921, took the baton from her mother when Rose was 78 years old, at the time Eunice, herself, was 44.

Eunice Shriver understood that **the disabled derive pleasure from participating in unrealized and realized areas of giftedness**. Mrs. Shriver had a vision, a love, and a respect for handicapped people.

R. Sargent and Eunice Shriver, who are heirs to the Kennedy fortune, proclaim that the recipients of "gold" are the amateur athletes who participate in the nonprofit work of Special Olympics. "Absolutely no one is getting richer [than the Special Olympian] in these activities," proclaims Mr. Shriver. Contrasting the splendor of the Special Olympics Games with the corporate demeanor of professional sports, "The professional athlete doesn't really play the sport anymore, but [he] just goes out there to do his job and earn his living." With an attitude of generosity, localities open their arms to host the local, regional, state and world Special Olympics Games. The 1999 World Summer Games in North Carolina hosted over 7,000 athletes in competition. Dentists donate time and services to give free examinations at the Games; corporations provide all the meals and snacks; and even individuals, such as Fidel Castro, who are not known for their magnanimity, send their delegation free of charge to the Games.

It all happens because thousands of volunteers, like the Shrivers, have dedicated themselves "not to set records, but to improve [the athletes] both physically and mentally."[95]

Athletes, families and volunteers have been instrumental in changing perceptions about mental retardation and building a bridge to "The Next Generation of Heroes." Participation in Special Olympics is basically free for the athletes. Before every competition, the special athletes recite their Special Olympics Oath:

"Let me win.

But if I cannot win,

let me be brave in the attempt."

With the combined efforts of thousands of athletes, family members and volunteers, Special Olympics is able to improve the quality of life for athletes and their families. The project is all about helping improve the lives of others and giving back to the community.

The bottom line in theories of inclusion and handicapped legislation is the Golden Rule: [96]

"Do unto others

as you would have them do unto you."

If we could get that simple instruction down pat, this book (and hundreds like it) would never need to be written; we wouldn't need disability legislation, nor programs like Special Olympics. **However, we are human and we are incredibly near-sighted, with respect to people and situations that are outside our zone of comfort.** Perhaps *most* people need a little extra help to come alongside the disabled population. It does not come naturally to be our brother's keeper.

Special Olympics provides a platform for the Golden Rule. As a movement, Special "O" relies on dedicated volunteers to provide year-round sports training and athletic competition for people eight years of age and older with mental handicaps. The Special "O" global community includes athletes, volunteers, coaches, family members and sponsors / supporters.

I propose this challenge: if you are not familiar with Special Olympics, check it out. If you *are* familiar with Special Olympics, consider getting involved. If you don't have the energy, the time, or the desire to consider volunteering for Special "O," then please consider opening your checkbook to them. I have seen Special Olympics' budgets and I have observed how they spend their money. Few organizations squeeze the value out of the dollar any better than Special Olympics. I believe that your contributions to Special Olympics will be better spent than any tax dollars on any kind of new, innovative program at any school or private workplace, anywhere! You *can* make a difference!

Try Special "O" – you'll like it!

Special Olympics, Inc.
1325 G Street, NW / Suite 500
Washington, DC 20005
Phone: (202) 628-3630
FAX: (202) 825-0200
website: >http://www.specialolympics.org<

~ ~ ~

APPENDIX

THE BASICS OF SSI

The following information is taken primarily [97] from the booklet, *Supplemental Security Income*, available at any Social Security Office, or on the Internet. [98]

This chapter explains what SSI is, who can qualify for it, and how to sign up for SSI. The information provided here is not intended to be exhaustive. Although most of the Social Security Administration (SSA) publications are written at about fifth grade level, the laws are *extremely* complex. For specific information, contact Social Security. [99] Contrary to public opinion, I have always found the employees at the Social Security offices wonderfully helpful and accommodating.

WHAT IS SSI?

Supplemental Security Income (SSI) is a federal entitlement program financed through general tax revenues, to provide income benefits to certain groups of very low-income people, including the aged, the blind, and people with disabilities.

SSI isn't just for adults. Monthly checks are also issued to disabled and blind children.

People who qualify for SSI usually receive Medicaid, which helps pay doctor and hospital bills. SSI recipients may also be eligible for food stamps. In some states, Low-Income Medicare Beneficiaries may receive state payment for Medicare premiums and other Medicare expenses, such as deductibles and co-insurance. See the leaflet, *Medicare Savings For Qualified Beneficiaries* (HCFA Publication No. 02184).

WHO QUALIFIES FOR SSI?

To qualify for SSI, the applicant must be 65 or older, or blind or disabled.

Blind means a person is either totally blind or has extremely poor eyesight. Children, as well as adults, may be eligible to receive benefits because of blindness.

Disabled means a person has a physical or mental problem that keeps him from working and is expected to last at least a year or to result in death. Children, as well as adults, may receive benefits because of disability. When deciding if a child is disabled, Social Security looks at how his or her disability affects everyday life. For more information about benefits for children, refer to the booklet, *Benefits For Children With Disabilities* (Publication No. 05-10026).

Sometimes, a person whose sight is not poor enough to qualify for benefits as a blind person may be able to receive checks as a disabled person if his or her condition prevents him or her from working.

How much an applicant qualifies for depends on where he lives. The basic SSI check is the same nationwide. However, many states add to that amount. (For example, the 1999 SSI amount for King County, in Washington state, was about $527 per month.) Call SSA at (800) 772-1213 to inquire about the amounts for specific localities.

RULES FOR QUALIFYING FOR SSI

INCOME AND RESOURCES

Qualifying for SSI also depends on a person's resources and his income. Income is money such as wages, Social Security checks and pensions, and may also include non-cash items received, such as food, clothing or shelter.

For married applicants, Social Security office also looks at the income and resources of the spouse. For children under 18, Social Security considers the parent's income and resources.

INCOME

To become eligible for SSI, a person must not be capable of Substantial Gainful Activity (SGA). As of July 1, 1999, SGA is defined as earning more than $700 per month. However, once eligibility is established, a person is allowed to earn more than $700 per month, with SSI being reduced on a sliding scale. SSI is also reduced by unearned income, such as Social Security Disability Insurance (SSDI).

RESOURCES

A person may be able to receive SSI with resources worth up to $2,000. A couple may be able to receive SSI with resources worth up to $3,000. Resources include items such as real estate, personal belongings, bank accounts, cash, and stocks and bonds.

Social Security doesn't count everything. Exempt resources include the applicant's home of residence and the land it is on, personal and household goods and certain life insurance policies, (usually) a car, burial plots and up to $1,500 in burial funds, and for applicants who are blind or have a disability, some items related to work or earning extra income may also be exempt.

A SPECIAL NOTE FOR PEOPLE WHO ARE BLIND OR WHO HAVE A DISABILITY

Blind or disabled people who apply for SSI may receive special services from their state. These services include counseling, job training, and help in finding work.

For more information about these rules, refer to the booklet, *Working While Disabled . . . How We Can Help* (Publication No. 05-10095).

FOR RESIDENTS OF A PUBLIC OR PRIVATE INSTITUTION

People who live in city or county rest homes, halfway houses or other public institutions usually cannot receive SSI checks. Some exceptions include people who live in a publicly operated community residence which serves no more than 16 people, those who live in a public institution, mainly to attend approved educational or job training, or people who live in a public or private institution and Medicaid is paying more than half the cost of the applicant's care.

Signing Up for SSI

How To Apply

Visit the local Social Security office. Or call (800) 772-1213 for an appointment with a local Social Security representative. Parents or guardians can apply for blind or disabled children under 18.

What To Bring

The following items are required for the application. If an applicant does not have all of the items listed, it is important to begin the application process anyway. The Social Security office can assist in obtaining necessary documentation.

√ Social Security card or a record of Social Security number

√ Birth certificate or other proof of age

√ Information about applicant's home, such as copy of mortgage, or copy of lease and landlord's name

√ Payroll slips, bank books, insurance policies, car registration, burial fund records, and other information about income and resources

√ If applying for disability, the names, addresses, and telephone numbers of appropriate doctors, hospitals, and clinics

√ Proof of U.S. citizenship or eligible noncitizen status

√ Checkbook or other bank account information (Social Security now deposits benefits directly into the client's account. Direct deposit is expedient, and protects benefits from loss, theft, and mail delay.)

A Word About Social Security Benefits

An individual may be eligible for Social Security benefits if he has worked long enough under Social Security. Often, people can receive both Social Security and SSI benefits. People qualify based on their own work history or that of a parent.

Social Security pays retirement benefits, disability benefits, and survivors benefits. Retirement benefits go mostly to people 62 or older and their families. Disability benefits go to people with disabilities and their families. Survivors benefits are paid to the families of workers who have died.

Some Social Security and SSI rules are the same. Some rules for SSDI are different than for SSI. Contact a Social Security office for specific information.

CONFIDENTIALITY ISSUES

SSA keeps personal information on millions of people. That information – such as Social Security number, earnings record, age, and address – is personal and confidential. Generally, SSA will discuss this information only with the applicant, or the natural parent or legal guardian of a child.

There are times when the law requires Social Security to give information to other government agencies to conduct other government health or welfare programs – such as Aid to Families with Dependent Children, Medicaid, and food stamps. Programs receiving information from Social Security are prohibited from sharing that information.

FOR MORE INFORMATION

For more information, visit or write any Social Security office. Or phone toll-free, 24 hours a day, (800) 772-1213. (Telephone service representatives are available between the hours of 7:00 a.m. and 7:00 p.m. on business days. Recorded information and services are available 24 hours a day, including weekends and holidays.) For Social Security's toll-free "TTY," representatives may be reached at (800) 325-0778, between 7:00 a.m. and 7:00 p.m. on business days.

Social Security has many publications that contain information about other Social Security programs. Contact Social Security to get a free copy of any of the following publications.

- *Social Security – Understanding The Benefits* (Publication No. 05-10024) – A comprehensive explanation of all the Social Security programs

- *Social Security — Retirement Benefits* (Publication No. 05-10035) – Explains Social Security retirement benefits

- *Social Security – Disability Benefits* (Publication No. 05-10029) – Explains Social Security disability benefits

- *Medicare* (Publication No.10043) – Explains Medicare hospital insurance and medical insurance

- *Social Security – Survivors Benefits (Publication* No. 05-10084) – Explains Social Security survivors benefits

> Social Security publications are also available to users of the Internet. These publications are available on the Social Security Administration website: >http://www.ssa.gov<

~ ~ ~

APPENDIX

A National Legal Precedent

Our coveted legal precedent defines Tourette Syndrome as a neurological disorder. Handed down on January 18, 1996, our Review Decision and Final Order reaffirmed and further strengthened the impact of the Initial Decision of May 22, 1995. Notwithstanding, Tourette Syndrome victims throughout the United States continue to battle for their legal rights. Insurance companies and states cling to the psychological disorder definition for Tourette Syndrome, and thereby exempt Touretters from receiving benefits they clearly deserve. Many Tourette families and attorneys remain unaware that this important neurological disorder precedent has already been established.

Included within this chapter is the text of our national legal precedent, Washington Docket No. 1293 A 1027. Quoted in their entirety are both the Review Decision and Final Order, and the Initial Decision.

~ ~ ~

STATE OF WASHINGTON

DEPARTMENT OF SOCIAL AND HEALTH SERVICES

OFFICE OF APPEALS

In Re:	) Docket No. 1293 A 1027
	)
TRISTA CONKLIN	) **REVIEW DECISION**
[address]	) **AND FINAL ORDER**
[address]	)
	) (DDD)
APPELLANT	)

NATURE OF ACTION

A hearing was held by Clayton F. Harrington, Jr., Senior Administrative Law Judge (ALJ). The initial decision or order was served on May 22, 1995. The Department filed a request for review on June 9, 1995, at the Spokane Office of Administrative Hearings. A copy was received by the Department's Office of Appeals on July 5, 1995. The request alleges:

There are numerous independent bases upon which the Initial Decision should be reversed. First, Tourctte's Syndrome is a mental / psychiatric disorder which disqualifies appellant for DDD services under WAC 275-27-026(6)(b)(ii).

Second, if Tourette's Syndrome is a neurological condition, appellant is disqualified for DDD services under WAC 275-27-026(6)(a). The fact that appellant's condition does not create a substantial handicap, and / or the fact that she has a normal range IQ, would each independently render her ineligible for DDD services under this subsection.

Third, the appeal was not timely filed. DDD provided notice to all person(s) required by law. Appellant failed to file her appeal within the required 28-day time period.

Fourth, appellant does not qualify for ICAP testing under WAC 275-27-026(6)(b)(ii), and it is improper to order retesting based upon an ICAP respondent's intentional inaccuracies. Appellant's normal IQ requires participation in special education, for reasons other than those enumerated, before she would be eligible for ICAP testing to determine DDD eligibility. The ALJ found that DDD properly administered and evaluated the ICAP and no other basis merits re-administration.

Fifth, it is improper to order DDD to allow Jean Conklin, appellant's mother, to be present for ICAP testing or to respond to ICAP questioning. An applicant's parents have no general right to be informed of and participate in their child's ICAP. No person has a general right to respond to ICAP questioning on bchalf of an appellant unless they meet the guidelines in the ICAP Examiner's Manual.

Finally, the DDD eligibility requirements have been carefully crafted to serve the needs of the greatest number of people with an increasingly limited amount of resources. DDD attempts to ensure that only applicants with the most severe need receive DDD services. It is impossible to provide all persons who request DDD assistance, with assistance. Therefore, DDD must carefully adhere to the requirements of the WAC.

For the reasons cited above, the Division of Developmental Disabilities (DDD), Department of Social and Health Services (DSHS), hereby respectfully requests that this appeal be dismissed as untimely or, in the alternative, that the ALJ's decision should be reversed.

The Appellant filed a response to the Department's petition for review.

FINDINGS OF FACT

The findings of fact in the initial decision or order are adopted under RCW 34.05.464(8), except as follows:

The following is added to Finding of Fact 20:

There are nine documents in evidence that relate to the Appellant's need for special education. These exhibits are SS. NN, LL, CC, EE, JJ, II, DD, and BB. These exhibits establish that the Appellant needed special education services because she is health impaired, has weaknesses in her ability to work under stress, has poor handwriting, note taking skills, concentration, and organization, that she needed perceptual training in visual-motor coordination and figure-ground relationships, that at age 15 years 5 months she was performing at 10% of the expected reading level, 1% of the expected math level, and 60% of the expected language level, and that she needed specially designed reading, math, spelling, and physical education classes. It is found that the Appellant's participation in special education classes was not based solely on a psychiatric impairment, serious emotional or behavioral disturbances or orthopedic impairment.

CONCLUSIONS OF LAW

1. The request for review was timely filed and is otherwise proper. WAC 388-08-464(3) and (4). Jurisdiction exists to review the initial decision or order and to enter the final agency order. WAC 388-08-464(2).

2. The findings of fact in the initial decision have been changed to include relevant or necessary facts, to conform to the record, and / or to support the conclusions of law in this review decision. RCW 34.05.461(3),(4). The Review Judge has the same decision-making authority as the Administrative Law Judge (ALJ), except that the ALJ's opportunity to observe the witnesses is given due regard. RCW 34.05.464(4). This authority includes the ability to modify or replace the factual findings of the ALJ. *Tapper v. Employment Security*, 122Wn.2d 397,404-406 (1993).

3. The Department has established good cause for the late-filed petition for review.

4. Since the appeal of this case began in 1993, a new regulation has been adopted. WAC 388-08-385 grants the defense of equitable estoppel to applicants or recipients of public assistance, as that term is defined at RCW 74.04.005(1). However, the Appellant is not an applicant for nor a recipient of public assistance. The ALJ's analysis of equitable estoppel in deciding whether the Appellant's appeal was timely filed, in Conclusion of Law 8, is not adopted. While the reasoning and arguments in that conclusion are sound, neither the ALJ nor the undersigned Review Judge can entertain the defense of equitable estoppel outside the public assistance arena. However, the issue of timely appeal from the Department's denial really is a non-issue. The Appellant could always have reapplied for DDD services. She would have undoubtedly been denied again, but she could have timely appealed the second denial. Review Judges at the Department's Office of Appeals are loathe to deny an applicant access to the administrative hearing forum on procedural

technicalities. The Department is not well served by arguing that an otherwise potentially eligible client should be denied services for all time because of misleading language and ambiguities in its own forms or because of the errors of third parties. It is concluded that the Appellant's request for hearing to appeal the Department's denial of DDD services was timely filed.

5. The undersigned has reviewed the extensive record developed at the hearing in this case and agrees with the ALJ's conclusion that Tourette's Syndrome is a neurological condition. The Appellant is potentially eligible for DDD services under WAC 275-27-026(6)(b)(ii), having established that her participation in special education was not due solely to a psychiatric impairment, a serious emotional / behavioral disturbance, or an orthopedic handicap. The ICAP retesting procedures ordered by the ALJ are not unreasonable and are affirmed.

6. The undersigned is troubled by what appears to be the Department's "moving target" basis of eligibility. First, the Appellant was denied DDD services because the Department claimed her ICAP scores were too high. Then, the Department advanced the argument that Tourette's Syndrome was not a neurological disease. Now the Department argues that the ICAP was administered in error because the Appellant doesn't meet the criteria of WAC 275-27-026(6)(b)(ii). The Appellant's frustration in dealing with the Department in determining her DDD eligibility is well founded.

7. The undersigned has considered the initial decision or order, the request for review, and the whole record or the parts cited by the parties. Any arguments in the request for review that are not specifically addressed have been duly considered but are found to have no merit or to not substantially affect a party's rights. The conclusions of law in the initial decision are adopted except as modified above. RCW 34.05.464(8). The procedures and time limits for seeking reconsideration for judicial review of this decision are in the attached statement.

DECISION AND ORDER

The initial decision or order is affirmed.

Served on the date of mailing, stamped above.

(stamped and mailed January 18, 1996, DSHS Office of Appeals)

(<u>signature: Christine Stalnaker</u>)
CHRISTINE STALNAKER
Review Judge

Attached: Reconsideration / Judicial Review Information

Copies have
been sent to :   Trista Conklin, Appellant

Jean Conklin, Representative

Joyce Malone, DDD Administrator 1

Deborah K. Danner, Assistant Attorney General

Clayton F. Harrington, Jr., Spokane OAH

~ ~ ~

Editor's notes: The REVIEW DECISION AND FINAL ORDER,
                 dated January 18, 1996, refers to the
                 Initial Decision, dated May 22, 1995.

                 The INITIAL DECISION is quoted in its
                 entirety on the following pages.

~ ~ ~

BEFORE THE WASHINGTON STATE OFFICE OF ADMINISTRATIVE HEARINGS FOR THE DEPARTMENT OF SOCIAL AND HEALTH SERVICES

In Re:	) Docket No. 1293 A 1027
	)
TRISTA CONKLIN	) **INITIAL DECISION**
[address]	)
[address]	)
	)
APPELLANT	)

Clayton F. Harrington Jr., Senior Administrative Law Judge, conducted the hearing on January 18, 1994. Appellant appeared, with her mother and representative, Jean Conklin. Gib Keithly, Administrator, represented the department's Division of Developmental Disabilities (DDD). An Initial Decision was filed June 10, 1994. A Review decision and Order of Remand was filed September 8, 1994, and a Decision on Reconsideration and Order of Remand was filed October 10, 1994. An additional hearing was held March 3, 1995, to address the issues raised in the Review Decision and the Decision for Reconsideration. Jean Conklin appeared for Trista Conklin. Joyce Malone, Administrator, appeared for DDD.

ISSUES

1. Is Tourette's Syndrome a neurological medical condition with associated mental disorders, or does the listing of Tourette's Syndrome in the Diagnostic and Statistical Manual of Mental Disorders, Third Revision, mean that Tourette's Syndrome cannot be a neurological condition?

2. Should the department's Division of Developmental Disabilities be required to readminister the Inventory for Client and Agency Planning test to Appellant to determine whether

Appellant is eligible for services through the Division of Developmental Disabilities if the caregiver-respondent in that test already administered is later found to have given responses which are not completely accurate?

3. Is there jurisdiction for a hearing where Appellant's representative was identified on the application for benefits as a person to be notified of the eligibility decision but was not notified of the department decision to deny eligibility until more than 28 days had passed from the date of that notice?

RESULTS

1. Tourette's Syndrome is a neurological medical condition with associated mental disorders. The listing of Tourette's Syndrome in the Diagnostic and Statistical Manual of Mental Disorders, Third Revision, does not prove or mean that Tourette's Syndrome is not a neurological condition.

2. The department's Division of Developmental Disabilities should be required to readminister the Inventory for Client and Agency Planning test to Appellant to determine whether Appellant is eligible for services through the Division of Developmental Disabilities if the caregiver-respondent in that test already administered is later found to have given responses which are not completely accurate.

3. There is jurisdiction for a hearing where Appellant's representative was identified on the application for benefits as a person to be notified of the eligibility decision but was not notified of the department decision to deny eligibility until more than 28 days had passed from the date of notice.

FINDINGS OF FACT

1. Appellant applied to the Division of Developmental Disability (DDD) August 16, 1993. DDD denied Appellant's application September 29, 1993. Notice of this denial was mailed to Appellant by certified letter dated October 4, 1993, which was received by Appellant October 6, 1993.

2. In the application Appellant noted that she lived with a caregiver, Ms. [name], in [address] Washington. She also wrote in the space provided for "SIGNIFICANT OTHER" the name and address of her parents, Dave and Jean Conklin, [address], Oregon. In Item 29, "WHO ELSE BESIDES APPLICANT SHOULD RECEIVE NOTIFICATION OF ELIGIBILITY / INELIGIBILITY DECISION?" Dave and Jean Conklin again were named. However, a copy of the denial letter was not mailed to Dave and / or Jean Conklin. The denial letter was mailed only to the applicant, Trista Conklin. Jean Conklin first received a copy of this letter from [the caregiver] approximately forty days following the date of delivery of the denial to Appellant. Ms. Conklin filed an appeal on behalf of Trista on December 7, 1993.

3. As part of the application process Ms. Karen Cheryl, a DDD intake worker, administered to Appellant an Inventory for Client and Agency Planning test (hereafter referred to as ICAP) on September 21, 1993. In administering the test DDD requested both Appellant and her caregiver, [name], be present to answer questions. Again, no notice of testing was given to Mr. or Mrs. Conklin.

4. For the purpose of determining eligibility for DDD services, the scores obtained from the four domains in the Adaptive Behavior Section of the ICAP test are used. For Appellant those scores were: Motor Skills domain, 65; Social and Communicating domain, 66; Personal Living domain, 75; Community Living domain, 79.

5. At hearing Ms. [caregiver] testified that she answered the ICAP test questions with the choice which would give the Appellant the highest level of performance for the questioned task, rather than say that she could not perform the questioned task. Thus, in the Community Living Skills section, to the question "correctly counts change from a five dollar bill after making a purchase" she responded "does very well", when in fact Appellant never counts change; to the question "operates potentially dangerous electrical hand tools and appliance with moving parts" she responded "does very well" when in fact Ms. [caregiver] would never let Appellant operate such a device because she shakes too much; to the question "writes down, if necessary, and keeps appointments made at least

three days in advance" Ms. [caregiver] responded "does very well", when in fact Appellant never does this; to the question "budgets money to cover expenses for at least one week" Ms. [caregiver] responded "does very well", when in fact Appellant does not budget money; to the question "balances a checkbook monthly", Ms. [caregiver] responded "does very well", when in fact Mrs. Conklin, not Appellant, was balancing Appellant's checkbook; even at the time of hearing Appellant testified that she keeps a running total in her checkbook, but does not reconcile monthly statements with the checkbook.

6. Ms. [caregiver] was influenced to answer questions in this way for several reasons. First, with Appellant sitting right next to her in the examination room, Ms. [caregiver] did not want to hurt Appellant's feelings.

Secondly, Ms. [caregiver] was aware that anxiety, and other highly elevated emotional states, cause Appellant's tics to increase in frequency and severity. That day, on the way over to the test site, Appellant was so agitated over the requirement of taking a test that she repeatedly kicked the dash of Ms. [caregiver]'s car with such force that she cracked it. Ms. [caregiver] did not want to risk more destructive tic behaviors by being honestly critical of Appellant's abilities.

A third reason for Ms. [caregiver]'s responses was that she did not understand the distinctions between the four rating choices presented. Since many of the questions appeared irrelevant or insultingly below Appellant's level of functioning she did not appreciate that the accuracy and quality of the information she provided was essential for a result which correctly described Appellant. Ms. [caregiver] testified that if she had responded to each question without regard to Appellant's feelings, without regard to any potential outbursts of negative tic behaviors, and seriously evaluating each question regardless of its apparent import, she would have responded differently (with lower performance indicated) in her answers on many of the questions.

As an example of the difference this would have made, at hearing Ms. [caregiver] and Mrs. Conklin reviewed some of the questions and determined that the raw score obtained in the Community Living Skills section should have been closer to 30 instead of the 49 actually scored. Similarly, questions in the Personal Living domain when answered by Ms. [caregiver] with the same considerations would have resulted in a much lower raw score. Since the raw score in the Motor Skills domain and the Social and Communication Skills domain already were below the maximum score allowed for eligibility to be established, Ms. Conklin and Ms. [caregiver] did not review the questions in these sections to determine if a different score would have been registered. The department representative conceded that if there was a change in the raw score to 30 from 49, that the resultant processed score in that domain would have been within the range in which DDD eligibility would have been approved.

7. Ms. [caregiver] was a caregiver for Appellant for a period of two months when they both lived together in Hood River, Oregon. Ms. [caregiver] then moved to Spokane, Washington, to be with her daughter and grandchild, and Appellant moved back to Hermiston, Oregon, where her family lived. In February, 1993, the Conklins and Ms. [caregiver] agreed that Appellant would move to Spokane, Washington, to again live with Ms. [caregiver] as a caregiver. At the time of the administration of the ICAP, Appellant had lived with Ms. [caregiver] approximately seven consecutive months.

8. At the time of hearing Ms. [caregiver] felt that she knew some of Appellant's likes and dislikes, such as her food preferences, but that she could not predict Appellant's behavior, particularly when tics would occur, what type of action or behavior the tic would take, nor the severity of the tic.

9. At the time the ICAP test was administered Appellant was nervous over the test and had nightmares the previous few nights. She felt greatly relieved when the test was finished.

10. During the ICAP test Appellant felt some of the questions were "babyish" and was "teed off" over the questions relating to toys, and staying in the yard. She did not understand some of the questions and neither she nor Ms. [caregiver] understood the distinctions between the four performance ratings.

11. The ICAP Examiner's Manual requires that the ICAP be completed by a respondent who has known a client for at least three months and who sees him or her on a day-to-day basis. The test is designed to be completed in a short period of time, stated to be "approximately twenty minutes", and is designed to be administered by individuals without extensive training in test administration. The test is designed to be administered *repeatedly* to clients for diagnostic, tracking and / or follow-up purposes.

12. Directions for administration of the test requires the test administrator to exercise judgment in determining which response best describes the client. It is the test administrator, not the client or caregiver, who determines the appropriate response to each question. However, the test administrator must instruct the respondent(s), and the respondents must understand, the primary criterion of independence is the statement, "*Does (or could do) task completely without help or supervision.*" All four performance ratings for each task are evaluated by applying this statement.

13. The rating "Does Very Well" indicates *complete* independence on an item. The client does the task completely and very well *without* any help or supervision from anyone. The client also must know when it is necessary to do the task without being asked or reminded.

14. The rating "Does Fairly Well" indicates the client performs the task reasonably well, without help or supervision. Although a task may not have been mastered, the client *can do all of the required parts of the task*. The client may need to be reminded or asked to do the task. This rating indicates that the client can successfully perform the task three-quarters of the time.

15. The rating "Does, But Not Well" indicates the client sometimes performs the task without help but does not do it well, and / or the results are not good. The client may need to be reminded or asked to perform the task. This rating indicates that the client can perform the task correctly, without help or supervision, not more than one-quarter of the time.

16. The rating "Never or Rarely" indicates the task is too hard for the client, or the client is not permitted to do the task because it is not safe. The client never or rarely performs all parts of the task without help even if asked. If a client attempts all parts of a task and is partially proficient on a task, the test administrator must make a judgment regarding the quality of the client's performance and select a rating of "Does, But Not Well," or "Does Fairly Well."

17. Appellant's full scale IQ is 86.

18. Appellant has been diagnosed by mental health professionals to have an Axis One diagnosis of Tourette's Disorder with Obsessive / Compulsive symptoms. Tourette's Disorder or Tourette's Syndrome is a listed mental disorder in the Diagnostic and Statistical Manual of Mental Disorders, Third Edition, Revised (hereafter referred to as the DSM 3R).

19. Medical professionals classify Tourette's Syndrome as a neurological condition also.

20. For Appellant this condition has existed since Appellant was at least five years old. As result of this condition Appellant has been eligible for and participated in special education when she was in school, and has received developmental disability services in the state of Oregon from the agency responsible to administer these services in Oregon just as DDD administers these same programs in the state of Washington.

21. Appellant does not have cerebral palsy, epilepsy, or autism and has not suffered any neurologic trauma.

22. On December 10, 1993, DDD filed a motion to dismiss Appellant's appeal based upon Appellant's filing her request for hearing more than twenty-eight days after receipt of the notice of the denial of her application. This motion is responded to in the conclusions of law following.

23. At hearing Mr. Keithly was asked if DDD would consider administering the ICAP to Appellant again. He responded that he would not authorize the test be administered again because

"I've seen this happen before where the test questions (were) handed out to people. They can analyze those questions to tell exactly what has to be done in order to, in essence, flunk the test. I've seen it done before. So I have a reluctance to do a re-test now immediately on the heels of the reviewed answer, questions here. I seriously question the validity of such a procedure."

24. It specifically is found here that Jean Conklin is a credible witness, and that her personal testimony is completely trustworthy. It is further found that Jean Conklin is a person with exceptionally high personal integrity.

CONCLUSIONS OF LAW

1. There is jurisdiction to hear this matter pursuant to Washington Administrative Code (WAC) 275-27-500.

2. Tourette's Syndrome is a neurological condition with associated mental disorders. The fact that Tourette's Syndrome is identified in the DSM 3R as a mental disorder does not preclude considering the condition as a neurological disorder nor mean that the condition is not a neurological condition. Accordingly, DDD should process Appellant's application for services under the category described as a neurological medical condition pursuant to Washington Administrative Code. (WAC) 275-27-026(6).

3. In reviewing all of the evidence and argument presented in this case the primary question in issue is how the results of the ICAP test administered by DDD to Appellant should be treated.

In reviewing the test's Examiner's Manual sections which describe how the test should be administered it is apparent to this Tribunal, and it is here concluded, that DDD staff properly administered and scored the test.

4. However, the testimony at hearing identifies a critical problem with the test results reached in this particular case. The problem is that [the caregiver] intentionally responded to test questions in a manner that was more considerate of Appellant's feelings and Ms. [caregiver]'s person and property than by describing Appellant's actual ability to perform identified tasks.

As a result the scores obtained from the test are not reliable. Since the circumstance regarding Ms. [caregiver]'s car and Trista's behaviors were first disclosed at hearing the test administrator was not aware of nor able to detect Ms. [caregiver]'s deception. It is for these reasons that the Review Decision the department argues is dispositive on this point is not pertinent.

5. The next issue presented is how to deal with these tainted test results. From the very beginning of this dispute between Appellant and DDD, and throughout this hearing process, Jean Conklin has requested that DDD simply retest Appellant, with herself being present to assist with the responses.

Mr. Keithly, the DDD representative, argued against retesting for the reasons that he believed that Jean Conklin, having reviewed the questions in the test, would intentionally misrepresent Appellant's abilities in a negative way so as to qualify her daughter for DDD services; that the ICAP test procedure would be invalid if it were administered repeatedly within short time intervals. Mr. Keithly does not disagree with the fact that the results obtained from the ICAP test administration in issue may be inaccurate. Rather, Mr. Keithly argues that the test was administered properly, and, therefore, the results must stand.

As noted above, this Tribunal finds no error on the part of the department in the administration of the ICAP test in issue, nor does this Tribunal find error in the department actions taken in response to those test results. However, this Tribunal also has found and concluded as a result of the evidence in this hearing that the test results in issue are not reliable. This Tribunal concludes, therefore, that DDD should readminister the ICAP test to Appellant, giving notice to Jean Conklin of the scheduled test date, and an opportunity for her to appear to respond to the test questions.

In reaching this conclusion this Tribunal notes in response to Mr. Keithly's arguments that Washington Administrative Code (WAC) 275-27-026(6)(b) requires DDD to administer the ICAP test to determine client eligibility at least every twenty-four months. As Mr. Keithly testified at hearing, necessarily, this would require the ICAP test to be administered repeatedly to those DDD clients qualifying under section 6 whenever their eligibility is reviewed. However, this Tribunal does not accept the DDD argument that a mentally competent adult would not be able to remember the ICAP test, the nature of the test questions or how to respond to the questions to obtain a "qualifying" result over a period of twenty-four months. This Tribunal also does not accept the insinuation in the DDD argument that Jean Conklin will intentionally misrepresent her daughter's capabilities in order to qualify her for DDD services. This Tribunal notes from testimony and the ICAP test Examiner's Manual that the test is designed to be administered repeatedly, and, also, that the test administrator ultimately is responsible to mark what appears to be the correct response to any give question. If there are any questions regarding the veracity of Jean Conklin's statements this Tribunal presumes the test administrator would be sufficiently skilled and trained to nevertheless obtain a reasonably accurate test result, or, in the alternative, to take whatever would be an appropriate action under the circumstances presented.

Moreover, in addressing this particular argument, this Tribunal notes that this is a de novo hearing, that some twenty-two months have passed since the date of application, and, under the time frame argued by the department the test can legitimately be readministered. For these reasons this Tribunal concludes the test should be readministered as well.

6. Another reason this Tribunal believes the test should be readministered is because at the time of application Jean and Dave Conklin were identified as "significant others" and as persons to be contacted about the eligibility decision. Yet at no time during the processing of the application, from evaluation to decision, did the department give the Conklins any notice of what was going on. While it was convenient and within acceptable test procedure rules to have had Ms. [caregiver] appear with Trista, this Tribunal believes the department had a duty to notify the Conklins of the testing requirement and give them at least the opportunity to decide who would appear with Trista for the test. For the department to solicit this type of information in the application form and then not act on it in a manner consistent with that which is implied by having it in

the printed application form is a misleading and deceptive practice. For this reason the test should be readministered.

7. Finally, this Tribunal concludes the test should be readministered because to hold otherwise in this particular case would be exceptionally harsh and punitive to Appellant, punishing her (by denying eligibility for DDD services) the errors committed by others for reasons which have nothing to do with obtaining or attempting to obtain DDD services. For these reasons this Tribunal concludes that DDD should readminister the ICAP test to Appellant.

8. The final issue presented is the question of the timeliness of the Appellant's appeal. The department takes the position that the notice sent to Appellant by certified letter advising of the denial of the application is all that was required by the department to satisfy its duty to give notice of its decision. The department argues in this regard that Appellant is a competent adult capable of handling her own business affairs. The department also argues that it did not err by not sending a notice to the Conklins because as a matter of law the Conklins were not entitled to notice of the decision. Therefore the appeal was not timely.

For the reasons identified in Conclusion of Law 6, this Tribunal believes the request for hearing should be considered timely. At the time of application Jean and Dave Conklin were identified in the application in a space identified as "significant others" and in another location as persons to be contacted about the eligibility decision. Why does the department print these questions on the application form if it has no obligation or intention of notifying the identified individuals of what actions the department is taking? Clearly, if someone in the position of Mrs. Conklin reads this question and puts her name in the identified space, as she testified, she is going to be relying on the department, not Trista or Ms. [caregiver], to notify her in a timely manner of what actions are being taken on the application. Yet at no time during the processing of the application, from evaluation to decision, did the department give the Conklins any notice of what was going on. This Tribunal believes that if the department places questions in its application soliciting the names of persons to be notified of the department decision that the department should be estopped from later arguing that the department has no duty to notify those persons of the department actions taken on the application. It is unconscionable and manifestly unjust for the department to solicit this type of information in an application form and then argue it has no duty to act in a manner consistent with the implication for soliciting it. If this information was not solicited by the department Mrs. Conklin would have made alternative arrangements to keep herself informed of what was going on with her daughter's application, and, in all probability, the appeal would have been filed within twenty-eight days of the date of the notice.

This Tribunal also takes issue with the department implication that the applicant for DDD services here is a competent adult capable of handling her own business affairs. The fact of this issue disproves this department assertion. At best Trista Conklin's abilities to function as an independent person are marginal. She is living with a caregiver because in the past she has not demonstrated an ability to make acceptable decisions regarding personal care. She has been a recipient of DDD services in the state of Oregon for this reason, among others.

This Tribunal believes, and here concludes, that Trista Conklin was not capable of understanding the implications of the notice given her. Therefore, for this reason the notice to Trista Conklin is invalid as a sufficient notice of the department action. The department reliance on the notice to Trista Conklin as being legally sufficient by itself is misplaced at best.

For these reasons this Tribunal concludes the request for hearing submitted by Jean Conklin which was received by the department December 7, 1993, is a timely request for hearing.

INITIAL DECISION

1. Appellant has filed a timely request for hearing.

2. The department's Division of Developmental Disabilities decision denying Appellant's application is vacated. The department is ordered to readminister the ICAP test to Appellant, and then

redetermine Appellant's eligibility. The department shall give to Jean Conklin sufficient advance notice of the ICAP test administration date so that she may appear and participate as a respondent in the test if she chooses to do so. The department shall give to Jean Conklin a legally sufficient written notice of its decision on the application for benefits.

FILED AND SERVED ON THE DATE OF MAILING.

(stamped and mailed May 22, 1995, OAH)

(<u>signature: Clayton F. Harrington</u>)

CLAYTON F. HARRINGTON JR.

Senior Administrative Law Judge

NOTICE OF APPEAL RIGHTS

This decision becomes the final administrative decision unless a party files a petition for review. A petition must be received within 21 calendar days of the mailing date of this decision at the Office of Appeals. A petition form and instructions are attached.

ATTACHMENTS

pc: Trista Conklin, Appellant
           Jean Conklin, representative for Appellant
           Joyce Malone, DDD Administrator I
           Edward J. Dee, Assistant Attorney General

~ ~ ~

WHAT WILL BECOME OF MY CHILD?

Fully three-quarters of parents never make a financial or life-plan for their son or daughter with a developmental disability. [100] The reasons stem from very human factors. One factor is fear of our own mortality. Writing a will, deciding who will assist our son or daughter, and deciding who may benefit from our estate confronts our very human fear of dying. It is a simple reality but not simple to overcome. Secondly, we fear that we will make the wrong decisions. A third factor is the anxiety we all feel when working with government agencies and attorneys. We worry they will not understand nor advocate for our child.

The current trend is for families to consider the disabled child's future in terms of a written plan. Generally called "Future(s) Planning," this technique is almost becoming a science today, and for very good reasons. Professionals and parents, alike, are understanding that if the parents plan, they can provide the disabled family member with what they most desire for him — a life lived fully and well.

> *"If you plan, you can provide an environment*
> *that best nurtures the independence and dignity*
> *of your family member.*
> *If you don't, you can never be sure*
> *whose choices will be heard*
> *and whose voice will be hushed."* [101]

Long-term planning for a disabled family member means looking into the future. Most every parent of a disabled child wants to insure that their son or daughter is well taken care of, lives in appropriate housing, and has sufficient money and other resources to meet day-to-day needs. Wise long-term planning also includes planning for one's own death and / or disability.

It can be difficult and painful to begin the planning process. It involves acknowledging that we *will* die, and that our children will probably outlive us. **It is a comforting thought to know that after the parent's death the disabled person will thrive, not just survive.** That can be the motivation to begin the planning process, to keep working on it, and then to complete it.

Futures planning became part of my understanding and my vocabulary when Trista was still in high school. The importance of the concept triggered all sorts of brave encounters on our part, and *every one* of them have been extremely productive for her benefit. It just "happened" that way for us because we have had the unspoken goal of getting everything set up for Trista while we are healthy and still have most of our faculties. Statistics tell Dave and me that we have between 20 and 30 years left on this earth. Hopefully the fruits of our labors will be that as we grow older and ultimately meet our demise, Trista will become progressively more independent of us, and her life will be safe, full, and secure.

With that goal always in the back of our minds, we have maneuvered through the maze of long-term planning for Trista, taking care of the project of the moment while concurrently self-educating for the next challenge.

> *"The best thing about the future*
> *is that it comes one day at a time."*
>
> Abraham Lincoln

The process was not something *we* planned and scheduled on a calendar. The years passed, needs presented themselves, and then something in Trista's life usually triggered our next move. We just walked in the light that we had at the moment, always looking for a brighter flashlight. SSI. Sterilization. Vocational Rehabilitation. Special Needs Trust. Guardianship. Housing. We knew what our child needed, and the technical solutions followed quite naturally as we kept our ears and eyes open. *That is* futures planning.

Not all parents have had the kind of life experiences that have propelled us through our futures planning maze. Even so, there are many books and workbooks written on this topic. [A brief futures planning resource bibliography is listed at the close of this section.]

In a nutshell, here are the primary considerations of futures planning:

Housing	Employment	Government Benefits
Friendships	Letter of Intent	Advocate or Guardian
Healthcare	Record-keeping	Finances / Resources

Legal Work: Special needs trust – Wills – Durable powers of attorney

Futures planning is much like preparing a good soup. By adding various basic ingredients and giving the mixture sufficient time to simmer, the flavors blend and the soup just naturally develops. It usually gets better as essential herbs and seasonings are added while it is simmering – until, at some moment in time, it becomes "just right." Likewise, there is no particular order of sequence in futures planning – the important thing is to just *get started, and keep working on it.*

> *"Nothing happens unless first a dream."*
>
> Carl Sandburg

~ ~ ~

Editor's Note: Three areas which have not been previously addressed in this volume deserve some special attention:

√ Letter of Intent
√ Special Needs Trusts
√ Brain Banks

The remainder of this chapter provides a brief introduction to these three very important topics.

LETTER OF INTENT

Simply put, the Letter of Intent is a document written by the parents, guardian, or concerned person. It describes the disabled person's history, his or her current status, and what they hope for him in the future. The letter "presents" and represents the loved one's choices, needs and preferences. The letter is ready at any moment to be used by all the individuals who will become involved in caring for the loved one, should the primary person(s) become ill, disabled, or pass away.

The letter of intent is not a legal document. However, the courts and others can rely on the letter for guidance in understanding the disabled child and the wishes of the significant people in that child's life. In this way, it is possible to "speak out" on behalf of the loved one, providing insight and knowledge about the quality of life desired in that person's future, based on the combined efforts of the family, the person with the disability, and concerned friends.

It spells out in black and white the loved one's background and history, as well as his present situation. It also describes the writer's wishes, hopes, fears, and desires for his future care, and describes the loved one's feelings about the present and his desires for the future.

While the writer is still living, the letter of intent can be used by lawyers and financial planners to draft the proper legal documents, to ensure that the writer's wishes are considered and carried out. Once the writer is no longer able to care for the child, the letter gives future caregivers information and insight into future care needs. Caregivers will not have to waste precious time learning the most appropriate behavioral supports or medical management techniques. If the child is independent and requires only occasional assistance, the letter can spell out exactly what is needed.

How much the disabled person is involved in the writing of the letter of intent will depend in large part upon his age and the nature and severity of the disability. After the writer has considered each part of the letter, it is suggested those areas be discussed with the disabled person. Ask for his input on favorite things to do, what type of employment he would enjoy, what people he trusts and likes to spend time with, what kind of future living arrangements would he like, and how he feels about the options being considered. The loved one may be worrying about what will happen to him when the parent is no longer there to provide assistance, and he *may* be relieved to talk about the future.

The letter is a crucial part of any life or estate plan because it speaks both *for* and *about* the person with a disability and his family. It can be written in longhand or typed. The major focus of the letter is not spelling and grammar – the major concern should be that anyone who reads the letter in the future can understand exactly what the writer meant, and what he would like to see happen in the disabled person's life. (Remember, if the disability involves a severe cognitive disability, the letter of intent is especially critical, as it will communicate vital information about himself that he cannot.)

Letter of Intent

Date:__________

To Whom It May Concern,

This letter is regarding my loved one, __________________, who has a developmental disability.

It is intended to describe our family history, current situation, and future hopes and dreams for ________. I would like future caregivers and other concerned and involved people to use this letter as guidance.

These are the significant family members and friends in ________'s life: (list names, addresses, telephone numbers and relationship)

These are the significant professionals in ______________'s life:
(example: DDD case manager, lawyer, pastor)

Brief Family History:
(names, birth dates, addresses of family members, significant
major information)

[Body of Letter, below, focuses on major areas of family member's
past, present and future life, summarizing your wishes, hopes, and
desires in each of the following topics:]

After my death, I would like ________ to live in the following
situation:

________ has the following Medical Problems and Health
Concerns: (what do future caregivers need to know?)

________ has the following Resources:
Social Security Insurance (SSI) ________
Social Security Disability Insurance (SSDI) ________
Medicaid ________   Medicare ________
Other Health Insurance ________
Other Income ________
Other Income ________
Other Resources ________

My family member needs the following behavioral supports:
Social (who will be there to support your loved one?)

Employment (is your son or daughter working?)

Education (what are some important facts about the school
situation?)

Behavioral Supports (how is your loved one supported to be
successful?)

The family wishes to stay involved in the following way:
(who will do what?)

Please consider and carry out our wishes.

Sincerely,

Name_______________________________________Date_________

Name_______________________________________Date_________

√ Let people know there is a letter of intent available to be consulted.
√ Give copies of the letter to people who may be affected by it.
√ Go over the letter with the disabled person.

~ ~ ~

Special Needs Trust

The only reliable method of making sure that an inheritance reaches the disabled person when he or she needs it is through the legal device known as a Special Needs Trust. The special needs trust is developed to manage resources, while maintaining the individual's eligibility for public assistance benefits. Simply put, the family leaves whatever resources it deems appropriate to the trust. The trust is then managed by a trustee on behalf of the person with a disability.

A special needs trust has stringent rules and regulations. It is imperative that the family insures that the attorney they work with to set up the trust is very knowledgeable about special needs trusts and government programs. It is true that the government says that a person with a disability cannot have a trust. However, a special needs trust does not belong to the person with the disability. The trust is established and administered by someone else. The person with the disability *does not* have a trust.

One should consider setting up an "Intervivos Special Needs Trust." "Intervivos" simply means that the trust functions now, while the parents are living. The trust is set up as a checking account at a local bank. Families can place funds in the trust periodically as a way of saving for the future, and also to help with current needs. It also allows relatives to give money to the trust without worrying that the money will jeopardize government benefits. [102]

Having a living special needs trust creates a secure financial scenario for the person with the disability.

~ ~ ~

RESOURCES: FUTURE(S) PLANNING

A FAMILY HANDBOOK ON FUTURE PLANNING
> Author: Richard Berkobien
> Published by The Arc of the United States

PLANNING FOR THE FUTURE: PROVIDING A MEANINGFUL LIFE FOR A CHILD WITH A DISABILITY AFTER YOUR DEATH
> Authors: L. Mark Russell, Arnold E. Grant, Suzanne M. Joseph, and Richard W. Fee
> Published by The American Publishing Company

SAFE AND SECURE: SIX STEPS TO CREATING A PERSONAL FUTURE PLAN FOR PEOPLE WITH DISABILITIES
> Author: Al Etmanski
> Published by Planned Lifetime Advocacy Network

Internet Resources:
> National Institute on Life Planning
>> >http://www.sonic.net/nilp/<
>
> The Arc of the United States
>> >http://www.thearc.org<

Helpful Organizations:
> Area Agencies on Aging (community agencies to promote, plan, develop, and manage a comprehensive long-term care system)
>
> Parent-to-Parent Support Programs (community-based programs which provide an opportunity for parents of children with disabilities to gain confidence and knowledge by sharing experiences with other parents)

Local Arcs (parent-founded advocacy and direct
service organization for people with
developmental disabilities and their families.
Offers problem solving and crisis intervention,
and helps families obtain services offered by
other agencies)

Parent Coalitions (helping parents and guardians
become effective advocates for their family
members and others who have developmental
disabilities)

Special thanks to The Arc–King County, for their unrestricted use of the information presented in this chapter. Most of the information provided has been compiled and made available through the efforts of Laurie Holscher and PATHWAYS TO FUTURE PLANNING, a project sponsored by the Arc-King County, and funded by a grant from the Washington Division of Developmental Disabilities and administered through TASH.

~ ~ ~

THE BRAIN BANK

Brain donation for research might sound to some people more like a joke than a truism. Because it is fairly new and it is not a widely publicized subject, brain donation can be a difficult subject to discuss. Nonetheless, **research over the past decade has shown that the study of human brain tissue is essential to increasing our understanding of how the nervous system functions.** Most recently, postmortem human brain research has played a significant role in the development of a genetic test for Huntington's disease, as well as a treatment for Parkinson's disease. Similarly, neurochemical and anatomical studies focusing on the biological nature of the severe mental illnesses are now emerging and bringing forth new hope for understanding the underlying brain mechanisms responsible for psychosis and other symptoms associated with these debilitating brain disorders.

In order to perform research into the neurological or psychiatric disorders, it is vital to collect normal control tissue as well. The Harvard Brain Tissue Resource Center has been established at McLean Hospital in Belmont, Massachusetts, as a centralized resource for the collection and distribution of human brain specimens for brain research.

Scientists from the nation's top research and medical centers request tissue from The Brain Bank for their investigations. Since the majority of these studies can be carried out on a very small amount of tissue, each donated brain provides a large number of samples for many researchers. However, in order to conduct valid experiments, it is necessary to supply researchers with a variety of brain specimens.

For comparative neurobiological investigations, brain tissue is being collected from:

- normal individuals with no neurological or neuropsychiatric disorders

- individuals diagnosed with a neurobiological disorder

- individuals diagnosed with schizophrenia or manic depressive illness

- parents, siblings and offspring of individuals diagnosed with schizophrenia or manic depressive illness

- individuals who have *no* blood-line familial diagnosis with a neurobiological disorder

Becoming a prospective tissue donor is easy and painless. Any person 18 years of age or older can simply complete a "Brain Donation Questionnaire" and send it off to the Brain Bank. The next most important thing to do after signing up is to inform the family that the donor is pre-registered for brain donation at the Harvard Brain Tissue Resource Center. Often a brain donation is a last minute decision on the part of the family. Generally, however, it is better if the family has already openly discussed the idea of donation in order to avoid misunderstandings and to facilitate the donation process.

At the time of death of the donor, the surviving family members will need to be available to verify the donor's intent-to-donate, and to offer authorization to the Brain Bank to acquire all medical records. At the time of death, an individual's body becomes the property of the spouse, or if there is no spouse, then the adult children or parent. **Although an individual can make a personal request to donate his / her brain, ultimately it is the surviving family members who have the privilege and responsibility of deciding whether this unique and valuable gift will be made.**

Various Types of Donation

There are different categories of tissue donation:

1. The "body donor" donates the entire body for medical education; however, the brain must remain with the body and cannot be used for research.

2. The "organ donor" donates organs for transplantation; however, the brain begins to decay immediately at death, and brain donation is generally not compatible with organ donation. However, each case is assessed individually at death.

3. The "brain donor" donates the brain for medical research and if interested, also has the option of donating eyes, skin, blood or bone tissue.

Please note that although these three options for donation are generally not compatible with one another, each case is handled and assessed individually.

At The Time Of Death

In order to initiate the process of brain donation, it is necessary to contact the Brain Bank at the time of impending death or immediately after the death of the donor. The Brain Bank associate will need the name and location of the donor and will work directly with the pathologist in charge. Most often, the brain should be removed and shipped to the Harvard Brain Tissue Resource Center within hours following the death of the donor. Only the donor's brain will be sent to The Brain Bank, so the donor's body will not be transported away from the local area. When questionable circumstances surround a death, a state medical examiner / coroner may be responsible for a postmortem investigation involving the brain tissue. However, the remainder of the brain which is not required for their evaluations may be donated to The Brain Bank upon request by the family. Generally, medical examiners will cooperate with the family's decision for brain donation. When an investigation by the medical examiner is not required, a pathologist in a nearby hospital can perform the brain removal using a protocol supplied by The Brain Bank.

Important Information

1. In all cases, the identity of each donor and potential donor will remain strictly confidential

2. Brain donation does not conflict with most religious perspectives, and it will not interfere with an open casket or other traditional funeral arrangements (call 1-800-BRAIN BANK for a brochure outlining Religious Perspectives)

3. A diagnostic neuropathological report will be sent to the family and pathologist involved with the case

4. Limited funds are available to cover the cost of brain removal for donors with schizophrenia or manic depressive illness, and the parents, siblings and offspring of individuals with these diagnoses

Forming A Brain Donation Network

Because brain donation for research is not a widely publicized subject, many physicians and pathologists are not familiar with brain banking. Contacting the pathologists at the local hospital and identifying the professionals in the locality who are sensitive to the need for brain donation can greatly facilitate the donation process. If identifying a cooperative pathologist becomes a problem, the National Alliance for the Mentally Ill at 1-800-950-NAMI (1-800-950-6264) can provide phone numbers for state and local chapters of the Alliance for the Mentally Ill in local communities. NAMI on the Internet lists individuals who may be helpful in identifying a cooperative pathologist in every state. NAMI website: >http://www.nami.org<

Steps Toward a Successful Brain Donation

For individuals interested in brain donation:

1. Have a family discussion about brain donation, and inform primary physicians of the decision

2. Complete and return the "Brain Donation Questionnaire," available from the Harvard Brain Tissue Resource Center, registering the potential donor(s)

3. Upon receipt of the Brain Donation Questionnaire, the Resource Center will send a wallet-sized "Donor Card." Carrying this card is not necessary but may facilitate the donation process

4. At the time of impending death or at death, call 1-800-BRAIN BANK (1-800-272-4622) and provide the following information:

> • date of birth of donor
>
> • time and cause of death (if known)
>
> • name and address of legal next-of-kin
>
> • neurological or psychiatric diagnosis (if applicable)

After the death of the donor, a "Postmortem Confirmation of Consent" form for donation must be signed by the next-of-kin. This form will be provided at the time of autopsy by the medical examiner, coroner or pathologist (if one has been identified) which authorizes the brain removal.

THERE ARE SEVERAL WAYS TO BEGIN THE DONATION PROCESS

To Contact the Harvard Brain Tissue Resource Center
McLean Hospital
115 Mill Street
Belmont, MA 02478

Phone: 1-800-BRAIN BANK (1-800-272-4622)

Internet: >http://www.brainbank.mclean.org:8080<

E-mail: BTRC@MCLEAN.ORG

Special thanks to The Harvard Brain Tissue Resource Center for providing unrestricted access to this information.

~ ~ ~

TELL ME ABOUT CEREBRAL PALSY

Cerebral palsy (CP) is a condition caused by damage to the brain, occurring before, during or after birth. Cerebral palsy is characterized by an inability to fully control motor function. Depending on which part of the brain has been damaged and the degree of involvement of the central nervous system, one or more of the following may occur: seizures, spasms, mental retardation, disturbance in gait and mobility, and impairment of sight, hearing or speech. It is estimated that 500,000 children and adults in the U.S., or about 16 out of every 5,000 people manifest one or more of the symptoms of cerebral palsy. Each year approximately 4,500 infants are born with the condition, and approximately 1,200 - 1,500 young children acquire cerebral palsy as a result of head injuries. [103]

In the 1860s, an English surgeon named William Little wrote the first medical descriptions of a puzzling disorder that struck children in the first years of life, causing stiff, spastic muscles in their legs and, to a lesser degree, their arms. These children had difficulty grasping objects, crawling, and walking. They did not get better as they grew up, nor did they become worse. Their condition, which was called Little's disease for many years, is now known as spastic diplegia. It is just one of several disorders that affect control of movement and are grouped together under the term cerebral palsy.

It seemed that many of these children were born following complicated deliveries, but in 1897, the famous psychiatrist Sigmund Freud disagreed. Noting that children with cerebral palsy often had other problems such as mental retardation, visual disturbances, and seizures, Freud suggested that the disorder might sometimes have roots earlier in life, during the brain's development in the womb. Despite Freud's observation, the belief that birth complications cause most cases of cerebral palsy was widespread among physicians, families, and even medical researchers until very recently.

In the 1980s, however, scientists analyzed extensive data from a government study of more than 35,000 births and were surprised to discover that such complications account for only a fraction of cases – probably less than 10 percent. **In most cases of cerebral palsy, no cause could be found.** These findings have profoundly altered medical theories about cerebral palsy and have spurred today's researchers to explore alternative causes.

Identification of infants with cerebral palsy very early in life gives youngsters the best opportunity for developing to their full capacity. Biomedical research has led to improved diagnostic techniques – such as advanced brain imaging and modern gait analysis – that are making this easier. Certain conditions known to cause cerebral palsy, such as rubella (German measles) and jaundice, can now be prevented or treated. Physical, psychological, and behavioral therapy that assist with such skills as movement and speech and foster social and emotional development, can help children who have cerebral palsy to achieve and succeed. Medications, surgery, and braces can often improve nerve and muscle coordination, help treat associated medical problems, and either prevent or correct deformities.

Much of the research to improve medical understanding of cerebral palsy has been supported by the National Institute of Neurological Disorders and Stroke (NINDS), America's leading supporter of biomedical research into cerebral palsy and other neurological disorders. [104]

The NINDS offers comprehensive introductory information on Cerebral Palsy at its Internet website. The following topics are covered extremely well:

- What is Cerebral Palsy?
- How Many People Have This Disorder?
- What Are the Different Forms?
- What Other Medical Disorders Are Associated With Cerebral Palsy?
- What Causes Cerebral Palsy?
- What Are the Risk Factors?
- Can Cerebral Palsy Be Prevented?
- What Are the Early Signs?
- How is Cerebral Palsy Diagnosed?
- How is Cerebral Palsy Managed?
- What Specific Treatments Are Available?
  - Physical, Behavioral, and Other Therapies
  - Drug Therapy
  - Surgery
  - Mechanical Aids
- What Other Major Problems Are Associated With Cerebral Palsy?
- What Research is Being Done?
- Where Can I Find More Information?
- Glossary
- Information Resources (comprehensive listing of addresses and telephone numbers for several agencies that focus on Cerebral Palsy)

For further information, contact NINDS:

National Institute of Neurological Disorders and Stroke
P.O. Box 5801
Bethesda, MD 20824
(800) 352-9424 or (301) 496-5751
>http://www.ninds.nih.gov/patients/disorder/cp/
cphtr.HTM#causes<

~ ~ ~

TELL ME ABOUT TOURETTE SYNDROME

Tourette Syndrome has received a great deal of positive media attention in the last ten years. I frequently encounter people who say they heard about Tourette Syndrome on *Dateline*, *ABC's 20/20*, *The Maury [Povich] Show*, or *The Practice*; or they saw the movie, *The Tic Code*; they read about it in Ann Landers, or they heard a media public service announcement (PSA) on a local TV or radio station.

In spite of so much media attention, many people with Tourette Syndrome go undiagnosed. Our phone frequently rings with desperate calls from parents who have been informed by the schools that their child might have Tourette. They can't find any information on the topic, and they don't know where to turn. I always refer them directly to the national office of the Tourette Syndrome Association in Bayside, New York.

This book is not intended to be an exhaustive work on Tourette Syndrome. Nonetheless, I would be remiss in not providing a basic framework of information about Tourette and related disorders.

Tourette Syndrome was named after an 18th century French doctor. Georges Gilles de la Tourette (born Georges Albert Edouard Brutus Gilles de la Tourette) made several valuable contributions to medicine and literature before being shot by a patient. His greatest achievements were in the study of hysteria and hypnotism. Dr. Tourette, a competent neuropsychiatrist, was particularly interested in therapy. [105]

Tourette Syndrome is an inherited neurological disorder characterized by repeated and involuntary body movements (tics) and uncontrollable vocal sounds. In a minority of cases, the vocalizations can include socially inappropriate words and phrases — called coprolalia. These outbursts are neither intentional nor purposeful. Involuntary symptoms can include eye blinking, repeated throat clearing or sniffing, arm thrusting, kicking movements, shoulder shrugging or jumping.

These and other symptoms typically appear before the age of 18 and the condition occurs in all ethnic groups, with males affected three to four times more often than females. Although the symptoms of TS vary from person to person and range from very mild to severe, the majority of cases fall into the mild category. Associated conditions can include obsessivity, attentional problems and impulsiveness.

Most people with TS lead productive lives and participate in all professions. Increased public understanding and tolerance of TS symptoms are of paramount importance to people with Tourette Syndrome. [106]

Tourette occurs in all nationalities and across all economic groups. Among school age children, TS occurs in one child per 1000. According to the Department of Health and Human Services, as many as one in 200 individuals are afflicted by Tourette, but many people continue to be misdiagnosed or remain undiagnosed. This is particularly true of people in inner-city, minority neighborhoods where access to medical care and information is limited or inadequate. [107] Tourette Syndrome is not a common household ailment: *it is still considered a rare disorder*.

~ ~ ~

Editor's notes: This chapter contains concise medical information. A GLOSSARY and INDEX are provided in this volume to further assist the reader.

Additional information on this subject is available on the Tourette Syndrome Association website. [108]

Special thanks to Tourette Syndrome Association for allowing the unrestricted use of their publications in this volume.

DIAGNOSIS AND TREATMENT

The following section is from the third revision of *A Physician's Guide to the Diagnosis and Treatment of Tourette Syndrome*, by Ruth Dowling Bruun, M.D., Donald J. Cohen, M.D., and James F. Leckman, M.D. The booklet includes up-to-date clinical information for TS families and physicians treating patients with this complex, frequently misunderstood neurobehavioral (neurobiological) disorder. [109]

DEFINITIONS of TIC DISORDERS

Tics are involuntary, rapid, repetitive and stereotyped movements of individual muscle groups. They are more easily recognized than precisely defined. Tic disorders are generally categorized according to age of onset, duration of symptoms, severity of symptoms and the presence of vocal and / or motor tics.

Transient tic disorders often begin during the early school years and can occur in up to 18 percent of all children. Common tics include eye blinking, nose puckering, grimacing and squinting. Transient vocalizations are less common and include various throat sounds, humming or other noises. Childhood tics may be bizarre: examples include palm licking, poking and / or pinching the genitals. Transient tics last only a few weeks or months and are usually not associated with specific behavioral or school problems. They are especially noticeable during times of heightened excitement or fatigue. As with all tic syndromes, boys are three to four times more often affected than girls. While transient tics by definition do not persist for more than a year, it is not uncommon for a child to have recurrent episodes of transient tics over the course of several years.

Chronic tic disorders are differentiated from transient tic disorders not only by their duration over many years, but by their relatively unchanging character. While transient tics come and go (sniffing may be replaced by forehead furrowing, and the furrowing may become finger snapping), chronic tics – such as facial contortions or blinking – may persist unchanged for years.

Chronic multiple tics suggest that an individual has several chronic motor tics (or, in rare cases, several chronic vocal tics). Often it is not an easy task to draw distinctions between transient tics, chronic tics, and chronic multiple tics.

Tourette Syndrome (TS) can be the most debilitating tic disorder and is characterized by multiform, frequently changing motor and phonic tics. The current diagnostic criteria, as defined by the Diagnostic and Statistical Manual of Mental Disorders IV, are as follows:

A: Both multiple motor and one or more vocal tics have been present at some time during the illness, although not necessarily concurrently.

B: The tics occur many times a day (usually in bouts) nearly every day or intermittently throughout a period of more than one year, and during this period there was never a tic-free period of more than three consecutive months.

C: The disturbance causes marked distress or significant impairment in social, occupational, or other important areas of functioning.

D: The onset is before age 18.

E: The disturbance is not due to the direct physiological effects of a substance (e.g. stimulants) or a general medical condition (e.g. Huntington's disease or postviral encephalitis).

While the criteria appear basically valid, they are not absolute. First, there have been rare cases of TS which have emerged later than age 18. Second, the concept of "involuntary" may be hard to define operationally, since many patients experience their tics as having a volitional component – either a capitulation to an internal sensory urge for motor discharge, or a more generalized psychological tension and anxiety, or both. Finally, the diagnostic criteria do not adequately portray the full range of behavioral difficulties that are commonly observed in patients with TS, such as attentional problems, compulsions, and obsessions.

DIFFERENTIAL DIAGNOSIS

Today, the full-blown case of TS is unlikely to be confused with any other disorder. In the past, however, Tourette Syndrome was frequently misdiagnosed or undiagnosed.

The differentiation of Tourette Syndrome from other tic syndromes may be no more than semantic, especially since recent genetic evidence links TS with multiple and transient tics of childhood, and can only be defined in retrospect.

At times it may be difficult to distinguish children with extreme attention deficit hyperactivity disorder (ADHD) from those with TS. On close examination, many ADHD children have a few phonic or motor tics, grimace, or produce noises similar to those with Tourette. Since at least half of patients with TS also have had attention deficits and hyperactivity as children, a physician may well be confused. However, the treating doctor should be aware of the potential complications of treating a possible case of TS with stimulant medication.

On rare occasions, the differentiation between Tourette Syndrome and a seizure disorder may be difficult. The symptoms of TS sometimes occur in a rather sharply separated paroxysmal manner and may resemble automatisms. Patients with TS, however, retain a clear consciousness during such paroxysms. If the diagnosis is in doubt, an EEG may be useful.

We have seen Tourette Syndrome in association with a number of developmental and other neurological disorders. It is possible that central nervous system injury from trauma or disease may cause a child to be vulnerable to the expression of the disorder, particularly if there is a genetic predisposition. Autistic and retarded children may display the entire gamut of TS symptoms. Whether an autistic or retarded individual requires the additional diagnosis of TS may remain an open question until testing (biological or otherwise) is available for definitive diagnosis of TS.

In older patients, conditions such as Wilson's disease, tardive dyskinesia, Meige's syndrome, chronic amphetamine abuse and the stereotypic movements of schizophrenia must be considered in the differential diagnosis. The distinction can usually be made by taking a good history or by blood tests.

Since more physicians are now aware of TS, there is a growing danger of over-diagnosis or over-treatment. It is up to the clinician to consider the effect that the symptoms have on the patient's ability to function (as well as the severity of associated symptoms) before deciding to treat with medication or other approaches.

SYMPTOMATOLOGY

The varied symptoms of TS can be divided into motor, vocal, and behavioral manifestations. (Table 1, page 287) Simple motor tics are fast, darting, meaningless muscular events. They can be embarrassing or even painful (such as jaw snapping). They are easily distinguished from simple muscular twitches or rapid fasciculations, e.g. of the eyelid or lip. Complex motor tics may be slower or more purposeful in appearance and more easily described by terms used for deliberate actions. (Table 2, page 288)

Complex motor tics can be virtually any type of movement that the body can produce, including gyrating, hopping, clapping, tensing arm or neck muscles, touching people or things, and obscene gesturing.

At some point in the continuum of complex motor tics, the term "compulsion" seems appropriate for capturing the organized, ritualistic character of the actions. The need to do and then redo or undo the same action a certain number of times (e.g. to stretch out an arm ten times before writing, to "even up," or to stand up and push a chair into "just the right position") is compulsive in quality and accompanied by considerable internal discomfort. Complex motor tics may greatly impair school work, e.g. when a child must stab at a workbook with a pencil or must go over the same letter so many times that the paper is worn thin. Self-destructive behaviors, such as head banging, eye poking and lip biting also may occur. The distinction between complex tics and compulsions may be a difficult one for the physician to make, and some "complex tics" may be alleviated by medications used for obsessive compulsive disorder.

Vocal tics extend over a similar spectrum of complexity and disruption as do motor tics. (Table 3, page 289) With simple vocal tics, patients emit linguistically meaningless sounds or noises, such as hissing, coughing or barking. Complex vocal tics involve linguistically meaningful words, phrases or sentences, e.g. "wow," "Oh boy, now you've said it," "Yup, that's it," "but, but . . ." Vocal symptoms may interfere with the smooth flow of speech and resemble a stammer, stutter or other speech irregularity. Often, but not always, vocal symptoms occur at points of linguistic transition, such as at the beginning of a sentence where there may be speech blocking at the initiation of speech or at phrase transitions. Patients suddenly may alter speech volume, slur a phrase, emphasize a word or assume an accent.

The most socially distressing complex vocal symptom is coprolalia, the explosive utterance of foul or "dirty" words, or more elaborate sexual, aggressive or insulting statements (e.g. racial slurs). Coprolalia is not simply obscene speech spoken in anger or to offend. Rather it is often sudden speech (typically just the first syllable of an inappropriate word) that interrupts an otherwise appropriate flow of words. While coprolalia occurs in only a minority of patients with TS (from 5 to 30 percent, depending on the clinical series), it remains the most well-known TS symptom. A diagnosis of TS does not require that coprolalia be present, and the majority of patients do not ever exhibit this symptom.

Some patients with TS may have a tendency to imitate what they have just seen (echopraxia), heard (echolalia), or said (palilalia). For example, the patient may feel an impulse to imitate another's body movements, to speak with an odd inflection or to accent a syllable in just the same manner as another person. Such modeling or repetition may lead to the onset of new specific symptoms that will wax and wane in the same way as other TS symptoms. Some patients also describe "triggers" that almost invariably prompt a tic, e.g. another person coughing in a certain way.

The symptoms of TS can be characterized as mild, moderate or severe by their frequency, their complexity and the degree to which they cause impairment or disruption of the patient's ongoing activities and daily life. For example, extremely frequent tics that occur 20 to 30 times a minute, such as blinking, nodding or arm flexion, may be less disruptive than an infrequent tic that occurs several times an hour, such as loud barking, coprolalic utterance or touching tics. The premonitory sensory urges tend to be present by 9 to 10 years of age. They are most commonly reported in the shoulder girdle, hands, throat and abdomen.

There may be tremendous variability over short and long periods of time in symptomatology, frequency and severity. Tics typically occur in "bouts," with many tics over a short interval of time. Patients may be able to inhibit or not feel a great need to emit their symptoms while at school or work. When they arrive home, however, the tics may erupt with violence and remain at a distressing level throughout the remainder of the day.

It is not unusual for patients to "lose" their tics as they enter the doctor's office. Parents may plead with a child to "show the doctor what you do at home," only to be told that the youngster "just doesn't feel like doing them" or "can't do them" on command. Adults will say, "I only wish you could see me outside your office," and family members will heartily agree.

Often a patient with minimal symptoms may display more severe tics when the examination is over. Thus, for example, the doctor may often see a nearly symptom-free patient who then leaves the office and begins to hop, flail, or bark as soon as he or she reaches the street.

In addition to the moment-to-moment or short-term changes in symptom intensity, many patients have oscillations in severity over the course of weeks and months. The waxing and waning of severity may be triggered by changes in the patient's life; for example, around holidays, children may develop exacerbations that take weeks to subside. Other patients report that their symptoms show seasonal fluctuation. However, there are no rigorous data on whether life events, stresses or seasons do, in fact, influence the onset or offset of a period of exacerbation. Once a patient enters a phase of waxing symptomatology, a process seems to be triggered that will run its course for several weeks or months.

In its most severe forms, patients may have countless motor and vocal tics during all their waking hours with paroxysms of full body movements, shouting or self-mutilation. At times the tics seem organized in orchestrated patterns that are characteristic of that individual. Despite this, many patients with severe tics manage to achieve adequate social adjustment in adult life, although usually with considerable emotional pain. **More than the severity of motor and vocal tics, the factors that appear to be of importance with regard to social adaptation include the seriousness of attentional problems, obsessive compulsive symptoms, the degree of family acceptance and support, intelligence and ego strength.**

In adolescence and early adulthood, patients with TS frequently come to feel that their social isolation, vocational or academic failure and embarrassing symptoms are more than they can bear. At times, a small number may consider and attempt suicide. Conversely, some patients with the most bizarre and disruptive symptomatology may achieve excellent social, academic and vocational adjustment. Fortunately, in many cases, tics diminish during the course of adolescence. However, in other cases (less than 10 percent), the tic symptoms can become even more severe in adulthood.

ASSOCIATED BEHAVIORS AND COGNITIVE DIFFICULTIES

Many, though not all, patients with TS experience a variety of behavioral and psychological difficulties in addition to tics. These behavioral features have placed TS on the border between neurology and psychiatry and require an understanding of both disciplines to comprehend the complex problems faced by many patients.

The most frequently reported behavioral problems are attentional deficits, obsessions, compulsions, impulsivity, irritability, aggressivity, immaturity, self-injurious behaviors and depression. Some of the behaviors (e.g. obsessive compulsive behavior and certain forms of ADHD) may be an integral part of TS, while others may be common in patients with TS because of certain biological vulnerabilities. Still others may represent responses to the social stresses associated with a multiple tic disorder or a combination of biological and psychological reactions.

OBSESSIONS AND COMPULSIONS

Although TS may present itself purely as a disorder of multiple motor and vocal tics, many TS patients also have obsessive compulsive (OC) symptoms that may be as disruptive to their lives as the tics – sometimes even more so. There is recent evidence that obsessive compulsive symptomatology may be another expression of the TS gene and, therefore, an integral part of the disorder. Whether this is true or not, it has been well documented that a high percentage of patients with TS have OC symptoms, that these symptoms tend to appear somewhat later than the tics, and that they may be seriously impairing.

The nature of OC symptoms in patients with TS is quite variable. Conventionally, obsessions are defined as thoughts, images or impulses that intrude on consciousness, are involuntary and distressful; and while they are perceived as silly or excessive, they cannot be abolished. Compulsions consist of the actual behaviors, often carried out in response to the obsessions, or in an effort to ward them off. Typical OC behaviors include rituals of counting, repetitively checking things over and washing or cleaning excessively. While many patients with TS do have such behaviors, there are other typical TS symptoms that seem to straddle the border between tics and OC symptoms. Examples are the need to "even things up," to touch things a certain number of times, to perform tasks over and over until they "feel right," and self-injurious behaviors. Although patients with TS can have the full range of OC symptoms, some symptoms such as contamination worries occur less frequently than among OCD patients without tics or TS.

ATTENTION DEFICIT HYPERACTIVITY DISORDER (ADHD)

Up to 50 percent of all children with TS who come to the attention of a physician also have attention deficit hyperactivity disorder (ADHD), which is manifested by problems with attention span, concentration, distractibility, impulsivity and motoric hyperactivity. Attentional problems often precede the onset of TS symptoms and may worsen as the tics develop. The increasing difficulty with attention may reflect an underlying biological dysfunction involving inhibition, and may be exacerbated by the strain of attending to the outer world while working hard to remain quiet and still. Attentional problems and hyperactivity can profoundly affect school achievement. At least 30 to 40 percent of children with TS have serious school performance handicaps that require special intervention, and children with both TS and ADHD are especially vulnerable to serious, long-term educational impairment.

Attention deficits may persist into adulthood, and together with compulsions and obsessions, can seriously impair job performance.

EMOTIONAL LABILITY, IMPULSIVITY AND AGGRESSIVITY

Some patients with TS (percentages vary greatly in different studies) have significant problems with labile emotions, impulsivity and aggression directed at others. Fits of temper that include screaming, punching holes in walls, threatening others, hitting, biting and kicking are common in such patients. Often they will be the patients who also have ADHD, making impulse control a considerable problem. At times, the temper outbursts can be seen as reactions to the internal and external pressures of having TS. A specific etiology for such behavioral problems is, at present, not well understood. Nevertheless, they create much consternation in teachers and great anguish for the patients and their families. The treating physician or counselor is often asked whether these behaviors are as involuntary as the tics, or whether they can be controlled.

Rather than trying to make such a distinction, it is perhaps more helpful to think of such patients as having a "thin barrier" between aggressive thoughts and the expression of those thoughts through actions. These patients may think of themselves as being out of control, a concept that is as frightening to them as it is to others.

Management of these behaviors is often difficult and may involve adjustment of medications, individual therapy, family therapy or behavioral retraining. The intensity of these behaviors sometimes increases as the tics wax, and decreases as the tics wane. Along with the tics and the ADHD symptoms, these additional disruptive symptoms can cause major social difficulties.

SELF-INJURIOUS BEHAVIORS

These may consist of complex tics (e.g. hitting or biting oneself), or they may be compulsions (e.g. moving a sore joint over and over, in order to achieve a certain painful sensation).

LEARNING DIFFICULTIES

There are many reasons why children with TS have difficulties in school and may require special educational assistance. Tics may interfere with writing, listening (as trying to control tics may require all of the student's concentration), or may be disruptive in the classroom. Associated symptoms such as ADD, ADHD, or obsessions and compulsions may impair attention. Medications may also impair attention and concentration. Finally, there are a number of specific learning disabilities which have been found to be frequently associated with TS. These include impairments in visual-perceptual and visual-motor skills, wide discrepancies between verbal and performance IQs, and other specific learning disabilities.

TABLE 1

RANGE OF SYMPTOMS
OF TOURETTE SYNDROME

MOTOR

Simple motor tics: fast, darting and meaningless.

Complex motor tics: may be slower, or may consist of stereotyped series of movements and may appear purposeful (includes copropraxia and echopraxia).

VOCAL

Simple vocal tics: meaningless sounds and noises.

Complex vocal tics: linguistically meaningful utterances such as words and phrases (including coprolalia, echolalia and palilalia), interruptions in the flow of speech, sudden alterations in pitch or volume.

BEHAVIORAL AND DEVELOPMENTAL

Often associated with attention deficit hyperactive disorder, obsessions and compulsions, emotional lability, irritability, impulsivity, aggressivity and self-injurious behaviors; various learning disabilities, social difficulties including peer rejection.

EXAMPLES of VOCAL SYMPTOMS

SIMPLE VOCAL TICS

Coughing, spitting, screeching, barking, grunting, gurgling, clacking, whistling, hissing, sucking sounds, and syllable sounds such as "uh uh," "eee," and "bu."

COMPLEX VOCAL TICS

"Oh boy," "you know," "shut up," "you're fat," "all right," and "what's that."

RITUALS

Repeating a phrase until it sounds "just right," and saying something over three times.

SPEECH ATYPICALITIES

Unusual rhythms, tone, accents, loudness, and very rapid speech.

COPROLALIA

Obscene, aggressive or otherwise socially unacceptable words or phrases.

PALILALIA

Repeating one's own words or parts of words.

ECHOLALIA

Repeating sounds, words, or parts of words of others.

Additional information on the following topics is also addressed in the booklet, *A Physician's Guide to the Diagnosis and Treatment of Tourette Syndrome:*

- Etiology
- Stimulant Medication
- Epidemiology and Genetics
- Non-Genetic Contributions
- Clinical Assessment of Tourette Syndrome
- Treatment of Tourette Syndrome:
    - Monitoring
    - Education and Reassurance
    - Pharmacologic Treatment of Tourette Syndrome
    - Psychodynamic Psychotherapy
    - Family Treatment
    - Genetic Counseling
    - Academic and Occupational Interventions

A Physician's Guide to the Diagnosis and Treatment of Tourette Syndrome
    by Ruth Dowling Bruun, M.D.
    Donald J. Cohen, M.D.
    James F. Leckman, M.D.

Available from the Tourette Syndrome Association
    (718)224-2999

Editor's note: This book is not intended as a substitute for the medical advice of physicians. The reader should regularly consult a physician in matters relating to his / her health care and particularly to any symptoms that may require diagnosis or medical attention.

Medications and Dosages

The following section is the text of *Current Pharmacology of Tourette Syndrome,* [110] by Roger Kurlan, M.D.

Chronic, multiple motor and vocal tics are the most prominent clinical features of Tourette Syndrome (TS) and represent the signs upon which the diagnosis of the disorder is currently based. Tic severity encompasses a wide spectrum. Although a number of patients with TS experience severe and disabling tics, recent family studies indicate that for most individuals with the disorder, tic severity is relatively mild, and medical attention is not required.

Tics may also be accompanied by a variety of associated behavioral disorders. For example, recent genetic work suggests that obsessions (recurrent, persistent ideas, thoughts, images, impulses) and compulsions (repetitive behaviors performed as rituals or in a stereotyped fashion) may be clinical manifestations of TS. Others have suggested that attention deficit disorder (short attention span, daydreaming, poor concentration) with hyperactivity (ADHD) also may be associated with TS. For some individuals, such behavioral disturbances may represent the predominant clinical manifestations of the disorder. In addition, patients with TS may display a variety of other psychopathological conditions (e.g. depression, anxiety, conduct disorder) and personality traits (e.g. irritability, argumentativeness, stubbornness, impulsivity) that may be part of the disorder or, alternatively, may represent psychological responses to living with a chronic illness.

Taken together, current evidence indicates that the clinical manifestations of Tourette Syndrome can be quite variable. It is, therefore, important to evaluate each individual closely to determine which aspects are most disabling. For example, school performance may be impaired by frequent tics, obsessional thinking, attention deficit, personality disorder, or various combinations of those difficulties. For most patients, one or two of the clinical aspects will predominate and can serve as specific target symptoms for therapy.

Ideally, patients with mild cases of TS who have made a good adaptation in their lives can avoid the use of any medications. Our impression is that the majority of patients with TS can manage well without drug therapy. Educating patients, family members and school personnel concerning the nature of TS; restructuring the school environment (e.g. small group teaching, one-on-one tutoring, allowing TS students to work at their own pace); and providing supportive counseling, are measures that may be sufficient to avoid medications.

Medication therapy should be considered if it is determined that the symptoms of TS are functionally disabling and not remediable to non-drug interventions. A variety of therapeutic agents are now available to treat the symptoms of TS. Each medication should be chosen on the basis of specific target symptoms and potential side effects. For example, in one patient, tic-suppression may be the important goal, while treatment of obsessive compulsive features may take precedence in another. Dosages should be titrated slowly in order to achieve the lowest satisfactory dosage. The maximum dosage utilized depends on achieving a "tolerable" suppression of symptoms. "Tolerable" is determined by the nature of the symptoms (for example, coprolalia is usually less tolerable than eye tics) and the ability of an individual to exercise voluntary modulation of his / her vocalizations and motor tics. Some children may have relatively few tics in school but a great many at home, thus allowing less overall use of medication. In our view, home is a haven where a child can have some relief from holding symptoms in check. It is vital that the patient and the family understand the ever-changing nature of TS, so that medications can be adjusted in a rational fashion, increasing when the symptoms upsurge and decreasing during periods of relative remission. It is essential for effective dosage adjustment that "target symptoms" are monitored at all times. For example, if an individual is treated with so much medication that all movements are suppressed, it can never be known when tics, which tend to wax and wane in severity during the course of the illness, decrease spontaneously. In the long run, our goal is to use as little medication as possible (i.e. "less is best").

PHARMACOTHERAPY OF TOURETTE SYNDROME AND RELATED DISORDERS

I. Tics

   A. Clonidine (Catapres)

   B. Neuroleptics

      1. Haloperidol (Haldol)

      2. Pimozide (Orap)

      3. Fluphenazine (Prolixin)

      4. Others

   C. Other Drugs

   D. Botulinum Toxin *

II. Obsessive Compulsive Disorder

   A. Clomipramine (Anafranil)

   B. Fluoxetine (Prozac)

   C. Sertraline (Zoloft)

III. Attention Deficit Hyperactivity Disorder

   A. Clonidine (Catapres)

   B. Stimulants

      1. Methylphenidate (Ritalin)

      2. Pemoline (Cylert)

      3. Dextroamphetamine (Dexedrine)

   C. Tricyclic Antidepressants

* Recent research has shown that for a small number of patients who prove resistant to the motor medications, injections of botulinum toxin might be helpful. [111]

ALTERNATIVE / COMPLEMENTARY THERAPIES FOR TOURETTE SYNDROME SYMPTOMS

> The following information is from the Tourette Syndrome Association. TSA has always maintained a policy of encouraging a free exchange of information concerning research and treatment of Tourette Syndrome. [112]

As with almost any chronic condition for which medications are imperfect, TSA is aware that there are some families with an interest in learning more about non-medication treatment regimens for the control of TS symptoms. It is important to note that, to date, there are no published studies, and therefore, no reliable data confirming the safety and / or efficacy of one or another of such treatments.

Having said that, there is a steady stream of single case reports describing a variety of environmental factors such as chemical additives in food or common allergens (dust, molds, and pollens) that seem to worsen TS symptoms in those individuals who may be vulnerable to such insults to their immune systems. TSA's national Medical Advisory Board members are interested in collecting these anecdotal reports. For those interested in reading more about the occurrence of allergies in people with TS, contact TSA for an article from TSA's Newsletter by Larry Scahill, MSN, MPH.

The Association for Comprehensive Neurotherapy (ACN) has a continuing interest in the topic of non-drug treatments for TS and other neurobiological conditions. This group regularly publishes the newsletter, *Latitudes*. While TSA is not formally affiliated with ACN, they have always referred those interested in alternative / complementary / integrative therapies to this network for further information.

Association for Comprehensive NeuroTherapy
1128 Royal Palm Beach Boulevard #283
Royal Palm Beach, FL 33411
Phone: (561)798-0472   FAX: (561)798-9820
E-mail: acn@latitudes.org
Website: >http://www.latitudes.org<

Insurance Coverage & Reimbursement

Because the symptoms of TS are neurobiologically-based, and often co-morbid with psychiatric disorders, patients with TS should expect their insurance to cover evaluation and treatment in a manner similar to that for any other medical condition.

The organizations listed below are concerned that some benefit plans do not provide adequate coverage for the assessment and treatment of Tourette Syndrome (TS). TS is a medical condition that improves with treatment, and TSA strongly encourages the inclusion of coverage for this disorder in benefit plans. The organizations listed below, endorse the impact and importance of covering assessment and treatment of Tourette Syndrome. [113]

AMERICAN ACADEMY OF CHILD AND ADOLESCENT PSYCHIATRY

AMERICAN ACADEMY OF NEUROLOGY

AMERICAN ACADEMY OF PEDIATRICS

AMERICAN ASSOCIATION OF CHILDREN'S RESIDENTIAL CENTERS

AMERICAN ASSOCIATION FOR PARTIAL HOSPITALIZATION

AMERICAN PSYCHIATRIC ASSOCIATION

CHILDREN AND ADULTS WITH ATTENTION DEFICIT DISORDERS

INSTITUTE FOR BEHAVIORAL HEALTH CARE

NATIONAL ALLIANCE FOR THE MENTALLY ILL

NATIONAL ASSOCIATION OF SOCIAL WORKERS

NATIONAL DEPRESSIVE AND MANIC DEPRESSIVE ASSOCIATION

NATIONAL ORGANIZATION FOR RARE DISEASES

NATIONAL TREATMENT CONSORTIUM, INC.

OBSESSIVE COMPULSIVE FOUNDATION

TOURETTE SYNDROME ASSOCIATION, INC.

TREATING ADHD

The organizations listed on the previous page are concerned that some benefit plans do not provide adequate coverage for the treatment of Attention Deficit Hyperactivity Disorder (ADHD). ADHD is a medical condition that improves with treatment, and TSA strongly encourages the inclusion of coverage for this disorder in benefit plans. The organizations listed on page 295 endorse the impact and importance of covering assessment and treatment of ADHD. [114]

TREATING OCD

Because Obsessive Compulsive Disorder (OCD) improves with treatment and is often co-morbid with psychiatric disorders, patients with OCD should expect their insurance to cover evaluation and treatment in a manner similar to that for any other medical condition.

Providers are concerned that some benefit plans do not provide adequate coverage for the children and adolescents with OCD. The organizations listed on page 295 endorse the impact and importance of covering assessment and treatment of OCD. [115]

FAQ about Tourette Syndrome [116]

Q. What is Tourette Syndrome?

A. Tourette Syndrome is a neurological disorder characterized by tics — involuntary, rapid, sudden movements or vocalizations that occur repeatedly in the same way.

The symptoms include:

1. Both multiple motor and one or more vocal tics present at some time during the illness although not necessarily simultaneously;

2. The occurrence of tics many times a day (usually in bouts) nearly every day or intermittently throughout a span of more than one year; and

3. Periodic changes in the number, frequency, type and location of the tics, and in the waxing and waning of their severity. Symptoms can sometimes disappear for weeks or months at a time.

4. Onset before the age of 18.

The term, "involuntary," used to describe TS tics, is sometimes confusing since it is known that most people with TS do have some control over their symptoms. What is not recognized is that the control, which can be exercised anywhere from seconds to hours at a time, may merely postpone more severe outbursts of symptoms. Tics are experienced as irresistible and (as the urge to sneeze) eventually must be expressed. People with TS often seek a secluded spot to release their symptoms after delaying them in school or at work. Typically, tics increase as a result of tension or stress, and decrease with relaxation or concentration on an absorbing task.

Q. How would a typical case of TS be described?

A. The term typical cannot be applied to TS. The expression of symptoms covers a spectrum from very mild to quite severe. However, the majority of cases are in the mild category.

Q. WHAT CAUSES THE SYMPTOMS?

A. The cause has not been established, although current research presents considerable evidence that the disorder stems from the abnormal metabolism of several brain chemicals (neurotransmitters), such as dopamine and serotonin.

Q. HOW IS TS DIAGNOSED?

A. A diagnosis is made by observing symptoms and by evaluating the history of their onset. No blood analysis or other types of neurological tests exist to diagnose TS. However, some physicians may wish to order an EEG, MRI, CAT scan, or certain blood tests to rule out other ailments that might be confused with TS.

Q. WHAT ARE THE FIRST SYMPTOMS?

A. The most common first symptom is a facial tic, such as rapidly blinking eyes or twitches of the mouth. However, involuntary sounds such as throat clearing and sniffing, or tics of the limbs may be initial signs.

Q. HOW ARE TICS CLASSIFIED?

A. There are two categories of tics: motor and vocal. Both of these are then subdivided into simple and complex.

SIMPLE:

        Motor – Eye blinking, head jerking, shoulder shrugging and facial grimacing

        Vocal – Throat clearing, yelping and other noises, sniffing and tongue clicking

COMPLEX:

        Motor – Jumping, touching other people or things, smelling, twirling about (and only rarely, self-injurious actions including hitting or biting oneself)

        Vocal– Uttering words or phrases out of context, and coprolalia (vocalizing socially unacceptable words)

The range of tics is very broad. Some symptoms are often so complex that family members, friends, teachers and employers may find it hard to believe that the movements and vocalizations are involuntary.

Q. How is TS treated?

A. The majority of people with TS are not significantly disabled by their tics or behavioral symptoms and therefore do not require medication. However, there are medications available to help control the symptoms when they interfere with functioning. The drugs include haloperidol (Haldol), clonidine (Catapres), pimozide (Orap), fluphenazine (Prolixin, Permitil), and clonazepam (Klonopin). Stimulants such as Ritalin, Cylert, and Dexedrine that are prescribed for ADHD may increase tics. Their use is controversial. For obsessive compulsive traits that interfere significantly with daily functioning, fluoxetine (Prozac), clomipramine (Anafranil), sertraline (Zoloft), fluvoxamine (Luvox), and paroxetine (Paxil) are prescribed. Risperidone (Risperdal) is a newer medication that is also being prescribed.

Dosages which achieve maximum control of symptoms vary for each patient and must be gauged carefully by a doctor. The medicine is administered in small doses, with gradual increases to the point where there is maximum alleviation of symptoms with minimal side effects. Some of the undesirable reactions to medications are weight gain, muscular rigidity, fatigue, motor restlessness, and social withdrawal, most of which can be reduced with specific medications. Side effects such as depression and cognitive impairment can be alleviated with dosage reduction or a change of medication.

Other types of therapy may also be helpful. Psychotherapy can assist a person with TS and help his / her family cope, and some behavior therapies can teach the substitution of one tic for another that is more acceptable. The use of relaxation techniques, biofeedback and exercise can reduce the stress that often exacerbates tic symptoms.

Q. Is it important to receive a TS diagnosis early in life?

A. Yes, especially in those instances when the symptoms are viewed by some people as bizarre, disruptive and frightening. Sometimes TS symptoms provoke ridicule and rejection by peers, neighbors, teachers and even casual observers. Parents may be overwhelmed by the strangeness of their child's behavior. The child may be threatened, excluded from activities and prevented from enjoying normal interpersonal relationships. These difficulties may become greater during adolescence, which is an especially trying period for young people and even more so for a person coping with a neurological problem. To avoid psychological harm, early diagnosis and treatment are crucial. Moreover, in more serious cases, it is possible to control the symptoms with medication.

Q. **DO ALL PEOPLE WITH TS HAVE ASSOCIATED BEHAVIORS IN ADDITION TO TICS?**

A. No, but many do have one or more additional problems which may include:

• Obsessions which consist of repetitive unwanted or bothersome thoughts.

• Compulsions and ritualistic behaviors, when a person feels that something must be done over and over and / or in a certain way. Examples include touching an object with one hand after touching it with the other hand to "even things up," or repeatedly checking to see that the flame on the stove is turned off. Children sometimes beg their parents to repeat a sentence many times until it "sounds right."

• Attention deficit disorder (ADD) with or without hyperactivity (ADHD) occurs in many people with TS. Children may show signs of hyperactivity before TS symptoms appear. Indications of ADHD may include difficulty with concentration, failing to finish what is started, not listening, being easily distracted, often acting before thinking, shifting constantly from one activity to another, needing a great deal of supervision, and general fidgeting. Adults may also exhibit signs of ADHD, such as overly impulsive behavior and concentration difficulties, and the need to move constantly. ADD without hyperactivity includes all of the above symptoms except for the high level of activity. As children with ADHD mature, the need to move is more likely to be expressed by restless, fidgety behavior. Difficulties with concentration and poor impulse control persist.

• Learning disabilities, which may include reading and writing difficulties, arithmetic disorders and perceptual problems.

• Difficulties with impulse control, which may in rare instances result in overly aggressive behaviors or socially inappropriate acts. Defiant and angry behaviors can also occur.

• Sleep disorders, which are fairly common among people with TS. These include frequent awakenings or walking or talking in one's sleep.

Q. DO STUDENTS WITH TS HAVE SPECIAL EDUCATIONAL NEEDS?

A. While school children with TS as a group have the same IQ range as the population at large, many have special educational needs. It is estimated that many may have some kind of learning problem. That condition, combined with attention deficits and the problems inherent in dealing with frequent tics, often calls for special educational assistance. The use of tape recorders, typewriters, or computers for reading and writing problems, untimed exams (in a private room if vocal tics are a problem), and permission to leave the classroom when tics become overwhelming are often helpful. Some children need extra help, such as access to tutoring in a resource room.

When difficulties in school cannot be resolved, an educational evaluation may be indicated. A resulting identification as "other health impaired" under federal law will entitle the student to an Individual Education Plan (IEP), which addresses specific educational problems in school. Such an approach can significantly reduce the learning difficulties that prevent the young person from performing at his / her potential. The child who cannot be adequately educated in a public school with special services geared to his / her individual needs may be best served by a special school.

Q. IS TS INHERITED?

A. Genetic studies indicate that TS is inherited. Several genes of major effect appear to be responsible for TS, causing different symptoms in different family members. A person with TS has about a 50 percent chance of passing the genes to one of his / her children with each separate pregnancy. However, that genetic predisposition may express itself as TS, as a milder tic disorder or as obsessive compulsive symptoms with no tics at all. It is known that a higher than normal incidence of milder tic disorders and obsessive compulsive behaviors occurs in the families of TS patients.

The sex of the child also influences the genetic expression of the condition. The chance that the genetically involved child of a person with TS will have symptoms is at least three to four times higher for a son than for a daughter. Yet only about 10 percent of the children who inherit the genetic predisposition will have symptoms severe enough to ever require medical attention. In some cases TS may not be inherited, and is identified. Those cases are called sporadic TS and the cause is unknown.

Q. IS THERE A CURE?

A. Not yet.

Q. IS THERE EVER A REMISSION?

A. Many people experience marked improvement in their late teens or early twenties. Most people with TS get better, not worse, as they mature, and those diagnosed with TS have a normal life span. As many as one-third of patients experience remission of tic symptoms in adulthood.

Q. HOW MANY PEOPLE IN THE U.S. HAVE TS?

A. Since many people with TS have yet to be diagnosed, there are no absolute figures. The official estimate by the National Institutes of Health is that 100,000 Americans have full-blown TS. Some genetic studies suggest that the figure may be as high as one in two hundred, if those with chronic multiple tics and / or transient childhood tics are included in the count.

> Editor's notes: TSA has an extensive Catalog of Publications and Videos that details many of the topics touched upon in these FAQs.
>
> Spanish and French versions of *FAQ ABOUT TOURETTE SYNDROME* are available on TSA's website. [117]

Myths about Tourette Syndrome [118]

Tourette Syndrome symptoms are highly unusual and thus easily misunderstood. Over the years, several misconceptions have become widespread. Among them are:

ALL PEOPLE WITH TS SWEAR AND USE OBSCENE LANGUAGE — *NOT TRUE!*

Only a small minority of people have this symptom (called coprolalia), and from among those who do, most mask the offensive words, for example using "F... FINE" instead of the four-letter word.

PEOPLE WITH TS SUFFER FROM MENTAL ILLNESS — *NOT TRUE!*

Mental illnesses affect people with TS no more frequently than in the general population. Also, involuntary TS movements may lead some to mistakenly assume that individuals with TS are either drunk, on drugs, or threatening.

PEOPLE WITH TS ARE POSSESSED BY THE DEVIL — *NOT TRUE!*

It has been said that some of the Salem "witches" were actually people with TS whose medical condition was tragically misunderstood. Even in modern times, with symptoms such as those associated with TS and other neurological disorders, well-meaning people have been known to rush to rites of excorcism.

PEOPLE WITH TS CAN CONTROL THEIR MOVEMENTS AND SOUNDS IF THEY REALLY WANTED TO, AND POINTING OUT THE SYMPTOMS WILL HELP PEOPLE STOP PERFORMING THEM — *NOT TRUE!*

TS symptoms are caused by a chemical imbalance in the wiring of the brain. The physical and vocal tics are completely involuntary, and can only be controlled for very short periods of time, and then they must be released.

PEOPLE WITH TS ARE FROM CERTAIN GROUPS — *NOT TRUE!*

TS is found among people from all ethnic groups.

PEOPLE WITH TS CANNOT HOPE TO LEAD PRODUCTIVE LIVES — *NOT TRUE!*

Most lead rich lives, participate in normal activities and have rewarding careers.

FAMOUS PEOPLE WITH TOURETTE SYNDROME [119]

SAMUEL JOHNSON (1709 – 1784)

Dr. Johnson, a famous British writer and lexicographer, was a leading literary figure in the second half of the 18th century. He wrote the *Dictionary of the English Language,* and *Lives of the Poets.* Many medical historians have speculated about his having Tourette Syndrome.

Dr. Samuel Johnson was noted by his friends to have almost constant tics and gesticulations, which startled those who met him for the first time. He also made noises and whistling sounds; he made repeated sounds and words and irregular or blowing respiratory noises. Further, he often carried out pronounced compulsive acts, such as touching posts, measuring his footsteps on leaving a room, and performing peculiar complex gestures and steps before crossing a threshold. His symptoms of (a) involuntary muscle jerking movements and complex motor acts, (b) involuntary vocalizations, and (c) compulsive actions constitute the symptom complex of Gilles de la Tourette Syndrome (Tourette's Syndrome), from which Johnson suffered most of his life. [120]

JIM EISENREICH (1959 –)

Baseball player Jim Eisenreich has TS, but he was only diagnosed as a young rookie in the majors, and only after his young career was in shambles because of a flare-up of his symptoms.

Once doctors recognized what he had and treated it, he began the long road back to the majors. Playing first for the Kansas City Royals, then the Phillies, the Marlins and the Dodgers, outfielder Eisenreich proved to be a dependable and valuable player.

Eisenreich is a wonderful model for young children with TS. He receives them in the dugout wherever he plays. He gives talks around the country about having TS, has made a public service announcement shown on the air, played in TSA charity golf and bowling tournaments, and participated in *Handling It Like a Winner*, an inspiring children's video.

MOZART (1756 – 1791)

It has been documented that Mozart's scatological letters were written to his cousin Maria Mozart, whom he may have loved. He was known to be hyperactive, have mood swings, tics, sudden impulses and a love of nonsense words. He was observed spinning, leaping, fidgeting and performing strange motor movements. Nevertheless, while speculation about whether a famous historical personality of Mozart's genius might have had a medical condition makes for intriguing reading, we can never know if it is true or not.

MAHMOUD ABDUL-RAUF (1969 –   )

Mahmoud Abdul-Rauf (formerly Chris Jackson) was the leading NBA free throw shooter of the '90s. As a guard on the Denver Nuggets, he came to the NBA from Louisiana State University where he was an instant sensation, scoring 48 points in his third game. Abdul-Rauf is featured in an independent documentary, *Twitch & Shout*, produced by two filmmakers with TS. It is said that Mahmoud's obsessive compulsive TS traits are the reason for his unbelievable proficiency at the foul line.

T SA's MISSION IS TO:

- IDENTIFY THE CAUSE
- FIND THE CURE
- CONTROL THE EFFECTS OF TS
- SERVE ALL WITH TS

TSA is a national nonprofit voluntary health organization with 54 chapters in the USA and over 30 contacts in other countries. Members include people with TS, their relatives and other interested, concerned supporters.

TSA was established in 1972 by a handful of New York families whose loved ones had Tourette Syndrome. They came together to help others seeking a proper treatment for a TS diagnosis. Although first described in 1885 by Georges Gilles de la Tourette, these founding families believed that there were only 50 known cases in all of recorded medical history!

As a result of TSA's medical and public education, the gap between symptom onset and a diagnosis has narrowed to the point where families are diagnosed more quickly than in the past, when it could take 10 years or more.

The Association is governed by a nationally representative, democratically elected Board of Directors. Treatment policies and medical information are overseen by their volunteer national Medical Advisory Board, and applications to TSA's research grant award program are peer reviewed by the Scientific Advisory Board.

National TSA remains the primary source of accurate and up-to-date information about TS, its treatment, relevant scientific research, and consumer services. TSA publishes a quarterly Newsletter (40,000 readers), maintains a crisis hotline, and produces valuable literature for people with TS and their families, medical and allied professionals, educators and legislators.

CLIENT SERVICES

To better serve all people with Tourette Syndrome, the Association maintains a crisis hotline, physician referral listings by state, and medical referrals in other countries. For specific help, contact the national office and request their information and referral specialist.

TSA also maintains a counseling program specifically for New York City Residents.

PUBLICATIONS AND VIDEOS

TSA publishes a wide variety of brochures and films relevant to the needs of families and people with TS, educators, counselors, insurers, lawyers, physicians and scientists. Media public service announcements (PSAs), print ads, and TV and radio spots are available for local placement. (TSA Publications are listed on page 309.)

TSA CHAPTERS IN THE USA

A complete listing of TSA chapters in the United states is available on the Internet. Information provided includes chapter names, contact phone numbers and addresses, and a US map showing chapter locations.

Telephone inquiries for TSA chapters: (718)224-2999

Website Listing: >http://neuro-www2.mgh.harvard.edu/
                    TSA/whoandwhat/usachapters.html<

INTERNATIONAL CONTACTS [122]

Individuals from the following countries have indicated their willingness to provide information and support to families in their respective countries. For foreign contact information, duplicate or translations of TSA publications, and information about permission to reprint, please contact TSA directly.

International Contacts (as of 5 / 99)

Argentina	Germany	Norway
Austria	Great Britain	Peru
Australia	Iceland	Puerto Rico
Belgium	India	Russia
Brazil	Iraq	Singapore
Canada	Ireland	South Africa
Chile	Israel	Spain
China	Japan	Sweden
Colombia	Korea	Switzerland
Denmark	Lithuania	Taiwan
Ecuador	Mexico	Zimbabwe
Finland	Netherlands	
France	New Zeland	

REFERRALS

Inquiries for referrals or other information may be directed to the Tourette Syndrome Association. They are well staffed and eager to help.

TOURETTE SYNDROME ASSOCIATION
42-40 Bell Boulevard
Bayside, New York 11361-2820
Phone: (718)224-2999
E-mail: tourette@ix.netcom.com
website: >http://neuro-www2.mgh.harvard.edu/TSA<

TSA Publications [123]

- √ Coping with Tourette Syndrome: A Parent's Viewpoint

- √ Coping with Tourette Syndrome in the Classroom

- √ An Educator's Guide to Tourette Syndrome

- √ Problem Behaviors and Tourette Syndrome

- √ Understanding Coprolalia

- √ Tourette Syndrome and The School Nurse

- √ A Consumer's Guide to Tourette Syndrome Medications

- √ Current Pharmacology of Tourette Syndrome

- √ Latest Issues of National TSA Newsletters

- √ National TSA Catalog of Publications

Tourette Syndrome Association
42-40 Bell Boulevard
Bayside, New York 11361-2820
Phone: (718)224-2999
E-mail: tourette@ix.netcom.com
website: >http://neuro-www2.mgh.harvard.edu/TSA<

ON-LINE TS + RESOURCES

The Internet has a wealth of information about Tourette Syndrome and related disorders (TS+). Many Touretters and Tourette families have created wonderfully informative websites. This list is not intended to be exhaustive, nor is it intended to be an endorsement of any information other than that provided by the Tourette Syndrome Association.

TOURETTE SYNDROME ASSOCIATION'S BOOKMARKS:
>http://neuro-www2.mgh.harvard.edu/TSA/onlineresources.html<

GREAT LINKS TO TOURETTE, AND OTHER DISABILITY-RELATED SOURCES:
>http://members.tripod.com/~tourette13/links.html<

ABUNDANT LINKS AT THIS SITE:
>http://www.ben2.ucla.edu/~bshapiro/gts.html<

General Links
TS Mailing Lists
TS Chat Room at Massachusetts General Hospital
TSA Chapters
Related Links
News Groups

150+ LINKS TO TS LINKS AND OTHER ASSOCIATED DISORDERS:
>http://www.tourette-syndrome.com/tourette-syndrome-links.htm<

Especially well organized,
shows compete http address
plus a summary of the website.

POTPOURRI OF MORE LINKS – WITH GOOD DESCRIPTIONS:
>http://www.tsanj.org/tsa/links.htm<

~ ~ ~

ABBREVIATIONS & ACRONYMS

Editor's note: A GLOSSARY is also provided, which
includes expanded definitions of some
of the terms listed below. *See* page 313.

ACN	Association for Comprehensive Neurotherapy
ADA	Americans with Disabilities Act
ADHD	Attention Deficit Hyperactivity Disorder
AFH	Adult Family Home
ALJ	Administrative Law Judge
Arc	The Arc (Arc is no longer an acronym. *See* GLOSSARY)
CAT scan	Computerized Axial Tomography (also known as CT scan)
CNS	Central Nervous System
COPE	Coalition in Oregon for Parents in Education
CP	Cerebral Palsy
DD	Developmental Disability (division in Oregon)
DDD	Developmental Disabilities Division (in Washington)
DSHS	Department of Social and Health Services
DSM IV	Diagnostic and Statistical Manual of Mental Disorders
EHA	Education for All Handicapped Children Act
FAPE	Free Appropriate Public Education
ICAP	Inventory for Client and Agency Planning
IDEA	Individuals with Disabilities Education Act
ITS	Intensive Tenant Support
JTPA	Job Training Partnership Act
LCCE	Lamaze Certified Childbirth Educator

LRE	Least Restrictive Environment
MBD	Minimal Brain Dysfunction
MRI	Magnetic Resonance Imaging
NINDS	National Institute of Neurological Disorders and Stroke
OCD	Obsessive Compulsive Disorder
PAVE	Parents Advocating for Vocational Education
PET	Positron Emission Tomography
PGA	Parent Graduation Alliance
Ph.D.	Doctor of Philosophy
PL 94-142	Public Law 94-142
PSA	Public Service Announcement
SAT	Scholastic Aptitude Test
SGA	Substantial Gainful Activity
SPECT	Single Photon Emission Computed Tomography
SSA	Social Security Administration
SSDI	Social Security Disability Insurance
SSI	Supplemental Security Income
TAG	Talented and Gifted
TASH	(TASH is no longer an acronym. *See* GLOSSARY)
TS	Tourette Syndrome
TSA	Tourette Syndrome Association
TS+	Tourette Syndrome Plus (Tourette Syndrome +)
WAC	Washington Administrative Code

GLOSSARY

Advocate – (noun) A partner, a sustainer; someone who assists; an ombudsman.

Akathisia – Inability to be still; a feeling of inner restlessness. A possible side effect of neuroleptic medications.

Americans with Disabilities Act (ADA) – Signed into law in 1990 by President George Bush.

Antidepressant – A prescription drug that relieves or minimizes depression.

Arc – (The Arc) A nationwide organization which works through education, research and advocacy to improve the quality of life for children and adults with mental retardation and their families, and works to prevent both the causes and the effects of mental retardation. (Arc is no longer an acronym; the full name was deemed socially incorrect several years ago.)

Arithmomania – Compulsive mental counting.

Associated behaviors – The spectrum of behaviors sometimes seen in association with Tourette Syndrome; includes OCD, ADHD, and poor impulse control.

Association for Comprehensive Neurotherapy (ACN) – An organization with a continuing interest in the topic of non-drug treatments for TS and other neuro-biological conditions.

Association for Retarded Citizens – *See* Arc. (The full name was deemed socially incorrect several years ago.)

Attention deficit hyperactivity disorder (ADHD) – A neurobiological disorder causing distractibility and inability to focus attention.

Basal ganglia – Structures deep in brainstem that relay messages between the prefrontal cortex and the lower motor and sensory areas.

Behavior therapy – Used with OCD and other conditions such as phobias; a person is exposed to anxiety-provoking stimuli while being prevented from performing the ritual or behavior previously used to reduce that anxiety.

Bi-polar disorder – Another name for manic-depression, a disorder involving extreme ups and downs in mood.

Brain Bank – A centralized resource for the collection and distribution of human brain specimens for brain research.

CAT scan – Computerized axial tomography, a series of computerized X-rays of the brain. (also known as CT scan)

Catapres – *See* clonidine.

Central nervous system (CNS) – Refers to activity of the brain and spinal cord.

Cerebral Palsy (CP) – A disability believed to be caused by damage of the centers of the brain before or during birth, or an by accident after birth, resulting in compromised control of the muscles, and marked by muscular in-coordination, spastic paralysis, and / or speech disturbances.

Chorea – Abrupt, quick, jerky movements of the head, neck, arms, or legs.

Chromosomes – Microscopic, rod-shaped bodies in cells which contain genetic material.

Clinical depression – Depression that requires treatment.

Clomipramine – An antidepressant medication used in Tourette Syndrome to treat symptoms of OCD.

Clonidine (Catapres) – A high-blood-pressure medication used in treatment of TS. It can be helpful in controlling tics and ADHD symptoms.

Coalition in Oregon for Parents in Education (COPE) – A statewide advocacy group for parents of special-needs children in Oregon.

Cognitive dulling – A common side effect of neuroleptic drugs; involves short-term memory loss and slowed thinking.

  Glossary

Co-morbid condition – Medical term meaning a medical condition that occurs along with another medical condition, although one condition does not directly cause the other.

Compulsion – The feeling of being compelled or forced to exhibit a behavior, even though the person experiencing the compulsion does not want to do it. For example, evening things up, washing hands, cleaning.

Congenital disorder – Describes a condition that is recognized at birth, or that is believed to have been present from birth. Congenital malformations include all disorders present at birth, whether they are inherited or caused by an environmental factor.

Coprolalia – Involuntary utterances of obscene or inappropriate statements or words.

Cylert – *See* pemoline.

Depression – Disorder producing depressed mood, appetite changes, sleep changes, and sometimes suicidal thinking. Can often be treated with medication.

Desipramine – A tricyclic antidepressant used in the treatment of ADHD associated with TS.

Developmental disability – A handicap or impairment originating before the age of eighteen, which may be expected to continue indefinitely, and which constitutes a substantial disability.

Diagnostic and Statistical Manual of Mental Disorders (DSM) – A manual published by the American Psychiatric Association (APA), which describes all of the diagnostic criteria and the systematic descriptions of various mental disorders.

Dopamine – One of the neurotransmitters (brain chemicals) involved in motor and vocal tics.

Down's syndrome – A disability due to chromosome defect (there are three number 21 chromosomes, instead of the usual two). Main physical features are slightly oblique slant to the eyes, a round head, flat nasal bridge, small round or knotty ears, and short stature. IQ range is usually 50-60. (formerly called mongolism) (medical name: trisomy 21)

Dyskinesia – A general term for involuntary movements.

Dyslexia – One type of learning disability that affects reading ability.

Echolalia – Involuntary repetition of words or phrases of others.

Echopraxia – Copying the gestures of others.

Education for All Handicapped Children Act (EHA) – Public Law 94-142. (*See* Public Law 94-142)

Exacerbate – To make worse, to intensify.

Etiology – The study of the cause of a disease or condition.

Extrapyramidal effects – Side effects of medications.

Fasciculations – Brief spontaneous contraction of a few muscle fibers, which is seen as a flicker of movement under the skin – most often associated with a disease of the motor neurons in the spinal cord or of the nerve fibers.

Flexion – The bending of a joint so that the bones forming it are brought towards each other.

Fluoxetine (Prozac) – An antidepressant used in TS to treat OCD and depression.

Free appropriate public education (FAPE) – A mandated provision of Public Law 94-142 of 1975.

Genes – Material within the chromosomes that determines specific traits, such as hair and eye color and stature.

Guardian – Person(s) legally responsible for another person's physical care, health, education, and welfare. Parents are naturally their children's guardians before the age of 18. Guardians can be appointed by judges or court commissioners in response to guardianship petitions filed in the Superior Court.

Guardianship – A legal proceeding in which a court determines that someone is unable to manage his or her personal and / or financial affairs, either wholly or in part. The law distinguishes between guardianship of the person and guardianship of the estate.

Guardianship of the Person – Affects decisions about medical matters, living arrangements, consent to habitation plans, and other personal matters.

Guardianship of the Estate – Affects control of the person's money and other possessions.

Haloperidol (Haldol) – A neuroleptic medication used to treat TS.

Huntington's Chorea – Involuntary movements accompanied by progressive dementia and widespread neuronal degeneration throughout the brain. Movements particularly affect the shoulders, hips and face; each movement is sudden but the resulting posture may be prolonged for a few seconds.

Inventory for Client and Agency Planning (ICAP) – The evaluation instrument used by the State of Washington to determine whether an applicant is eligible for services through the Division of Developmental Disabilities (DDD).

Involuntary movements – Actions beyond one's control.

Individuals with Disabilities Education Act (IDEA) – An important part of ADA, signed into law in 1990.

Intensive Tenant Support (ITS) – One level of residential support; provides financial and service benefit for eligible disabled clients in the Washington state DDD system. It is the most well-funded level (and therefore the most coveted), and offers the highest level of support for clients.

Intervivos Special Needs Trust – A type of Special Needs Trust where the trust functions while the parents are living. Families can place funds in the trust as a way of saving for the future, and also to help with current needs. Consult a knowledgeable attorney for specifics.

Issue – Term used in mental health, meaning problem.

Lamaze Certified Childbirth Educator (LCCE) – A childbirth educator trained and certified by Lamaze International.[124]

Least Restrictive Environment (LRE) – A provision of PL 94-142 of 1975, which refers to a child's placement in a school environment in which the handicapped child will have the least obstructions to learning.

Letter of Intent – A document written by the parents, guardian, or concerned person, which describes the disabled person's history, his or her current status, and their hopes, desires, and wishes for him in the future.

Magnetic Resonance Imaging (MRI) – A scan of the brain or other part of the body that employs magnetic and low-energy radiowaves. No radioactive materials or dyes are needed.

Medicaid – People who qualify for SSI usually receive Medicaid, which helps pay doctor and hospital bills.

Methylphenidate (Ritalin) – A stimulant drug often prescribed for ADHD; can cause increase in tics of Tourette Syndrome.

Minimal Brain Dysfunction (MBD) – An older "summary" term which generally referred to a combination of hyperactivity, attention deficit problems, and learning problems; usually spoken with reference to children.

Monozygotic twins – Identical twins.

Neuroleptic – A class of medications, e.g. haloperidol, pimozide.

Neurotransmitter – Any of the chemicals carrying nerve impulses across the synapse (gap) between adjacent neurons (nerve cells).

Norepinephrine – One of the brain's neurotransmitters involved in the formation and function of dopamine and serotonin.

Obsession – An unwanted recurring thought or impulse that is without purpose.

Obsessive compulsive disorder (OCD) – A disorder in which uncontrollable thoughts and compulsive behaviors impair functioning.

Orap – *See* pimozide.

Otolaryngologist – A specialist of the ear and larynx.

Oxytocin (Pitocin) – A hormone naturally produced in the posterior
pituitary gland; has uterine stimulant properties, especially
on the gravid uterus in normal labor. Indicated for the
medical rather than the elective induction of labor; when
properly administered (intravenously), it stimulates uterine
contractions similar to those in normal labor, when delivery
is in the best interest of the mother and fetus. [125]

Palilalia – Repeating one's own words or phrases.

Parents Advocating for Vocational Education (PAVE) – A statewide
advocacy group for parents of special-needs children in
Washington.

Pemoline (Cylert) – A psychotherapeutic drug which stimulates the
central nervous system, although its mechanism of action is
not known in children with attention deficit disorder (formerly
called hyperactivity). Children under six should not receive
this medication. Uncontrolled movements of the lips, face,
tongue, and the extremities and wandering eye may also occur.

Perinatal Cause – (as pertaining to cerebral palsy:) A cause of the
disorder occurring shortly before birth and 1 to 4 weeks
after birth.

Pimozide (Orap) – A neuroleptic drug used to help reduce tics of TS.

Pitocin – *See* oxytocin.

Polyp – A growth, usually benign, protruding from a mucous
membrane, giving rise to obstruction, chronic infection,
and discharge. Polyps are usually removed surgically.

Positron Emission Tomography (PET) – An imaging technique using
small amounts of radioactive material that produces a cross-
sectional view of specific chemical activities in the brain.

Public Law 94-142 (PL 94-142) – Also known as the Education
for All Handicapped Children Act (EHA) of 1975.
Mandated free appropriate public education (FAPE) for
all children with disabilities, ensured due process right,
mandated individual education plans (IEPs), and least
restrictive environment (LRE), and became the core of
federal funding for special education.

Premonitory urges – Sensations immediately preceding an involuntary movement or vocalization.

Pro sé – A legal term meaning "his own person, without the benefit of an attorney."

Prozac – *See* fluoxetine.

Remand – To send back.

Remission – A complete absence of symptoms for a period of months to years. Sometimes occurs with TS.

Ritalin – *See* methylphenidate.

Serotonin – One of the brain's neurotransmitters, believed to be involved in depression and OCD.

Side effects – Secondary, unwanted effects of using a medication.

Single Photon Emission Computed Tomography (SPECT) – Device which measures brain function through blood flow and glucose metabolism.

Social Security Disability Insurance (SSDI) – A program that workers, their employers, and the self-employed pay for with Social Security taxes. People qualify based on their own work history or that of a parent.

Special Needs Trust – A legal instrument developed to manage resources, while maintaining the individual's eligibility for public assistance benefits. The only reliable method of making sure that an inheritance reaches the person with the disability when he or she needs it.

Staffings – A child-centered meeting, scheduled for the purpose of educating school staff. Generally conducted by a staff member, but may also be led by the parent advocate.

Stimulant – A psychotropic drug, such as methylphenidate (Ritalin) or dextroamphetamine (Dexedrine, Oxydess, Spancap), often used to control hyperactivity in children.

Substantial Gainful Activity (SGA) – Defined by the Social Security Administration as earning more than $700 per month, as of July 1, 1999.

Supplemental Security Income (SSI) – A federal entitlement program financed through general tax revenues to provide income benefits to certain groups of very low-income people, including the aged, the blind, and people with disabilities.

Synapse – The gap between neurons, across which messages are carried by neurotransmitters.

Talented and Gifted (TAG) – Organized as a division of The Council for Exceptional Children in 1958.

Tardive dyskinesia – Involuntary movements of the mouth, tongue, and lips. Some medications prescribed for Tourette Syndrome can contribute to the development of this condition.

TASH – An international association for people with disabilities, their family members, other advocates, and professionals fighting for a society in which inclusion of all people in all aspects of society is the norm. (Founded in 1974, TASH is no longer an acronym; the full name was deemed socially incorrect several years ago.)

The Arc – *See* Arc.

Tic – An involuntary movement (motor tic) or involuntary vocalization (vocal tic).

Titration – Process of determining how much of a medication is required to produce a desired reaction.

Tourette Syndrome (TS) – A chronic, physical disorder of the brain which causes both motor tics and vocal tics, and begins before the age of eighteen.

Tourette Syndrome Plus (Tourette Syndrome +) (TS +) – A term generally used by Tourette families, to describe the sum of a patient's Tourette Syndrome and related disorders and / or dysfunctions (such as Tourette Syndrome *plus* attention deficit disorder, and obsessive compulsive disorder, and hyperactive disorder, and low functional level).

Tracheostomy – A surgical operation in which a hole is made into the trachea (windpipe) through the neck to relieve obstruction to breathing. A curved metal, plastic or rubber tube is usually inserted through the hole and held in position by tapes. With the tube in place, it is often necessary for secretions to be sucked out of the bronchial tree.

Trichotillomania – A compulsion to pull out one's own hair in order to relieve anxiety.

Vacate – In legal use, to annul; to make void.

Waxing and waning – A naturally occurring increase and decrease in severity and frequency of TS symptoms.

~ ~ ~

Editor's notes: A portion of this glossary has been provided by the Tourette Syndrome Association.

This book is not intended as a substitute for the medical advice of physicians. The reader should regularly consult a physician in matters relating to his / her health care and particularly to any symptoms that may require diagnosis or medical attention.

Endnotes

1. *[p. 2]* Proverbs 17:22

2. *[p. 4]* Luke 4:23

3. *[p. 4]* "Something Good is Going to Happen to You," by Ralph Carmichael, © 1969 Bud John Songs, Inc.

4. *[p. 8]* *The Pill Book*, by Stern, Chilnick, Silverman, Simon. Bantam Books, 1992, page 304.

5. *[p. 8]* *See* GLOSSARY (oxytocin)

6. *[p.10]* Extensive Glossary and Index sections are included for technical terminology. *See* GLOSSARY, page 313; ABBREVIATIONS & ACRONYMS, page 311; INDEX, page 333.

7. *[p. 12]* Quotation collected along the journey. Author unknown.

8. *[p. 18]* *See* APPENDIX – DEPRESSION – MY CLOSE COMPANION, page 209.

9. *[p. 22]* *COPE Newsletter.* Reprinted with permission.

10. *[p. 25]* >http://www.geocities.com/HotSprings/Sauna/4441/cause.html< *See also* APPENDIX – TELL ME ABOUT CEREBRAL PALSY, page. 271.

11. *[p. 26]* Quotations collected along the journey. Authors unknown.

12. *[p. 28]* *The Pill Book*, by Stern, Chilnick, Silverman, Simon. Bantam Books, 1992, page 544.

13. *[p. 34]* *The Pill Book*, by Stern, Chilnick, Silverman, Simon. Bantam Books, 1992, page 665.

14. *[p. 35]* Village Missions / Stonecroft Ministries. PO Box 9609, Kansas City, MO 64134-0609. (816)763-7800. >http://spokane.net/coos/vm/stoncrft.htm<

15. *[p. 35]* Jean Zeiler's life story has recently been published. *Like a Pebble Tossed – The Legacy of a Prayer*, by Jean Lovelace Zeiler and Mayo Mathers, ACW Press, 5501 North 7th Avenue, #502, Phoenix, AZ 85013. ISBN # 1-892525-03-8.

16. *[p. 37]* Aglow International, PO Box 1749, Edmonds, WA 98020-1749. (425)778-9615. >http://www.aglow.org<

17. *[p. 38]*   *See* APPENDIX – WHAT I BELIEVE, page 214.

18. *[p. 38]*   *See* APPENDIX – WHAT I BELIEVE, page 213.

19. *[p. 39]*   *The Pill Book*, by Stern, Chilnick, Silverman, Simon. Bantam Books, 1992, page 666.

20. *[p. 43]*   Willow Louisa Cosand. (b) August 9, 1967 (d) March 2, 1984.

21. *[p. 43]*   *See* APPENDIX – CREATING YOUR ADVOCACY FILE page 215.

22. *[p. 46]*   M. A. "Buck" Ryan, Deputy Headmaster, 1973-1987, Parkway Middle School, Haverhill, Suffolk, England.

23. *[p. 48]*   *Tourette Syndrome Association, Inc. Newsletter* , Vol. 25, #3, Winter, 1997. Used with permission.

24. *[p. 51]*   *The Pill Book*, by Stern, Chilnick, Silverman, Simon. Bantam Books, 1992, page 404.

25. *[p. 51]*   To obtain Public Service Announcements for use in your locality, contact the Tourette Syndrome Association. (718)279-9596. For more information on the TSA, *See* APPENDIX - TELL ME ABOUT TS, page 275.

26. *[p. 54]*   *Tourette Syndrome Association, Inc. Newsletter*, Spring 1996, page 5. Used with permission.

27. *[p. 56]*   *See* APPENDIX – CREATING YOUR ADVOCACY FILE page 215.

28. *[p. 57]*   *See* APPENDIX – CREATING YOUR ADVOCACY FILE page 215.

29. *[p. 62]*   Exodus 17:12

30. *[p. 62]*   *See* APPENDIX – CREATING YOUR ADVOCACY FILE page 215.

31. *[p. 63]*   *Oregon Family Support News*, Spring, 1999. Used with permission.

32. *[p. 64]*   *COPE Newsletter*, Winter, 1989. Used with permission.

33. *[p. 65]*   *COPE Newsletter*, Winter, 1989. Used with permission.

34. *[p. 66]*   Quotations collected along the journey. Authors unknown.

35. *[p. 68]*   >http://ideapolicy.org/IDEA%20'97/idea_97_hist<

36. *[p. 69]*   U.S. Department of Education, 1996.

37. *[p. 70]*   Former Oregon Representative Barbara Jordan.

38. *[p. 71]*   "Do They Mean Us?" (an article on racism in the British police ranks), *The Mail on Sunday*. Feb. 28, 1999, page 9.

39. *[p. 71]*   Visit our website: HEART FOR ROMANIA. >http://www.hermiston.k12.or.us/heartsite/index.htm<

---

40. *[p. 90-91]* From "Working Together: A Training Handbook for Parent-Professional Collaboration," by Richard Vosler-Hunter and Kaye Exo. Portland (OR) State University, 1987, as reprinted in *COPE Communicator*, Winter, 1989. Used with permission.

41. *[p. 92]* *COPE Communicator*. Used with permission.

42. *[p. 93]* From the *Washington State School for the Deaf Newsletter*.

43. *[p. 95]* Proverbs 25:4, Malachi 3:3

44. *[p. 96]* Contributed by Jos Gisberts, Linne, The Netherlands.

45. *[p. 102]* *Teaching and Learning through Multiple Intelligences*, by Linda Campbell, et.al., 1996, by Allan and Bacon. ISBN # 0-205-16337-8, page xv.

46. *[p. 103]* *It Works, It Works, It Really Works! Life Changing Truths Found Only in Christ,* by Joey Duff and Jean Conklin, Carico Press, 1999, page 47. ISBN 0-9673440-1-8.

47. *[p. 104]* Reprinted from the Council for Exceptional Children's *Exceptional Times*, August, 1989, as appeared in *COPE Communicator*. Used with permission.

48. *[p. 106]* Genesis 1:27

49. *[p. 107]* *COPE Communicator*, March-April, 1997. Used with permission.

50. *[p. 110]* "Life Course," Furstenberg, Peterson, Nord, and Zill, 656ff. Cited on page 76 of *The Abolition of Marriage*, by Maggie Gallagher.

51. *[p. 110]* Between 1970 and 1996, the proportion of children under 18 years of age living with one parent grew from 12 percent to 28 percent. *1998 Census Bureau Report*.

52. *[p. 110]* Malachi 2:16

53. *[p. 112]* Quotation collected along the journey. Author unknown.

54. *[p. 112]* 1976 Nobel Prize winner for his contributions to economic theory. "A Happy Marriage of Minds," *NRTA Bulletin*, vol. 40, no. 5, May, 1999, page 19.

55. *[p. 120]* Quotation collected along the journey. Author unknown.

56. *[p. 121]* "President's Message," *Tourette Syndrome Association, Inc. Newsletter*, vol. 26, no. 3, Winter, 1998, page 2.

57. *[p. 122]* Story by Matthew Hill, Judge, Supreme Court, State of Washington, as appeared in *National Parent-Teacher*.

58. *[p. 125]* After an SSI application has been denied excessively, SSI can withhold money for attorney fees out of the retroactive benefits due (up to a maximum of 25 percent or $4,000, whichever is less). The attorney must petition the agency for approval of his fee. Upon approval, SSA then releases the check directly to the attorney. Any balance remaining is then paid to the beneficiary. SSA Code of Federal Regulation (CFR) vol. 20, sect. 404.1720.

59. *[p. 125]* Richard McNerney, Attorney at Law, Pridgeon, Stimac & Associates, 515 W. Olive Street, Newport, OR 97365, (541)265-2217.

60. *[p. 126]* "Authorization to Release Medical Records" forms are available at any medical office, or you can draft your own form on your letterhead (include your mailing address and phone number). Use the 5 W's: *Who* (list child's full name and date of birth), *What* (the records you are requesting), *When* (the inclusive dates you wish), *Where* (where you want the records sent), and *Why* (why you are requesting the records). *Sign* the request, and *date* it.

61. *[p. 129]* SSA Rule: SI 01150.001B.4: Resources. Transfer at Less than FMV July 1, 1988.

62. *[p. 134]* >http://neuro-www2.mgh.harvard.edu/TSA/AboutTS/faq.html<

63. *[p. 137]* Philippians 4:7

64. *[p. 143]* Quotation collected along the journey. Author unknown.

65. *[p. 148]* *See* APPENDIX - A NATIONAL LEGAL PRECEDENT, page 235.

66. *[p. 149]* *See* APPENDIX - A NATIONAL LEGAL PRECEDENT, page 235.

67. *[p. 153]* Hillel, Judaic scholar. (70? bc – ad 10?)

68. *[p. 154]* *PLUK News*, Nov. 1992, as reprinted by *COPE Communicator*. Used with permission.

69. *[p. 156]* *See* APPENDIX – HURRAH FOR SPECIAL "O", page 225.

70. *[p. 166]* Quotation collected along the journey. Author unknown.

71. *[p. 167]* *COPE Communicator*, March-April, 1997. Used with permission.

72. *[p. 172]* Larry A. Jones, 2118 8th Avenue, Seattle, WA 98121, (206)405-3240, FAX (206)405-3242. E-mail: lawjones@oz.net

73. *[p. 174]* *See* APPENDIX – CREATING YOUR ADVOCACY FILE page 215.

74. *[p. 175]* Chief Joseph (1840? – 1904), Nez Percé (pierced nose) Indian Tribe of the American Northwest.

75. *[p. 176]* *The Poetry of Robert Frost*, by Edward Connery Latham, Henry Holt & Co., NY, 1969.

76. *[p. 179]* Nancy Horn Cloud, great granddaughter of Sioux leader Red Cloud, *How the West Was Won*, a Time-Life audiotape. Based on *The Old West: The Indians*, by the editors of Time-Life Books, Time, Inc., 1973, page 92.

77. *[p. 184]* Genesis 2:18

78. *[p. 187]* Dr. Brien Vlcek, M.D., Director, Child Neurology, Swedish Medical Center / Neuroscience Institute, 801 Broadway – Suite 711, Seattle, WA 98122, (206)215-6050, FAX (206)215-6660.

79. *[p. 203]* From the Candlelighter's Childhood Cancer Foundation, Vol. 8, No. 32. Reprinted by *COPE*. Used with permission.

80. *[p. 205]* *Public Papers of the Presidents of the United States. Richard Nixon. Containing the public messages, speeches, and statements of the president.* January 1 to August 9, 1974. Washington. US Government Printing Office. 1975, page 632.

81. *[p. 207]* Philippians 1:6

82. *[p. 208]* Jeremiah 31:3. *See also* page 214.

83. *[p. 208]* "It Is No Secret," by Stuart Hamblen. © 1950, by Duchess Music Corp., NY. Our thanks to Mrs. Susie Hamblen for permission to quote her husband's song. *See also* page 214.

84. *[p. 209]* "Ask the Medical Advisory Board," Lawrence Scahill, MSN, Ph.D., *Tourette Syndrome Association, Inc. Newsletter*, Vol. 27, #1, Summer, 1999. Used with permission.

85. *[p. 209]* >http://www.angelfire.com/md/deridden/facts.html< Deridden Web Operations, L. A. Taylor. Used with permission.

86. *[p. 211]* L. A. Taylor, Deridden Web Operations. Used with permission. >http://www.depression.8m.com<

87. *[p. 211]* >http://www.save.org/index.html< (Tracy Pierson) SA\VE (Suicide Awareness \ Voices of Education) is an organization dedicated to educating the public about suicide prevention. Used with permission.

88. *[p. 213]* "What is Aglow?" Aglow International, PO Box 1749, Edmonds, WA 98020-1749. (425)778-9615. >http://www.aglow.org< Used with permission.

89. *[p. 214]* Quote by Shirley Crane, Hermiston, Oregon.

90. *[p. 214]* Mark 9:23

91. *[p. 218]* An excellent comprehensive resource on related topics: *Since Owen – A Parent-to-Parent Guide for Care of the Disabled Child*, by Charles R. Callanan, John Hopkins University Press, 1990. ISBN 0-8018-3963-5.

92. *[p. 219]* *See* APPENDIX – WHAT WILL BECOME OF MY CHILD? page 255.

93. *[p. 223]* "Hurtful Behavior...when friends and families turn away." *The Link*, August, 1996. Reprinted by the *COPE Communicator*, Nov.-Dec. 1996. Used with permission.

94. *[p. 225]* *See* page 101, SPECIAL GIFTS AND SPECIAL EDUCATION.

95. *[p. 226]* Quote by Richard Shriver, "Shriver Lauds Special Olympics," The *Yale Daily News*, by Richard Seltenrich, April 6, 1995. >http://www.yale.edu.ydn/paper/4.6/4.6.95storyno.CE.html<

96. *[p. 227]* Matthew 7:12

97. *[p. 229]* Other resource material integrated into this chapter: "Supplemental Security Income (SSI) and Social Security Disabiity Insurance (SSDI) for People 18 Years and Older. June 1999," The Arc of King County, Seattle, WA, (206)364-6337. Used with permission.

98. *[p. 229]* SSA Publication No. 05-11000 (1/97), available from Social Security On-Line: >http://www.ssa.gov<

99. *[p. 229]* For more information, visit or write any Social Security office. Or phone toll-free, 24 hours a day, (800)772-1213.

100. *[p. 255]* *Pathways to Future Planning Workbook*, by Laurie Holscher, Arc–King County, 10550 Lake City Way Suite A, Seattle, WA 98125. (206)547-2075. Used with permission.

101. *[p. 255]* New York State Developmental Disability Planning Council, 1997, as reprinted in *Pathways to Future Planning Workbook*, Step 1, page 3, by Laurie Holscher, Arc–King County, 10550 Lake City Way Suite A, Seattle, WA 98125. (206)547-2075. Used with permission.

102. *[p. 262]* "Special Needs Trust," *Pathways to Future Planning Workbook*, Step 3, page 7, by Laurie Holscher, Arc–King County, 10550 Lake City Way Suite A, Seattle, WA 98125. (206)547-2075. Used with permission.

103. *[p. 271]* United Cerebral Palsy of Prince George's and Montgomery Counties, Wm. Irwin Buck Center, 3901 Woodhaven Lane, Bowie, MD 20715. (301)262-4993. >http://www.ucppgmc.com/research.html<

104. *[p. 272]* National Institute of Neurological Disorders and Stroke, PO Box 5801, Bethesda, MD 20824. (800)352-9424, (301)496-5751. >http://www.ninds.nih.gov/patients/ disorder/cp/cphtr.HTM#causes<

105. *[p. 275]* >http://neuro-www2.mgh.harvard.edu/TSA/ tsamain.nclk< All information from the TSA website is used with permission.

106. *[p. 276]* >http://neuro-www2.mgh.harvard.edu/TSA/AboutTS/ whatists.html< Used with permission.

107. *[p. 276]* *Tourette Syndrome Association, Inc. Newsletter*, Vol. 27, #1, Summer, 1999. Used with permission.

108. *[p. 276]* Tourette Syndrome Association, Inc. on the Internet: >http://www.2.mgh.harvard.edu/TSA<

109. *[p. 277]* *A Physician's Guide to the Diagnosis and Treatment of Tourette Syndrome* (3rd edition), by Ruth Dowling Bruun, M.D., Donald J. Cohen, M.D., James F. Leckman, M.D. >http://neuro-www2.mgh.harvard.edu/TSA/medsci/ guidetodiagnosis.html< All information from the TSA website is used with permission.

110. *[p. 291]* The entire text of this publication is available from the Tourette Syndrome Association, Inc. (718)224-2999.

111. *[p. 293]* Roger Kurlan, M.D., Associate Professor, Department of Neurology, University of Rochester School of Medicine, Rochester, NY. >http://neuro-www2.mgh.harvard.edu/ TSA/medsci/medicationsanddosages.html< All information from the TSA website is used with permission.

112. *[p. 294]* >http://neuro-www2.mgh.harvard.edu/TSA/medsci/ alternative.html< Used with permission.

113. *[p. 295]* >http://neuro-www2.mgh.harvard.edu/TSA/medsci/ TS.html< Used with permission.

114. *[p. 296]*   >http://neuro-www2.mgh.harvard.edu/TSA/medsci/
ADHD.html< Used with permission.

115. *[p. 296]*   >http://neuro-www2.mgh.harvard.edu/TSA/medsci/
OCD.html< Used with permission.

116. *[p. 297]*   >http://neuro-www2.mgh.harvard.edu/TSA/AboutTS/
faq.html< [includes a genetic update from David Pauls,
Ph.D. (Yale Child Study Center)] Used with permission.

117. *[p. 302]*   >http://neuro-www2.mgh.harvard.edu/TSA/AboutTS/
faq.html< Used with permission.

118. *[p. 303]*   >http://neuro-www2.mgh.harvard.edu/TSA/AboutTS/
myths.html< Used with permission.

119. *[p. 304]*   >ttp://neuro-www2.mgh.harvard.edu/TSA/tsamain.nclk<
Used with permission.

120. *[p. 304]*   "Medical History of Dr. Samuel Johnson's Movement
Disorder," by T. J. Murray, *British Medical Journal*, 1979,
vol. 1, pages 1610-1614.

121. *[p. 306]*   >http://neuro-www2.mgh.harvard.edu/TSA/whoandwhat/
nationaltsa.html< Used with permission.

122. *[p. 308]*   >http://neuro-www2.mgh.harvard.edu/TSA/whoandwhat/
international.html< Used with permission.

123. *[p. 309]*   >http://neuro-www2.mgh.harvard.edu/TSA/allourstuff/
tsapublications.html< Used with permission.

124. *[p. 317]*   Lamaze International, 1200 19th Street, NW, Suite 300,
Washington, DC 20036-2442. (800)368-4404.

125. *[p. 319]*   "Oxytocics," *Facts and Comparisons*, Michael R. Riley,
Publisher, St. Louis, MO, 1996, pages 118, 1171.

~ ~ ~

Coping Tips & Treasures

Editor's note: The list below is a quick *alphabetical reference* to locate specific coping helps and treasures that are featured throughout this volume.

~ ~ ~

INDEX

NOTE: **BOLD NUMERAL (00)** DENOTES ARTWORK OR PHOTO

alcohol abuse 212. *See also*
     symptoms (of depression)
allergens 294
alternative therapies 294
Americans with Disabilities Act.
     See IDEA
Americans with Disabilities Act (ADA)
     68, 151, 224, 311, 313
amphetamine. *See* methylphenidate
Anafranil. *See* clomipramine
anatomical studies 265
Anfinson, Lawrene Nixon 205
anger, angry 108, 301
anguish 285
anointed (book) 4
antidepressant (s) 129, 210,
     313, 316. *See also* depression
anxiety 212, 291
apology 107
appeal (hearing) 144, 235
appropriate 68, 224
Arc 77, 191, 264, 311, 313
Arc of Spokane 119, 173, 185
Arc-King County 264, 328
argumentativeness 291
arithmomania 313
arm
     jerking 288
     thrusting 275
assimilate (assimilation) 70
Assistant Guardian 174
associated
     behaviors 283, 291, 300, 313
     conditions 276
     mental disorders 241, 248
Association for Comprehensive
     Neurotherapy (ACN)
     294, 311, 313
athletic competition 225

attention
     deficit (s) 283, 285
     deficit disorder (ADD)
          39, 286, 291, 300
     deficit hyperactive disorder
          (ADHD) 117, 279, 284,
          285, 286, 287, 291,
          293, 296, 299, 300,
          311, 313, 314
     span 34, 51, 285
     problems 278, 283. *See also*
          associated conditions
attorney 146, 255, 262
Attorney General's Office
     146, 152
Authorization to Release Medical
     Records 126, 326
autism 69, 279

B

Baker Senior High School 5
baptism in the Holy Spirit
     38, 213, 214
barking 289
Bartee, Paulette Carter **30**
basal ganglia 313
battle (s) 177
battle-weary 175
Beaten Before You Start 222, 331
behavior therapy 299, 313
behavioral
     domain 58
     manifestation (s) 280, 287.
          See also Table 1
     problems 285, 309
     retraining 286
     supports 258, 261
belief 38.
     See also Doctrinal Statement
Bell curve 79

Deanna (sibling) v, 196, 197
    See also Hasen, Deanna; Ruth
death 255, 263, 266
Debbie (sibling) v, 197, 198, 202.
    See also Marty
debilitating brain disorders 265
decisions 107
Declaration of Independence 105
Deep Thoughts about Hard Times
    26, 331
defiant 301
DeGroote, Sue 35, 36, 37
demeanor 155
demonic possession 303
denial letter 243
Department of Social and Health
    Services. *See* DSHS
depression 18, 130, 178, 209 -
    212, 291, 299, 313, 316
depressive illnesses 209, 210
Depressed ??? (checklist) 212, 331
desipramine 315
despondency 209. *See also*
    symptoms (of depression)
Developmental Disabilities
    Division (Washington) (DDD)
    143, 144, 149, 161, 185, 215,
    220, 235, 241, 248, 311
Developmental Disability division
    (Oregon) (DD)
    123, 143, 220, 311
developmental
    disability 315
    symptoms 287.
        See also Table 1
Devore, Paul 121
Dexedrine. *See* dextroamphetamine
dextroamphetamine (Dexedrine)
    299. *See also* stimulants

diagnosis
    49, 279, 291, 298, 299, 306
Diagnostic and Statistical Manual
    241, 242, 247, 278.
        See also DSM 3R, DSM IV
dignity 255
diploma 78
disability 255
disability information 218, 229
disabled 158
disappointment 159
disclaimer 52
discord 166
discrimination 70
Disorient Express 178
disqualification 215
distractibility 34, 285
diversity 70
Division of Vocational Rehabilita-
    tion (DVR) 118
divorce 110
Doctrinal Statement 213
Document of Natural Rights 105
documentation. *See* record-keeping
"Don't mess with my kids!" 63
dopamine 298, 315
dosages 299
Downey, Blaine 56
Down's syndrome
    183, 191, 197, 315
dream 257
driver's education 142
drug
    abuse 211. *See also*
        symptoms (of depression)
    therapy. *See* medications
DSHS 311
DSM 3R 248. *See also* Diagnostic
    and Statistical Manual

medication (s)
280, 286, 291, 292, 299, 309
Meige's syndrome 279
Memory Box 216
mental
health professionals 149
illness 265, 303
retardation
69, 183, 191, 225, 271
mentally challenged 158
metabolism 298
methylphenidate (Ritalin)
28, 31, 32, 299, 318, 320.
See also stimulants
minimal brain dysfunction (MBD)
27, 34, 50, 312, 318
Minimal Cerebral Dysfunction 27
miracle (s) 108, 154
misconception 303
misdiagnosed illness 211
Mission Impossible 70
modified
curriculum 79
diploma 84, 88.
See also diploma
monozygotic twins 318
More Tips for Siblings 203, 331
Morris, Ruth 181, 182, 183. *See also* Deanna (sibling); Ruth
Morrison, Gladys, R.N. 10
Mothers from Hell 113
motivation 113
motor
symptoms 288.
See also Table 2
tics 40, 278, 280, 283, 291, 298. *See also* Table 1
motoric hyperactivity 285
mountain 205
mouth twitches 298

moving target (approach) 143, 239
Mozart 305
MRI 298, 312, 318
Multiple Intelligences, Theory of
102, 225
multiple tics 284
muscular rigidity 299
muscular twitches 280
myths 303

N

nasty-grams 56, 149, 170. *See also* school correspondence
National Alliance for the Mentally Ill (NAMI) 268
National Institute of Health 276
National Institute of Neurological Disorders and Strokes (NINDS) 272, 318, 329
National Legal Precedent: Final Order 149, 153, 235, 331
Natural Rights 105
Nelson Mandela's 1994 Inaugural Speech 114, 331
neurobiological 266, 295, 313. *See also* brain bank
neurochemical studies 265
neuroleptic 293, 318
neurological
disease. *See* neurological disorder
disorder (condition) 143, 149, 236, 241, 242, 247, 248, 265, 272, 275, 279, 297
neuropsychiatry 275. *See also* de la Tourette, Georges Gilles
neurotherapy 294
neurotransmitter 298, 315, 318
news groups 310

MEET THE AUTHOR

J EAN (PIPES) CONKLIN

Jean is the younger daughter of a railroader. She was a tomboy and her father's sidekick. The two Pipes girls sold nightcrawlers to help pay for their college education, and Jean spent her first 19 years in La Grande, Oregon. Hoping to land a job in a big city, she transferred from her hometown college to Oregon State University, to major in home economics communications. When she became engaged to David Conklin, who wanted to live in rural Oregon, her plans were modified. Jean has been a lifelong east Oregonian, far from the metropolis of her dreams. Her high school teaching career was short lived, but she has continued her interest in communications, having worked in radio, magazine writing, website development, desktop publishing, and now book writing and publishing.

At age 52, Jean says, "I think it is wonderful becoming an 'older woman!' " She is fully retired from 27 years of management responsibilities for residential and commercial real estate rentals, and from 20 years as a self-employed interior designer. Her husband of 32 years recently retired as an elementary physical education specialist. Dave was also a teacher activist, working for teacher rights and the improvement of public education. They share a passion for helping the less fortunate here and abroad. Their website for *Heart for Romania* illustrates the work of their non-profit humanitarian aid foundation, which is dedicated to sharing God's love with the people of Romania. >http://www.hermiston.k12.or.us/heartsite/index.htm<

Dave and Jean Conklin have two grown daughters, Trista and Tia, and a fine son-in-law – and they are proud grandparents of two little boys. It can be said that Jean is a "Macintosh addict," her body-clock prefers the nighttime, she is a perfectionist and an optimist, she prefers solitude, and she enjoys "being domestic," RV-ing, writing and traveling. A fearless carpenter / handy woman and a mean typist, Jean also loves to pound the ivories and sing on the church worship team.

Jean's first book – *IT WORKS, IT WORKS, IT REALLY WORKS! LIFE-CHANGING TRUTHS FOUND ONLY IN CHRIST* – has just been released. Written about her friend, Joey Duff, the volume is a very readable, personal, and inspirational work laced with straight-talk, humor and scriptures. ISBN 0-9673440-1-8.

photo by Craig Satter

Order Form

_____ copy / copies of *Music in the Midst of Chaos*
One Family's Saga on the Human Rights Battlefield
by Jean Conklin

@ \$16.95 = \$ _________

_____ copy / copies of *It Works, It Works, It **Really** Works!*
Life-Changing Truths Found Only In Christ
by Joey Duff and Jean Conklin

@ \$11.95 = \$ _________

Add Postage \$ _________

\$3.20 for the first book, plus .50 for each additional book

Total enclosed **\$** _________

Name____

Address____

City___________________________________ State__________

Zip____________________ Phone # (_________)_____________

Make checks payable to Good Shepherd Publications,
and mail, along with this order form, to:

Carico Press

225 SW Butte Drive
Hermiston, OR 97838-1628

www.booksbyjean.com (541) 567-1566

VISA, MasterCard, Discover® Card, American Express

http://www.gspbooks.com/Carico.htm